I0893259

# Jacques Rivette

**Contemporary Film Directors**

Edited by James Naremore

The Contemporary Film Directors series provides concise, well-written introductions to directors from around the world and from every level of the film industry. Its chief aims are to broaden our awareness of important artists, to give serious critical attention to their work, and to illustrate the variety and vitality of contemporary cinema. Contributors to the series include an array of internationally respected critics and academics. Each volume contains an incisive critical commentary, an informative interview with the director, and a detailed filmography.

*A list of books in the series appears at the end of this book.*

# Jacques Rivette

Mary M. Wiles

UNIVERSITY
OF
ILLINOIS
PRESS
URBANA,
CHICAGO,
AND
SPRINGFIELD

In memory of my father,
Charles Preston Wiles

Frontispiece: Jacques Rivette
Photographer Moune Jamet. Courtesy
of Collection Cinémathèque Française.



∞ This book is printed on acid-free paper.

Library of Congress Cataloging-in-Publication Data
Wiles, Mary M.
Jacques Rivette / Mary M. Wiles.
p. cm. — (Contemporary film directors)
Includes bibliographical references and index.
Includes filmography.
ISBN 978-0-252-07834-7
1. Rivette, Jacques, 1928– Criticism and interpretation.
I. Title.
PN1998.3.R584W55 2012
791.4302'33092—dc23 2011026050

# Contents

# Preface and Acknowledgments

Cinema spent its earlier years distinguishing itself from theater: Jacques Rivette's cinema paradoxically achieves renewal precisely through reference to different forms of theatricality. Academic discussions in the past have consistently situated Rivette on the periphery of the French New Wave movement, as his films have been perceived to be at variance with those of his contemporaries. Film critics have measured his work solely against the zeitgeist of the New Wave, which vaunted spontaneity and freedom from theatrical convention. More recently, studies published in France and Britain, most notably Hélène Frappat's seminal work, *Jacques Rivette, secret compris* (*Jacques Rivette, Secrets Understood/Included*; 2001) and Douglas Morrey and Alison Smith's excellent monograph, *Jacques Rivette* (2009), have argued for Rivette's centrality, both as a leading figure of the postwar French avant-garde and as a filmmaker whose work anticipated the postmodernist concern with process, participation, and the performative. In the discussion that follows, I move backstage to observe Rivette's cinema more closely from the perspective of the theater; each section focuses on a different dimension of theatricality in his films.

The following commentary provides a loosely chronological overview of Rivette's films from the New Wave to the present day. In the first section, I examine the evolution of Rivette's early career and his work on short films that already reflect his interest in the connection between theater and cinema. I then move on to analyses of Rivette's feature films. In the second section, I show how Rivette's first feature film, a classic of the New Wave, draws on existentialist theater to address questions of personal culpability and conspiracy. The third section traces the evolution of the tableau as a dimension of theatricality in film adaptations. In the fourth section, I look at how Rivette engages with realism, reflexivity, and European experimental theater in his films from the 1960s and early 1970s. In the fifth section, I show how direct sound and music construct a theatrical dimension in films from the mid-1970s and early 1980s. The sixth section looks at how varied modes of theatricality contribute to the reinvention of film genres, from the 1990s to the commencement of the new millennium. In the seventh section, I trace the evolution of an occult theatricality across three decades. The final section examines Rivette's return to the tableau in his most recent Balzac adaptation, and also his subsequent departure for the theatrical arena of the circus.

In this project that has concentrated on those feature films that foreground theatricality, I have also attempted to show how Rivette's enduring interest in the relation between cinema and theater continues to evolve over the years, expanding to encompass the relation between cinema and various arts, particularly painting, literature, music, and dance. Painting that forms the subject matter of *La belle noiseuse* (1991), an adaptation of Honoré de Balzac's nineteenth-century novella, is thus approached as an additional pictorial dimension of the theatricality that defines Rivette's earlier adaptation of Denis Diderot's *La religieuse.* Rivette's work with film adaptation has continued to provide him with the means to explore the relation between literary, pictorial, and theatrical representations. Music that becomes part of the operatic conception of *Scènes de la vie parallèle* (Scenes from a Parallel Life; 1976) possesses a special significance in nearly all of Rivette's films. A musical score provides a source of inspiration for the director and his theater production in *Paris nous appartient* (Paris Belongs to Us; 1961); again, the compositional practices of Pierre Boulez provide a source of inspiration for the serial form of *Out 1: Noli me tangere* (Out 1: Touch Me Not; 1970). Yet the regenerative role of music is, perhaps, most evident in *Haut bas fragile* (Up Down Fragile; 1995) where a missing melody motivates a young woman's search "backstage," where she is finally able to retrieve her sense of selfhood.

While the following book is organized according to varied dimensions of theatricality in Rivette's work, I have attempted to demonstrate that each film has distinctive themes that ally it with others, while highlighting those inaugural moments that anticipate issues addressed in later films. The themes of conspiracy and investigation that are developed in Rivette's first feature film will be revisited and reworked in film after film throughout his career; the commitment to feminism already in evidence in his second feature film, *Suzanne Simonin, la religieuse de Denis Diderot* (The Nun; 1965–1966; released 1967), which focuses on the freedom of a woman to choose her own destiny, has remained a constant in his films. The examination of the male-female couple in the radically experimental *L'amour fou* (Mad Love; 1969) continues to be explored from within disparate generic and stylistic contexts over the years, perhaps most evocatively in the recent releases *Ne touchez pas la hache* (Don't Touch the Axe; 2007), which explores themes of erotic desire and possession, and *36 vues du Pic Saint-Loup* (Around a Small Mountain; 2009), which chronicles the journey of its heroine, Kate (Jane Birkin), who becomes involved with an Italian traveler while on summer tour with her family's circus troupe.

Rivette is known internationally as a director who presents unusual, persuasive portraits of female friendship and engages with the possibility of desire between women. I look at the powerful, subversive roles that Rivette's female heroines play in films interconnected not only through their relationship to film genres but also through other diverse associations, such as the relation between women and the occult, the resonance of the female voice on stage and off, the representation of the female body in dance and performance, and the depiction of friendship between women. Upon close analysis of these films, it becomes evident that Rivette's authorial signature is not merely discernible in the way in which theatricality inflects his films, but also in the manner in which women's lives are portrayed.

The majority of the films that I discuss are currently available either on DVD or video. Earlier films released in the late 1960s and 1970s, the four-hour versions of *L'amour fou* and *Out 1: Spectre* (1974), have never been commercially available on film or video; the thirteen-hour *Out 1: Noli me tangere* was never released theatrically. These three films are rarely screened outside the European film festival circuit and are only available at select film archives in Europe and North America, yet they form the core of Rivette's work with theatricality, temporal duration and reflexive textuality, and so I felt that it was imperative to include them in this discussion. Subtitled versions in English of *Duelle* (Duel; 1976), *Merry-Go-Round* (1977–1978; released 1983), and *Le Pont du Nord* (1982) remain commercially unavailable and, although these films represent an important part of Rivette's work, I have kept discussion of them to a minimum. I should add that I have chosen to include an extensive analysis of *Noroît* (Northwest Wind; 1976) (even though no subtitled version in English is available) not only because it is the sole film in the oeuvre that announces itself as an adaptation of a play, but also because it bears traces of an operatic theatricality. I have had the opportunity to see all of Rivette's films, with the exception of the three silent 16 mm shorts, *Aux quatre coins* (On Four Corners; 1949), *Le quadrille* (1950), and *Le divertissement* (1952); for an illustrated, in-depth discussion of these films, I highly recommend Frappat's illustrated biography of Rivette's early life and film career in *Jacques Rivette, secret compris.* Owing to spatial constraints, I have given more attention to some feature films than to others and radically limited discussion of certain films, including *Hurlevent* (Wuthering Heights; 1985) and *Jeanne la pucelle* (Joan the Maid; 1994), in particular, that bear a less obvious relation to theater. I am hopeful that this introductory study of Rivette's career will prompt further study of films that I have not treated in detail in this volume.

All translations from the French are my own, unless otherwise noted, and with the exception of the interview with Rivette published in this volume, which Dr. Yolanda Broad and I translated together. The titles of Rivette's films are given in both the original French and in their English translations on initial citations, and subsequent references are made with the French-language title. The release date of each film is the date cited in the text unless otherwise noted; the dates of the actual film shoot are included in the filmography. Note that in the filmography, I use the term "mise-en-scène," rather than the term "direction," out of respect for Rivette's own nomenclature that reflects his deeply held conviction that film is a collective, rather than a solitary, endeavor.

| | |

This book has greatly benefited from the contributions of a variety of key individuals. My discussions with Maureen Turim, who directed my doctoral dissertation on Rivette, provide the impetus behind this volume. My former colleagues Nora Alter and Robert Ray helped establish the correspondence between James Naremore, the series editor, and myself. I would like to express my gratitude to Jim for this exciting series that places independent filmmakers like Rivette on center stage, and also for inviting me to play a part in it. Additionally, special thanks go to Joan Catapano, editor in chief, for her patience, encouragement, and support and also assistant editor Daniel Nasset, who joined the editorial team late in the process. I am especially grateful to Jonathan Rosenbaum for his excellent feedback; his expertise on Rivette and detailed observations were invaluable. Additionally, I am indebted to the expertise of Dr. Yolanda Broad for her assistance with the translation of the interview with Rivette that is published in this volume. I owe a special debt to Véronique Manniez, who facilitated the subsequent interview with Rivette in December 2009; her knowledge, willingness to help, and words of encouragement sustained me throughout the final stages of this project. I thank the following friends and colleagues for their counsel, support, and encouragement: Nora Alter, Matthew Ayton, Martyn Back, Robin Bond, Mike Budd, Margaret Burrell, Rolando Caputo, Jennifer Clark, Léa Colin, Patrick Evans, Walt Evans, Peter Falkenberg, Eric Freedman, Christophe Gallier, Bruce Harding, Susan Hayward, Susan Hegeman, Douglas Horrell, Katherine Jensen, Jeongwon Joe, Daniel King, Michel Marie, Martine Marignac, Sharon Mazer, Douglas Morrey, Scott Nygren, Phil Powrie, Robert Ray, Susan Reilly, Émilie Sitzia, Rose Theresa, Jim Tully, and Alan Wright.

I am grateful to the Cinema Studies program and the College of Arts at the University of Canterbury in Christchurch, New Zealand, for research support. I would also like to thank David Schwartz of the American Museum of the Moving Image, Lise Zipci and Émilie Lacourt of Films du Losange, and Pierre Grise Productions. I am also grateful to the staff members at the British Film Institute and the Iconothèque at the Bibliothèque du Film in Paris for their help and assistance in acquiring images.

My interview with Jacques Rivette took place in Paris in June 1999. I was struck by his brisk, determined gait as he entered the café at Place de la Bastille (which for the French is always associated with the storm of revolution) and also by the unkempt shock of gray, curly hair that at once evoked photographic portraits of Jean Cocteau. Rivette's genuine goodwill, self-deprecating sense of humor, and patience with my French put me at ease very quickly. Just as one would anticipate, Rivette remains a candid and thoughtful critic, whose love for the cinema is always in evidence. My commentary on Rivette's work is drawn from published sources, especially from interviews; I have not sought confirmation from Rivette for any interpretation or statement made in this volume. In sum, Rivette recalls this line from Cocteau's poem, *Léone,* which is recited by the dancer Pierrot in *Duelle*: "I only see the underside of the fabric I am weaving."

| | |

Earlier versions of the material on *Haut bas fragile* appeared as "Re-staging the Feminine in Jacques Rivette's *Haut bas fragile*" in *Studies in French Cinema* 1.2 (2001): 98–107, ed. Susan Hayward and Phil Powrie; and earlier versions of the material on *Noroît* appeared as "Sounding Out the Operatic in Jacques Rivette's *Noroît*" in *Between Opera and Cinema,* ed. Rose Theresa and Jeongwon Joe, in Critical and Cultural Musicology, ser. ed. Martha Feldman (New York: Garland/Routledge Press, 2002), 199–222; and different versions of the material on *Out 1: Noli me tangere* appeared in "In 'Permanent Revolution': Jacques Rivette's *Out 1: Noli me tangere*" in the *Australian Journal of French Studies* 47.2 (2010): 146–59, ed. Douglas Morrey and Brian Nelson.

# Jacques Rivette

# Moving Backstage

## The Films of Jacques Rivette

### The Apprentice Years: *Aux quatre coins, Le quadrille, Le divertissement*, and *Le coup du berger*

In the spring of 1957, Jacques Rivette had just completed his first short 35 mm film, *Le coup du berger* (A Fool's Mate; 1956), and was in the planning stages of his first feature, *Paris nous appartient,* while continuing to write incisive critical pieces for the Paris film journal *Cahiers du cinéma.* Not yet thirty years old, Rivette was already a veteran film critic and an aspiring director who had worked as an apprentice on the set of Jacques Becker's *Ali-Baba et les quarante voleurs* (Ali-Baba and the Forty Thieves; 1954) and Jean Renoir's *French Cancan* (1955). Rivette was born on March 1, 1928, and raised in the Norman city of Rouen in a family "where everyone is a pharmacist" (qtd. in Rosenbaum, *Texts* 91). He commenced an undergraduate humanities degree in Rouen, but his scholastic work was placed on indefinite hold when he discovered Jean Cocteau's diary of the filming of *La belle et la bête* (Beauty and the Beast;

1946), a fortuitous event that he later affirmed marked the beginning of his vocation as a filmmaker. Rivette knew that to realize his ambition, he must move to Paris. In 1949, he packed a copy of his first 16 mm short film, *Aux quatre coins* (On Four Corners; 1949), and left his native town determined to pursue a filmmaking career. The afternoon that Rivette arrived in Paris, he made his first contact, the young actor Jean Gruault, who was at the time managing a bookshop not far from Place St. Sulpice. Gruault invited Rivette to a screening that same evening of Robert Bresson's *Les dames du Bois de Boulogne* (Ladies of the Park; 1945), which was being introduced by a film critic, Maurice Schérer, who would later adopt the pseudonym "Éric Rohmer." In the months that followed, Rivette frequented the Cinémathèque on Avenue de Messine and the Latin Quarter *ciné-club*, where he became acquainted with Gruault's circle of friends, which included Suzanne Schiffman, François Truffaut, and Jean-Luc Godard.

Gruault ultimately became Rivette's scriptwriter on *Paris nous appartient,* the film that Truffaut alludes to in his semiautobiographical *Les quatre cent coups* (The Four Hundred Blows; 1959), which in May 1959 premiered at the Cannes Film Festival. Truffaut won the Best Director Award that year, a distinction that has led critics to identify this work as the inception of a *nouvelle vague* (new wave). Yet the French press' earlier enthusiastic description of such films as Claude Chabrol's *Le beau Serge* (Bitter Reunion; 1957–1958, released 1959) and *Les cousins* (The Cousins; 1959) as a *nouvelle vague* testified to what certain film historians like Alan Williams describe as the "growing national interest" in youth culture, which was expressed in the media throughout the 1950s (329). The metaphor of a "new wave" was appropriated by those eager to identify the inaugural films made by the ex-Cahiers critics as a youth culture phenomenon. Indeed, the directors were soon dubbed and became known internationally as "the young Turks."

Rivette recalls that in the early 1950s they met every day at *Cahiers* and collaborated on each other's 16 mm productions. In 1950, Godard produced and acted in Rivette's second short 16 mm film, *Le quadrille,* which was subsequently projected at successive screenings at the Latin Quarter *ciné-club*. In the summer of 1952, Rivette filmed *Le divertissement,* another 16 mm production, which its cameraman Charles Bitsch described as "a Rohmeresque Marivaudage between young men and women," foreshadowing scenes in more recent films such as *La bande des quatre* (qtd. in Frappat, *Secret* 98). Around this time, Rivette was also acquiring valuable experience by assisting as a cameraman on Truffaut's *Une visite* (A Visit; 1954) and Rohmer's *Bérénice* (1954). By 1956, Chabrol had formed his own production company, AJYM Films, and in alliance with producer Pierre Braunberger, he produced the company's first film, *Le coup du berger*, directed by his friend Rivette. Film scholar Michel Marie affirms that this 35 mm film was "the first professional production accomplished by the New Wave," as the previous shorts directed by Rivette, Truffaut, Rohmer, and Godard had been shot in 16 mm, a format that was considered "non-professional" (59).

Rivette filmed *Le coup du berger* in Chabrol's smoke-filled apartment, where Godard, Truffaut, Robert Lachenay (Truffaut's childhood friend), Jean-Claude Brialy (in the role of the lover), and Jacques Doniol-Valcroze (in the role of husband) gathered to discuss each shot setup. Rivette retained Bitsch as a cameraman and was assisted on the set by Jean-Marie Straub, who later became a key figure in the evolution of the New German Cinema. The film was completely post-synchonized, as was *Paris nous appartient*, because, as Marie points out, in the 1950s, "direct sound still posed cumbersome and difficult conditions for recording dialogue (to say nothing of the need for more retakes), all of which ran counter to the needs set by the small budgets of the New Wave" (95). *Le coup du berger* owes its title to a chess move that Rivette had heard about. Its story is centered on a young woman (Virginie Vitry) who attempts to deceive her husband about the origins of a mink coat that her lover has given her as a present. She does not foresee, however, the secret alliance that has formed between her husband and her own sister (Anne Doat). While aspects of the film's story about lovers' schemes predict Rivette's future work, as Hélène Frappat points out, the film lacks the mediation of theatrical mise-en-scène that lends his later films their contemplative reflexivity (*Secret* 99).

The theatrical dimension that sets Rivette's work apart from others' in the New Wave film movement surfaces in his first feature-length film, *Paris nous appartient*. The film's release in 1961 provoked *Le Monde* critic Yvonne Baby to query, "Why have you situated *Paris nous appartient* in the milieu of the theater?" to which Rivette responds, "Maybe it is because of my affection for Jean Renoir's *Le carrosse d'or* (The Golden

Coach; 1952), but I like films that use theater as their décor and I would like, sooner or later, to make a film about actors" (14). The notion of "theatricality" as a dramatic performance is crucial to understanding Rivette's work, especially the most obviously staged texts—the plays within the films. The majority of films within Rivette's oeuvre make direct references to a play or plays: *Paris nous appartient* refers to Shakespeare's *Pericles* and *The Tempest*; the revolutionary *L'amour fou* stages Jean Racine's *Andromaque*; the legendary experimental work *Out 1: Noli me tangere* cites Aeschylus's *Prometheus Bound* and *Seven Against Thebes*; *Céline et Julie vont en bateau* (Celine and Julie Go Boating; 1974) is based, in part, on the dramatization of Henry James's novella, *The Other House*; the third part of a four-part film series *Les filles du feu* (Girls of Fire) or *Scènes de la vie parallèle, Noroît* announces itself as an adaptation of Cyril Tourneur's *The Revenger's Tragedy*; *L'amour par terre* (Love on the Ground; 1984) is centered on dramaturge Clément Roquemaure's mysterious play; *La bande des quatre* (Gang of Four; 1989) is set in a theater school; *Va savoir* (Who Knows?; 2001) incorporates the mise-en-scène of Luigi Pirandello's *Come tu mi vuoi* (As You Desire Me). Although *Suzanne Simonin, la religieuse de Denis Diderot,* an adaptation of Denis Diderot's eighteenth-century novel, bears no apparent relation to theater, Rivette constructed the film from a theater performance at Studio des Champs Elysées, which he directed. The recent *Haut bas fragile* relies on the theatrical performance style associated with early cinema and the taxi-dance halls of the 1920s and 1930s.

Predictably, the formal innovations Rivette experimented with in his early work were generally dismissed by Anglophone film historians and critics as contrived and artificial—in a word, as "theatrical." In his assessment of *Paris nous appartient,* James Monaco in *The New Wave* dismisses the film for its forced, "theatrical" tone: "*Paris nous appartient* seemed to be exactly the kind of film one would expect a critic to make, full of what seemed like forced, false intellectual mystery: thin, monotonous, and lacking resonance" (308). Film historian Roy Armes upholds Monaco's appraisal in his assertion, "The tone never varies, the dialogue is flat and the photography, although competent, is never striking. The film's major defect is its failure to create any sort of dramatic tension" (182). The perception of the film common among these New Wave historians seemed to perpetuate the idea that the film's affected "theatrical" tone was the source of its commercial failure. The terms of their critique invoke the tenets of Truffaut's landmark article for *Cahiers* entitled, "A Certain Tendency of the French Cinema," in which he formulated the zeitgeist of the New Wave by opposing it to "theatrical" Tradition of Quality productions of the 1950s. Truffaut denounced the dialogue of such films, which was derived from literary classics and adapted by scriptwriters Jean Aurenche and Pierre Bost to complement the metteur en scène's use of "scholarly framing, complicated lighting-effects, 'polished' photography" that inevitably resulted in an artificial studio style (230). The New Wave aesthetic was critically formulated in opposition to the Tradition of Quality cinema, its filmmakers applauded for their ability to wipe the slate clean of the artificially "staged" look that threatened to compromise film's status as an autonomous art.

This discussion of Rivette envisions an alternative to the type of film criticism that locates the theatricality of his films as their determining flaw. Such a casual dismissal of the director reveals a fundamental misunderstanding of his acute awareness of the diverse notions of theatricality that inform his work. Indeed, Rivette's penetrating critical pieces composed for *Cahiers du cinéma* that reflect his understanding of the profound interrelation between the arts are as internationally recognized as his films. Rivette owes his critical acuity, in part, to the mentorship of film theorist André Bazin, whose formulation of an ontology of cinema broke new theoretical ground, providing justification for a cinema based on the principles of realism. Bazin's theory of cinematic realism preoccupied the postwar intellectual and artistic community, yet it was the debate concerning the interrelation between theater and cinema that most deeply concerned Rivette. In his seminal essay from 1951, "Theater and Cinema," Bazin responded to those French critics who had been using the notion of the "'irreplaceable presence of the actor'" to construct an unbridgeable aesthetic moat between theater and cinema (96). Bazin challenges such commonplaces of theatrical criticism to introduce a strangely paradoxical notion of presence, which he argues in cinema is both delayed and deferred: "It is false to say that the screen is incapable of putting us 'in the presence of' the actor. It does so in the same way as a mirror—one must agree that the mirror relays the presence of the person reflected in it—but it is a mirror with a delayed reflection, the tin foil of which retains the image" (97). Bazin shrewdly transfers the problem of the actor's presence from the ontological to the psychological level, thus dismissing the notion of the actor's presence as an issue that definitively sets theater apart from cinema.

He proceeds to locate cinematic specificity in decor, attributing its unicity to a founding lack, for "one could say that in the best films something is missing. It is as if a certain inevitable lowering of the voltage, some mysterious aesthetic short circuit, deprived us in the cinema of a certain tension which is a definite part of theater" (98). Yet this lack to which Bazin refers does not refer simply to the cinema's formal properties but to the perceived historical, literary, and cultural lack, the inferiority complex that cinema bears beneath the weight of its ancestor, the theater. Bazin points to metteurs en scène like magician Georges Méliès, who at the beginning of the twentieth century used the old art of theater in the new cinema, with the actors facing the public (78). Such examples permit Bazin to conclude that primitive cinema served as both an extension and a refinement of the theater. This observation serves as the theoretical impetus for his formulation of cinematic specificity—the independent stance of the cinema as a mature art form (87). By focusing on cinema's inferiority complex with respect to the theater, Bazin is able to liberate cinema from theater, locating its specificity within a dramaturgy of nature where the actor is no longer required. Bazin thus reclaims a realist cinema from its association with the theatrical tableau by aligning it with the quotidian and the authentic. Theatricality, by comparison, is shown to be a closed and conventional space, a *locus dramaticus* where theatrical ritual is cut off from the real world, a stage where the plasticity of the body is perceived as central to the scene. Bazin's realist stance led him to advocate filmed theater, championing those theatrical adaptations in which the artificiality of the original *locus dramaticus* was respected, and thus recorded simply, rather than transformed through formative cinematic trickery.

Bazin's theoretical speculations on the relation between the theater and the cinema remain extremely pertinent to our discussion that focuses primarily on theatricality in Rivette's films. The theatricality that remains the hallmark of Rivette's oeuvre can be viewed, in some sense, as an implicit response to Bazin. Bazin prioritized the place of realist cinema by insisting on the integrity of stage space and decor within theatrical adaptations. Rivette returns to the theatrical tableau to rediscover a true realism. Rivette affirms:

> All films are about the theatre, there is no other subject. That's choosing the easy way, of course, but I am more and more convinced that one must do the easy things and leave the difficult things to pedants. If you take a subject, which deals with the theatre to any extent at all, you're dealing with the truth of the cinema: you're carried along. It isn't by chance that so many of the films we love are first of all about that subject, and you realise afterwards that all the others—Bergman, Renoir, the good Cukors, Garrel, Rouch, Cocteau, Godard, Mizoguchi—are also about that. Because that is the subject of truth and lies, and there is no other in the cinema: it is necessarily a questioning about truth, with means that are necessarily untruthful. Performance as the subject. Taking it as the subject of a film is being frank, so it must be done. (qtd. in Aumont et al. 26–27)

Rivette does not seek to theatricalize cinema, transforming it into a lesser descendent of theater; rather, as film theorist Jacques Aumont affirms, he permits cinema to follow its dramatic inclination, while paradoxically placing this on display ("Patron" 234). Rivette uses theater to assist him in achieving what he believes to be cinema's true vocation—to encounter the real. For Rivette, the theater is not cinema's enemy but its ally in a more difficult mission, which, in Aumont's terms, is to achieve—against the facility of the cinematic machine—a true realism ("Patron" 236).

Rivette's form of reflexivity must be distinguished, however, from the materialist cinema promoted primarily by British Marxist critics during the 1960s and 1970s. Marxist critics at the British journal *Screen* applauded films that foregrounded their own rhetorical codes designed to reproduce the real, specifically through the preferred Brechtian strategy of emphasizing the means of representation at the expense of mimesis. In contradistinction to the reflexivity of materialist cinema, Rivette's films participate in the wider political, artistic, and social trends of postwar France with its renewed interest in such categories as aesthetics, subjectivity, and experience as a response to the postwar crisis in the realm of representation. The arrival of television in the 1950s, which was accompanied by the inundation of high capitalist Hollywood spectacle, precipitated the contemporary crisis in representation that film theorist Youssef Ishaghpour associates with the world-historical "decline of the aura" (61).[1] The theatrical tendency characteristic of cinematographic modernity emerged in response to this "*banalizing* trend," which entailed an accelerated loss of meaning and reduction of image information to the ephemeral (Debord 38). The theatrical tendency of Rivette's cinema protested the reintegration of art into the mundane world of utilitarian consumerism by promising a restoration of aura through recourse to secularized ritual. The theatricality of Rivette's cinema challenges the cultural dominant through a return to ritual and myth. A focus on theatrical ritual and its potential for cinema thus unites our discussion of Rivette's work, while ensuring specific points of reference for each section in which a film or group of films is examined.

## From Shakespeare to Sartre: *Paris nous appartient*

*Paris nous appartient* (Paris Belongs to Us; 1961), a founding masterpiece of the New Wave, is about a university student, Anne Goupil (Betty Schneider), and a struggling Paris theater director, Gérard Lenz (Giani Esposito), who are rehearsing Shakespeare's play, *Pericles, Prince of Tyre*. Their questionable commitment to the production and to each other leads them into a sinister maze of madness, duplicity, and death from which there is finally no escape. Lines from Shakespeare's *Pericles,* a drama derived from a classical Greek tale of murderous intrigue, high seas piracy, and an imperiled kingdom, repeatedly resonate from within their *locus dramaticus,* seeming to echo the modern-day machinations of an international cold war conspiracy that has taken hold of the entire city and its denizens. In its concurrent staging of classical and cold war conspiracy scenarios, the film draws an implicit parallel between antiquity and the contemporary world, between theater and cinema, between the dramaturge and the film director, and in this way re-presents the quotidian world of postwar Paris with the force of ancient ritual.

As *Paris nous appartient* begins, we watch from the window of a train as it moves through the bleak suburbs south of Paris to approach the Gare d'Austerlitz. The scene positions the spectator to identify with the point of view of a tourist arriving from beyond the borders of the city, a refugee seeking the city as a safe haven, or a Parisian native returning home. The point of view remains unsourced; thus, the film opens with an enigma. Rivette reflects in 1959: "To the extent that there is mystery at the heart of the cinema (as there is mystery at the center of everything, in general, and of all the arts, in particular), . . . I believe that the mystery at the heart of cinema is, to use the expression of André Bazin, ontological: in the cinema, there is a process through which one can apprehend reality that, on the one hand, will only be able to apprehend appearances, but that, on the other hand, through appearances, can also apprehend an interiority" (qtd. in Collet, *Le cinéma* 57–58). The "mystery" at the heart of Rivette's cinema becomes a quality of the world itself when we attribute to him Bazin's conception of an ontological realism, which was based on the existentialist ideas of Jean-Paul Sartre (Andrew 105–6). For existentialists such as Sartre, Emmanuel Mounier, and Maurice Merleau-Ponty, reality perpetually unfolds: the mind participates in its experience. Thus, mystery is the quintessential attribute of the real and a value attained when consciousness sensitively confronts the world (Andrew 106).

An intricate plot follows the film's enigmatic opening. Having recently arrived in Paris from the provinces, Anne is seated before the open window of her flat in midsummer trying to focus on Shakespeare's *The Tempest* when she overhears the sound of a woman crying. A distraught Spanish woman in the neighboring flat forewarns Anne of a conspiracy that has already resulted in the death of a close friend Juan and several others. Later at a café, Anne meets her half-brother Pierre (François Maistre), to whom she discloses this strange incident. That evening, Anne accompanies Pierre to a soirée where the mysterious circumstances surrounding the death of Juan, a Spanish musician, are again the subject of speculation. Some guests debate whether Juan's stabbing was the result of murder or suicide. While milling about, Anne encounters the distracted theater director Gérard Lenz, a drunken, loud-mouthed journalist Philip Kauffman (Daniel Croheim), who is in flight from the McCarthy trials, and his friend, the svelte Terry Yordan (Françoise Prévost), Juan's old flame.

Juan's death has not only deeply affected those in his immediate circle but has potentially gutted Gérard's production of *Pericles*. An audiotape of original guitar music that Juan had recorded with Terry was to have offset the poorly funded production, and the vexed director bemoans the fact that it has gone missing. He runs into Anne again when she arrives on his set one afternoon, accompanied by her friend Jean-Marc (Jean-Claude Brialy), an actor in the play. Gérard asks Anne if she would read for the role of Marina, the imperiled princess in *Pericles*. She agrees, and later decides to help Gérard by tracking down the missing audiotape. Anne discovers from a conversation with Juan's former mistress Aniouta Barsky that it might be in the possession of a financier Dr. de Georges. She follows up on this lead, and on others, but does not succeed in locating the tape until much later, when she overhears it unexpectedly at Terry's flat. Meanwhile, Gérard has enlisted the support of De Georges and a new producer, Raoul Boileau, enabling the troupe to recommence rehearsals in the well-established Théâtre Sarah Bernhardt. Gérard admits to Anne that he has been forced to make concessions and has had to cut her from the production.

To distract her from her woes, Pierre invites Anne to a private screening of Fritz Lang's German expressionist classic, *Metropolis* (1927). This grandiose, modernist allegory, which reflexively mirrors the story of *Paris nous appartient,* envisions the city of the future as a New Tower of Babel imperiled by a conspiracy that threatens to unleash the dark, explosive forces contained within the regulated systems of modern technology (Gunning 55–56). As the parable of Babel sequence unfolds before us, the film strip breaks, causing a loud eruption during the silent projection that calls attention to the cinematic apparatus as a machine as potentially volatile as the city of 'Metropolis' itself. Anne's evening is definitively ruined when Philip phones to inform her that Gérard is dead, apparently having committed suicide. After a distressing visit to Gérard's flat, Anne calls a taxi, planning to meet Terry and Pierre, and others, at a remote country estate. Once there, Anne unexpectedly has a hallucinatory vision of Terry shooting Pierre, who falls onto a snowy embankment. Shortly thereafter, Terry arrives at the house alone without Pierre and subsequently confesses to the accusatory Anne that he is dead. Terry refuses to accept responsibility, however, explaining that Pierre's demise was actually Anne's own fault because she had wanted "the sublime." Philip and Terry drive away to an unknown destination, and an actor from *Pericles* confides to Anne that he intends to continue with the production. The film closes as Anne watches geese disperse over a still lake.

Throughout the film, Rivette's camera embraces the incertitude of seemingly random passageways, the unexplained occurrence, and the unanswerable query. The camera takes a circuitous path to introduce the film's main character, Anne, as it cranes across rooftops into the window of her room, where she is reciting Ariel's song from *The Tempest*. Our entry into the room, like Ariel's, is motivated by sound, and thus we are situated as eavesdroppers. Post-synchronized sound permits Rivette throughout the film to focus on the interplay between sound and image. In the opening scenes, dialogue lines reverberate as though from within an echo chamber in which words migrate and change meaning. In response to Pierre's query in the café scene, Anne's exasperated exclamation of "I can't bear it anymore" echoes the Spaniard's response to Anne's inquiry in the previous scene. Anne's repetition of the Spanish woman's line and the posture she assumes, "I no longer have the courage," point to the identification of the women with each other. Moreover, the meaning of the phrase becomes reflexive within the context of the café conversation, not only as an indication of Anne's inability to repeat her theatrical "script" but as a self-conscious pointing to the character Anne's repetition of the scripted line of another character. Pierre takes up Anne's role of eavesdropper, asking her what her Spanish neighbor had said, to which Anne paradoxically replies, "Nothing I can repeat." Reasserting her identification with the Spaniard, Anne adds, "It didn't make any sense. I think she's crazy, like me." The café scene closes with a final repetition and literary citation. As they leave the café, Pierre's partner Ida remarks, "Let's not waste time," which becomes a line Anne repeats and rephrases as a Proustian reference, "And lost time, one never retrieves it."

While Anne is positioned by the film as an eavesdropping witness, an outsider who will persistently seek to pin down the meaning behind the mystery, she is simultaneously situated as a participant, an insider whose discourse repeats, without her knowledge or control, partial phrases that the Spaniard reveals. The psychoanalytic implications of this aural repetition are elaborated with reference to Sigmund Freud's analysis of a case of female paranoia (1915) in which a woman embracing her male lover is frightened by a click or knock.[2] Believing herself to have been photographed in a compromised situation, she reproduces, without understanding, the memory of the primal scene. The uncanniness of this situation derives not only from the hallucinated repetition of an unconscious memory in the woman's present sexual life, but in the splitting of her identification as a witness and a participant across the two scenes insofar as the paranoia of being observed originated in the unconscious memory of observation. While the character Anne points to her own paranoiac disposition, "I think she's crazy like me," the uncanniness of the situation is set in place by a structure of repetition not recuperable as an aspect of character psychology. The effect of an echo chamber produced by the reflexivity of the film's dialogue and by literary citations places the spectator simultaneously in the position of a participant who identifies with character psychology and a witness forced to reflect on the character as a fictional construct within a dramatic situation.

This ceremonial participation that the film demands resembles a Sartrean dramatic rite. In "The Author, the Play, and the Audience," Sartre observes in 1959, "I want the audience to see our century from outside, as something alien, as a witness. And at the same time to participate in it, since it is in fact making this century. There is one feature peculiar to our age: the fact that we know we shall be judged" (76). Rivette reinvents Sartrean theatricality in *Paris nous appartient,* specifically through the notion of "situation." Sartre borrowed the concept of "situation" from Charles Dullin, whose theater school *L'atelier* shaped an entire generation of artists, including such luminaries as Jean-Louis Barrault, Antonin Artaud, Jean Vilar, and Jean Marais (Bradby 5). Drawing on the strategies of situationist theater that Sartre proposed as a safeguard against realistic, psychological theater, Rivette positions the spectator as a witness who encounters a dramatic situation and as a participant engaged in it.

A crane shot captures Anne once again; this time poised by the window of a painter's atelier. Like Anne, we again participate as eavesdroppers on a scene in which we are made privy to the mysterious circumstances surrounding Juan's death. His portrait, which has already been sold and which we never see, is replaced by the painter's blank canvas, which serves as the structuring absence of the scene. The phantom quality of Juan would seem to point toward what historian Louis Stein in *Beyond Death and Exile* has termed the "shadow war," the specter of the Spanish Civil War that appeared sporadically up until the point of Francisco Franco's death (223). Much of this clandestine struggle left no documentation, according to Stein, because "most of the records of the guerrilla fighters, as well as those of local and regional committees, were seized by the authorities and impounded or destroyed" (223). Invaluable documents were irretrievably lost. The painter's blank canvas serves as the center of gravity of the scene and the film itself, pointing not only to the absence of the character Juan but also to the absence of an accurate historical portrait of the period he represents.

Juan's story is based on myth, the figure of the republican guerrilla cloaked in an aura of mystery. The frustrated painter whose task has been to penetrate surface appearances in order to portray his model's essence gesticulates angrily "Fictions! Mysteries!" in response to José, the Spanish guitarist who questions "the truth" of Juan's identity. The guitarist plays a melancholic refrain, a hollow echo of Juan's original composition that one guest (Claude Chabrol) dubs the "Music of the Apocalypse." The guitarist calls attention to his own imitative refrain unapologetically with the remark "It's all that's left." Minna compares Juan to Spanish dramaturge García Lorca, whose verses such as *Cancion del jinete* (Song of the Horseman) drew inspiration from the lyricism of popular Andalusian songs. Others suggest that Juan, like Lorca, might have faced a fascist firing squad had he lived. A disillusioned Romanian seated inconspicuously to the side (Rivette in an exceptional cameo role), despairs of the others' cavalier response to "the crushed revolution," alluding to the Hungarian Revolution of 1956. In this scene, Juan becomes a nostalgic reference standing for the portrait of the political artist tragically doomed by a situation of crisis. Stein attempts to account for the mythic force that the figure of the Spanish republican generated within the minds of the masses: "Were they the Don Quixotes of the twentieth century, immersed in a fantastic dream and wearing tattered rags for armor? Were they simply zealots and revolutionaries who didn't know when to acknowledge defeat? Or were they heroes, anonymous idealists whose exploits, told and retold in the villages, would keep hope alive?" (228). While the absence of Juan's portrait implicitly poses questions destined to remain unanswered, his possible suicide presents the disturbing image of a final retreat into despair.

The mythic force of the republican warrior, Juan, evokes that of the Sartrean existentialist hero, who is tied to a situation of crisis that requires sacrifice. In his own plays, Sartre favored extreme initial situations, often opening them with crisis. Sartre's *Les mains sales* (Dirty Hands; 1948), which questions the nature of collaboration and personal culpability, is a work that informs *Paris nous appartient*; the drama, like the film, opens with the characters' speculations surrounding a political murder and closes with the suicide of its existentialist hero Hugo. Sartre's later drama *Les séquestrés d'Altona* (The Condemned of Altona; 1960) examines the connections between modern history, capitalist expansionism, and violence through its depiction of the sequestration and suicide of a Nazi torturer named Frantz and his collaborationist bourgeois father. Here, the Sartrean hero within the situation of crisis bears obvious resemblance to the myth of the Spanish revolutionary, who takes whatever risks are deemed necessary at whatever the cost and accepts responsibility for his actions. The portrait of the existentialist hero intersects with that of the republican warrior, for both are viewed on the sociohistorical landscape as solitary figures forced by a crisis to choose and accept the risks involved.

The absent portrait of the exiled Juan provides space for the elaboration of a new mythopoesis from the perspective of postwar Paris, for the Spanish guerrilla's unrealized dream of liberation stands in a parallel relation to that of the French Left. The wartime heroics of the maquis and those Leftists in the Resistance were commemorated by General Charles de Gaulle, and then forgotten. Like the Spanish maquisards, those members of the French Left who fought in the Resistance were forced to live as though "in exile" within a nation whose destiny they had shed blood to protect but were ultimately powerless to control. It was, perhaps, the intact myth of the indomitable Spanish warrior that inspired the French Left to rise up in May '68 in an attempt to reclaim their country from the tyranny of global capitalism. The resonance of Spanish myth is evident several years later in Alain Resnais's *La guerre est finie* (The War Is Over; 1966), which concerns three days in the life of an aging revolutionary, Diego (Yves Montand), who thirty years after the Spanish Civil War is still working for the overthrow of the Franco regime. Diego visits Paris, where his political strategies and commitment to the struggles of the past are challenged by a band of student terrorists.

Unlike Resnais's young terrorists, the guests at the soirée are eavesdroppers, witnesses to an abject, mysterious scene that will have traumatic resonance. The serious tone of the company at the soirée is reflected in the reasons they cite for his death: the nihilism of Spanish exiles who had given up the struggle, the stagnant Paris climate, the secretive machinations of the elusive femme fatale Terry, who embodies the seductive allure of Western capitalism. Juan's death echoes Lorca's, which in turn echoes that of Vladimir Mayakovsky—the celebrated poet of the Bolshevik Revolution. Like the spectator, the guests eavesdrop to pin down details; yet they are simultaneously situated as participants and collaborators in the mysterious circumstances surrounding Juan's death and implicate each other by turn. The guilty paranoia of the guests augments the uncanny effect already formally present in the film's opening scenes. On the surface, the film's title, "Paris Belongs to Us," implies plenitude and possession, while providing an ironic evocation of the sense of loss and exile central to the atelier scene and the film. Rivette's title offers a shifting historical referent—at once retaking Paris from the collaborationist Vichy government, but more directly, Francoist Spain—to which the film's opening epigram borrowed from Catholic playwright Charles Péguy, "Paris belongs to no one," provides a measured response. Indeed, the film's obsessive focus on the mythic figure of the republican warrior might be read as the expression of a national trauma: the guilt and shame that is experienced after the fact for the collaborationist role that France played under Maréchal Pétain and then continued to play in the fascist consolidation of power in Spain after World War II. It could also be that the film's commemorative allusion to the Spanish Civil War, appearing not long after France's defeat in Indochina and at the height of the Algerian conflict, is reinvented in and for the historical moment, displacing the contemporaneous crises to an "elsewhere" (Higgins 108). Indeed, the artist's inability to represent the crisis in communication and the cascade of whispered innuendos at the soirée could testify to the intense censorship that the Algerian conflict provoked and that was in full force at the time the film was made.

The story that follows the resonant atelier scene focuses on Gérard and his recruitment of Anne for *Pericles*. It draws on the subcultural, communal student ethos of the Théâtre National Populaire. During the 1950s, the T.N.P. functioned as a young theater devoted to a new generation of workers and students (Serrière 182). Under the directorate of Jean Vilar, its repertoire reflected the tradition of the Elizabethans and the ancient Greeks, for whom theater represented an open forum for the public debate of civic concerns (Bradby 93). The film's focus on Shakespeare and the powerful appeal of the Bard to both Gérard's troupe and the student Anne clearly reflect the spirit of the T.N.P. cultivated by Vilar; yet it simultaneously predicts the end of this era. The film shows that, by the end of the decade, young people were either discarding the postwar dream of a popular theater to secure more lucrative positions in new media technologies or were, like Gérard, being co-opted by capitalist speculators.

The staging of Shakespeare in the film provided Rivette with the opportunity to explore the interrelationship between theater and cinema. In a 1996 interview with Aliette Armel, Rivette describes Shakespeare as "a myth," which he envisioned as "a continent that we know to be gigantic, extraordinary," but that remains "*Terra incognita*" (64). Rivette places stress on theatrical space, which, he explains, is for him, "the primary scene, the unconscious of the cinema" (qtd. in Armel 62). The scene in which Anne rehearses the role of Marina from *Pericles* playfully cultivates the interchange between theater and cinema. Anne's role of Marina, the abandoned waif who becomes the unwitting object of a murderous conspiracy, rhymes with her cinematic script in Rivette's production. This duplication of theatrical and cinematic scripting is paralleled by the scene's formal elements. As Anne repeats her lines, "Is this wind westerly that blows," a prop man stands at her side with a blowing fan that is used to simulate a sea breeze. The fan would be used to create the effect of realism at the cinema, but in this scene, its ungainly appearance on the stage foregrounds theatrical artifice. This scene holds up theatrical and cinematic conventions to the light, permitting the spectator to reflect on profilmic representation as an artificial construct.

After the rehearsal, Terry pulls up to the theater in a flashy convertible coupe to pick up Gérard, leaving Anne behind in the street with Philip. Suddenly, a shot of another car rapidly approaching, followed by the sounds of screeching brakes and a woman screaming, explodes into the quiet, contemplative space of the city square. The cut transports us, in effect, from a leisurely Paris afternoon to an expressionistic Los Angeles night, a moment that pays homage to the celebrated opening sequence of Robert Aldrich's film noir, *Kiss Me Deadly* (1955). In it,

Figure 1. Anne's audition in *Paris nous appartient.*

private eye Mike Hammer's (Ralph Meeker) expensive sports car that closely resembles the one Terry drives is run off the road, and his crazed female passenger is inexplicably tortured and killed. Hammer's maniacal search, which anticipates Anne's subsequent trajectory, through a shadowy maze of anonymous streets, stairwells, and apartments for "the great whatsit" that he presumes to be the source of a conspiracy ultimately uncovers an atomic bomb. Aldrich's "closed in" world "in decay," which Rivette refers to in his 1955 essay, "Notes on a Revolution," is reflected in the universe of *Paris nous appartient,* which similarly offers "an account of moral suffocation, whose only way out must be some fabulous destruction" (qtd. in Hillier 96). Shell-shocked after the so-called auto accident, Philip rushes off with Anne through the bright neon streets, having witnessed the suspected murder of "another" anonymous victim run down in the street. Anne listens attentively to Philip's paranoid rants about an international conspiracy and his prophesies of the director Gérard's demise.

The cold war conspiracy that Philip describes to Anne draws on the explosive energy of *Kiss Me Deadly,* yet the obsession with crime, criminals, and criminal conspiracies began in the early 1840s when a collective paranoia captivated Parisians of all classes (Burton 51). Publications such as the *Gazette des tribunaux* and *Les mystères de Paris* amplified the terror, until Parisians readily subscribed to the notion that the city had succumbed to a menacing criminal conspiracy aimed not just at its inhabitants but also at the very structure of society (Burton 51). Encrypted forms of communication and a private language characterized this dangerous underworld, a composite of criminal and working classes. *Paris nous appartient* inverts this urban myth, transforming an insidious proletariat underclass into an invasive cosmic force governed by the panoptic eye of Protean rulers, whose perspective hovers over the city. Wandering through the bustling Paris shopping district, the paranoiac Philip is situated as an eyewitness to a conspiracy that is unfolding everywhere around him. Rushing from the crowd past department store windows, Philip remarks to Anne, "The real masters are hidden and govern in secret. They have no names," a comment inflected with the certainty of being controlled by social, political, and economic forces that are no longer visible or identifiable. Conspiracy here may serve as an oblique reference to the postwar networking of American, British, and French nation-states, whose concerted effort to counter international communism by admitting Francoist Spain into the United Nations necessitated their "accidental" abandonment of the revolutionary cause of Spanish republicans.

Rivette challenges the meaning of mystery in *Paris nous appartient,* for in his film "mystery" becomes associated not simply with a conspiracy plot but with the city itself, which is transformed into "that sphinx called Paris" that Alfred Delvau describes in *Les dessous de Paris* (1862) (9). As Philip discovers a dark walkway, he confides to Anne: "The world is not as it seems. What seems true is only an appearance. I seem to speak in riddles, but some things can be told only in riddles." Like the mid-nineteenth-century *flâneur* who stands apart as a privileged witness, Philip becomes a "chronicler" and "philosopher" of the city, who claims to decipher its hieroglyphic and arcane signs, commenting, "What I'm saying, some have guessed. But I KNOW it"

(Benjamin, "Paris" 37). Yet as his observations reenact the rapture of the *flâneur,* a chorus of women's voices filters into his conversation with Anne, recirculating Ariel and the sea-nymphs' song from *The Tempest*. At this moment, Philip is recast within Anne's theatrical script from the film's opening scene. The unmotivated intervention of this song, which remains illegible and indecipherable to Philip, places him as an unwitting participant in, rather than an informed witness to, the mysteries that the sphinxlike city holds.

*Flânerie* finds its historical echo in Philip's autoscopic nightmare of self-replication, his production and reproduction of a series of self-portraits that adorn his hotel wall. Anne discovers him incapacitated on the floor of his hotel room, unable finally to decipher the signs of the city before him. Haunted by memories of the Paris boulevards, he remains destined to perpetually clone images of himself. Like the nineteenth-century criminal, Philip sees himself as "a cloak without a body," a Proteus whose lack of self-individuation leads him to obsessively identify with the imagined being of others: "I cling to people I meet, you or anyone. I look at them. They exist" (Balzac qtd. in Burton 52). Like the canny criminal Jacques Collin of Honoré de Balzac's *Splendeurs et misères des courtesans* (1838–1847), Philip remains an invisible witness to those he observes, possessing omniscient powers of observation over hotel inhabitants that serve as a microcosm of the city. He instructs Anne to "Look at people who pass. They live in the real world," while consecutive images of hotel occupants illustrate his activity of observing and recording: "Finnish, 18 years old. Ambition, happiness. Works as a model, hopes for better." Philip's protean capability will paradoxically deprive him of the possibility of entering into relationships with these other selves and will instead condemn him to the solitude of self-replication. The hotel inhabitants he observes are themselves simultaneously engaged in an identical process of self-dilation. When Anne later enters the Finnish model's room, extreme close-ups of the portfolio photographs lining her wall offer a dizzying spectacle of self-replication, her identity transformed into dilated images of body parts. The proteanization of Paris life is produced and reproduced ad infinitum in *Paris nous appartient*, where the principle of character identity collapses into an endless echo of the criminal self.

In his capacity to project himself into his "characters" and in his desire to move from the analysis of particulars to a synthetic knowledge of the whole, the dramaturge Gérard participates in the same epistemological universe as the protean criminal. On the Pont des Arts overlooking the Ile de la Cité, a district historically associated with the criminal underclass, Gérard displays to Anne his knowledge of the synthetic structure of *Pericles,* explaining to her, "it's made up of rags and pastiches, but it hangs together on another plane, from a global point of view." As the two stroll across the bridge, Gérard offers her a part in his play, recalling an earlier scene in which Philip, crossing the identical bridge, urges Anne to play the part of criminal investigator in the conspiracy that threatens Gérard. The film scripts the spectator in the same manner that Anne is cast in Gérard and Philip's scenario, seducing us into a "brotherhood" of participatory identification with a "family of the damned" that creates the conspiratorial web of the film itself. Louis Moreau-Christophe in *Le monde des coquins* (1863) writes of the nature of the criminal conspiracy in *Paris nous appartient*: "Still today, in France, an association of rogues forms a kind of brotherhood, a guild, a family pact—the family of the damned—whose members are united through unbreakable ties of criminal solidarity" (qtd. in Burton 53). The close conformance of the film's organization to the underlying structure of the conspiracy myth that preoccupied the mid-nineteenth-century French imagination seems overdetermined. Its reinscription in *Paris nous appartient* must be read as an echo of the moral panic and national trauma that had resurfaced once again in Paris like a postwar aftershock. It can simultaneously be understood as symptomatic of the identity crisis at the heart of French film as an art and a technology.

Jacques Attali, like Claude Lévi-Strauss, argues that music and musicians themselves provide a substitute for myth in contemporary culture. Attali affirms that music enables us to envision a new world, which will supersede the everyday and establish a new order; it is "the herald of the future" (11). For this reason musicians, Attali argues, are "dangerous, disturbing and subversive," and consequently, their history is irrevocably tied to that of repression and surveillance (11). The ambiguous role of the musician is analogous to that of the film director, as both are playing a double game. Both musician and director serve in the duplicitous role of "reproducer and prophet" (Attali 12).

Playing his part in the Parisian underworld of criminals and outcasts, the exiled musician Juan, like the director Rivette, is a participant in a society that he cast in a political light (Jean-Luc Godard surfaces in a cameo appearance as Juan's "cohort" to serve as a "fence" or middleman in this network of criminal contacts). Yet, the musician, like the director, is simultaneously destined to serve as historian and reflect through aesthetic ritual the deeper values of society. The myth of music and musician paradoxically provides the impetus to the film's narrative economy, which is propelled by the paranoiac activity of eavesdropping and surveillance. The paranoia, panic, and identity crisis central to the film predict the accelerated shift into late capitalism, which is reflected in the consolidation of American, British, and French nation-states and the consequent abandonment of the Spanish republican cause. The censorship put into place by the surveillance apparatus of the late capitalist state, in which multinational corporations and the media play a collaborative role, is forecast by the economist De Georges, who brands Juan's music as "rubbish, pure filth" and the musician as "a walking anachronism." Juan's music is replaced by the high-tech simulated sound effects of waves and seagulls that are imposed on the director by the capitalist entrepreneurship of Boileau, who ultimately oversees and polices the production. Yet the plaintive melody at the heart of the heroine's quest is not irretrievably lost, for Anne is at last privy to the mysterious music when Terry unexpectedly produces the original tape and plays it, its quiet sonority imparting a melancholic, pensive dimension to Anne's discovery.

The conspiracy plot of *Paris nous appartient* that centers on the retrieval of taped music dramatizes the listening in on, transmitting, and recording at the heart of the modern cinema and, in this manner, discloses the surveillance potential of the apparatus. *Paris nous appartient* exposes the Protean potential of the cinematic apparatus to play a collaborative role in the conspiracy that serves the interests of capital. The concerns of capital are consistent with surveillance and silencing that preclude the politics of a prophetic music. The final scene of the film returns us to the theater in a circular fashion with the recitation of the actor's line from the unfinished production of *Pericles*: "Is this wind westerly that blows? . . ." Philippe Arthuys's haunting musical refrain counterpoints the final repetition of the theatrical script; both reproduce the enigma with which the film began and re-present the "mystery" at the heart of Rivette's cinema.

### From the Literary Text to the Tableau: *La religieuse*, *Hurlevent*, *La belle noiseuse*, and *La belle noiseuse: Divertimento*

In some sense, Rivette's second feature film, *Suzanne Simonin, la religieuse de Denis Diderot* (The Nun; 1965–1966; released 1967) represents his refusal to adapt novel to film. He approaches the original artwork, Denis Diderot's eighteenth-century epistolary novel, through the theater; his inaugural theatrical production of *La religieuse* at Studio des Champs-Elysées defines his conceptualization of the film adaptation. To extend one of Bazin's most well-known metaphors in which he likens the cinema to an usher's flashlight, Rivette's style of direction on the film set of *La religieuse* might be likened to a flashlight's fugitive beam, for according to his featured performer Anna Karina, he was "always behind the camera, . . . darting in and out of all the corners," placing "himself alongside the actors," while "always looking at this or that detail" (qtd. in Frappat, *Secret* 132). In *La religieuse,* Rivette's cinematic flashlight cuts through the theatrical footlights to transfigure the original work.

The novel's story is based on the historical figure Marguerite Delamarre, who was locked up from early childhood—first at the convent of the Visitation de Sainte-Marie, and then at the abbaye de Longchamp. Modeled on Delamarre, the character Suzanne Simonin was Diderot's concoction that had been created to play a joke on a friend, the Marquis de Croisemare, to whom he composed letters written by a young nun who had escaped from her convent. These letters provided Diderot with the foundation for his novel, *La religieuse,* fashioned as an autobiographical account of the life of the imprisoned nun. Diderot's novel inspires Rivette's austere portrait of eighteenth-century life in France. As the film opens, Suzanne (Anna Karina) stands at the precipice of sacred and secular worlds. Her mother Madame Simonin's sin of illicit love has condemned her illegitimate daughter to convent life. Suzanne initially refuses her mother's selfish demand that she take the veil, but later assents and enters Longchamp Convent. There, she meets a kind-hearted Mother Superior, Madame de Moni (Micheline Presle), who inspires her to take her holy vows.

The untimely death of the saintly Mme. de Moni is a terrible loss for Suzanne, for once deprived of her protector at Longchamp, she becomes prey to violent abuse at the hands of a harsh new Superior. She resorts to the courts in an effort to have her vows rescinded, but to no avail. Suzanne is instead transferred to a worldly convent, where she is at the disposal of a new Mother Superior, Madame de Chelles (Liselotte Pulver), drawn from Adélaïde d'Orléans, a notorious abbess, who falls passionately in love with her. Mme. de Chelles insists on an open, idyllic order; yet the shift to a softer, calmer atmosphere belies the madness and darker, more intense passion that is unleashed as Mme. de Chelles's desire for Suzanne becomes uncontrollable. Aided by Dom Morel (Francisco Rabal), her confessor, Suzanne escapes. Prey to the corrupt forces of the outside world, she finds herself trapped within a world of salon prostitutes, and in a final desperate gesture, kills herself.

Rivette first envisioned Diderot's novel as a theatrical production. On February 6, 1963, Rivette made his theatrical debut at Studio des Champs-Elysées directing Jean Gruault's adaptation of *La religieuse*.[3] His choice of a classical, rather than an avant-garde, approach to mise-en-scène was designed to render the young nun's story in the simplest and most elegant manner possible. Rivette modeled the production on the works of eighteenth-century dramatist Pierre Carlet de Marivaux, creating a pleasant, decorative, tidy production with intermittent moments of violence. Yet the play's light, courteous presentation belied its scandalous, confrontational content, which for Rivette was above all feminism, a young woman's claim of freedom from her family, and even more broadly, the right of the individual to choose his/her own destiny, viewed from the perspective of 1760. Though the play was not a financial success, the experience was crucial to Rivette's evolution as a director. Faced with the challenge of transposing the theatrical mise-en-scène and Karina's charismatic presence to the screen, Rivette understood the necessity of conceptualizing a different scenario for the film adaptation, which would take into account the way in which the theater simplified and accentuated all traits. Rivette would also modify his approach to the actors while filming them to account for the audience's greater proximity to their performances. The film that resulted was very different in its method and in its tone, less pleasant, less gentle, harsher, and coarser.

Neither Rivette nor its producer Georges de Beauregard could have envisioned, however, the reception of the film by the censors. A total ban was placed on *La religieuse* in April 1966 for France and for exportation, propelling the film into the press. In one interview with *Figaro littéraire,* Rivette voiced his astonishment: "It was as though they had guillotined us" (Le Clec'h). After the ban was lifted a little more than a year later, on July 6, 1967, the film enjoyed tremendous commercial success, becoming a *succès à scandale*. In the interim, *La religieuse* had sustained harsh criticism from certain quarters, such as Guy Daussois from *Le populaire,* who had criticized its portrayal of characters, which he found to be "marked by a schematization and oversimplicity that is rarely encountered, with absolutely no human depth." Yet Rivette's "schematic" characterization was actually inspired by Diderot, who in *The Paradox of Acting* had advocated character typing as part of a presentational, pantomimic acting style in an effort to construct a morally vital theater (15).

The idealist notion of pure forms that underlies the greater part of Diderotian aesthetics informed not only Rivette's method of acting but also his critical perspective on cinema and painting. As cultural historian George Lellis observes, this critical tendency is, perhaps, most evident in Rivette's review of *Voyage in Italy* (1953) in which he compares the work of neorealist director Roberto Rossellini with that of Henri Matisse, emphasizing the purity of geometry and forms (18). Rivette affirms:

> All you need do, to start with, is look: note, throughout the first part, the predilection for large white surfaces, judiciously set off by a neat trait, an almost decorative detail; if the house is new and absolutely modern in appearance, this is of course because Rossellini is particularly attracted to contemporary things, to the most recent forms of our environment and customs; and also because it delights him visually. This may seem surprising on the part of a *realist* (and even neo-realist); for heaven's sake, why? Matisse, in my book, is a realist too: the harmonious arrangement of fluid matter, the attraction of the white page pregnant with a single sign, of virgin sands awaiting the invention of the precise trait, all this suggests to me a more genuine realism than the overstatements, the affectations, the pseudo-Russian conventionalism of *Miracle in Milan;* . . . (qtd. in Hillier 193)

As Lellis notes, the Platonist overtones of this passage become pronounced later in the essay where Rivette describes Rossellini as possessing "this faculty of seeing through beings and things to the soul or the ideal they carry within them, this privilege of reaching through appearances to the doubles which engender them" (qtd. in Hillier 198). The Platonist philosophical assumptions that inflect Rivette's discussion of painting and film connect his early critical perspective to Diderotian aesthetics.

Diderot's theories of theater and painting are reflected in the composition of his novel, *La religieuse,* and Rivette's adaptation of it. For Diderot, theatrical presentation could be conceptualized as a series of pictorial tableaux (Barthes 70; Lellis 34). Unsurprisingly, he envisioned his novel's construction similarly, as "filled with pathos-laden *tableaux,*" as a work "to be perused ceaselessly by painters; and if it were not forbidden by modesty, its true epigraph would be *son pittor anch'io*" (qtd. in Fried 199–200, n. 119). The Diderotian literary intertext informs Rivette's adaptation, where black wipes underscore scene changes to give each a fixed tableau definition. Certain critics have suggested that the Diderotian tableau actually anticipates film (Lellis 35; Vexler 49). Lellis, for instance, maintains that Diderot's notion of the tableau, in which "the composition of the actors and the visual elements" plays an essential role in the production of meaning, is "pre-cinematic" (34–35). To support this claim, he cites Diderot, who writes, "Oh! If we could have theaters where the decors would change every time the place of the scene had to change" (35). It is impossible to know whether Diderot was actually conceptualizing in "pre-cinematic" terms when he describes such "magical" scenic transitions; yet it is tempting to speculate that Diderot was already thinking of the successive tableaux of his novel as the interface to a new art form—film. Centuries later, Rivette returns to Diderot's notion of the tableau in *La religieuse* to discover a source of fascination dependent upon a theatrical and pictorial aesthetic.

Rivette's discovery of the Diderotian tableau, already associated with the novel *La religieuse,* is coincident with his movement toward Barthesian structuralism in the mid-1960s. Diderot also served as a touchstone for cultural critic Roland Barthes, who affirms in his seminal essay, "Diderot, Brecht, Eisenstein," that Diderotian aesthetics rest on "the identification of theatrical scene and pictorial tableau" (70). Rivette's decision to interview Barthes in 1963, the year that he assumed the position of editor in chief of *Cahiers*, reflected his ongoing effort to expand the journal's repertoire to include key figures from the Paris literary, philosophical, and artistic community, such as composer Pierre Boulez, anthropologist Claude Lévi-Strauss, and even Sartre (although the conversation never occurred). Barthes's response to Rivette and his colleague Michel Delahaye in this crucial interview signals the shift in *Cahiers* in the direction of a new kind of formal filmic analysis upheld by the theoretical apparatus of semiology, which had already taken hold in the field of literary criticism. For Barthes, film is closely allied to literature in its material and its techniques. He dismisses the notion of a Brechtian cinema because, he observes, the theatrical image "does not offer itself up in the same way" as the cinematographic image to "segmentation, duration, or perception" (qtd. in Hillier 282). He maintains that film, like literature, should provoke answers rather than give them, assuming "that very particular responsibility of form which I have called the technique of *suspended meaning*. I believe that the cinema finds it difficult to deliver clear meanings and that, in the present phase, it ought not to do so. The best films (for me) are those, which are best at *suspending meaning*" (my italics, qtd. in Hillier 282). In the modern world that Barthes denounces as "fatally bound to meaning," freedom in artistic production, he concludes, should consist "not so much in *creating* meaning as in *suspending* it; . . ." (qtd. in Hillier 281). Rivette's *La religieuse* assumes this particular form that Barthes describes as a "suspension of meaning" in the contemplation of successive tableaux, for, in Barthes's words, the film resembles "a gallery, an exhibition; . . . ," which "offers the spectator 'as many real tableaux as there are in the action moments favourable to the painter'" (70; Diderot qtd. in Barthes 70).

Rivette's *La religieuse* opens with pictorial tableaux that reveal the drawings of Longchamp Convent and a portrait of the Abbess of Chelles in 1719, making it clear that the film's story finds its source in actual historical places and personages. The sound of an insistent knocking or banging unexpectedly commands our attention; this is immediately followed by three measured knocks recalling the way in which *les trois coups* (the three knocks) traditionally alerted French theater audiences to the curtain rising. The camera travels over a seated audience and stops before an iron grille through which we see Suzanne Simonin, who enters the brilliantly lit up space of the sanctuary. The grille that separates the congregation from those officiating in the ceremony creates a visible barrier similar to the invisible fourth wall that separates the proscenium stage from the audience. It is from behind the grille that Suzanne initially refuses her holy vows; the vertical iron bars point to the self-enclosed space of the chancel as an undisguised acting area. Within this initial scene, the codes of theater—architectural, cultural, gestural—are encrypted within the film text. The chancel is actually a proscenium stage where religious vows are repeated like a rehearsed script, transforming the ceremony itself into a botched theater performance that closes with the hurried fall of the curtain. The injection of codes of theater transforms the film scene into a striking vision—a tableau. In the film's opening moments, Rivette constructs an institutional space associated with a potentially paralyzing theatricality, which we observe, for we are situated outside the film as if in theater seats, rather than unreflectively identified with the camera's point of view.[4]

Suzanne's arrival at Longchamp Convent follows her fateful decision to acquiesce to her mother's demand and take the veil. To signify the transition from the world of her bourgeois family to the ascetic world of the convent, Rivette strips away all decorative excess from his set; the decor that remains amounts to a bed, a few wooden chairs, a night

Figure 2. A tableau: Suzanne Simonin refuses her vows in *La religieuse.*

table, and curtains, which conceal the darker recesses of convent life as much as they dramatically reveal its ceremonial religiosity. Drawing on his previous experience as metteur en scène at the Studio des Champs-Elysées, Rivette returns to the sparse decor of theatrical staging to focus on what Bazin describes as theater's domain—the human soul (106). The soul of Suzanne Simonin is the focus of Diderot's novel, and thus, Bazin would argue, her story belongs within the theatrical sphere: "Like the ocean in a sea shell the dramatic infinities of the human heart moan and beat between the enclosing walls of the theatrical sphere. This is why this dramaturgy is in its essence human. Man is at once its cause and its subject" (106). Rivette relies on theatrical staging to give human priority to the dramatic structure of his film.

The profound "stillness" of the film, as Douglas Morrey and Alison Smith have observed, recalls that of Robert Bresson's *Les anges du péché* (Angels of Sin; 1943), a somber study of sacrifice and redemption within a Dominican convent (181). The institutionalized space of Bresson's convent devoted to the rehabilitation of women convicts mirrors that of Longchamp, which is similarly defined by the rigid, linear corpus of nuns who line the chapel pews. Rivette uses the slow horizontal panning and tracking motion of his camera to accentuate this linearity. Lines of blue habits that file through the space of Longchamp Convent are also reinforced by architectural structures: the horizontal and vertical lines of the grille that separate Suzanne from the secular world, the Christian crosses that adorn the convent walls, or the crisscross maze of endless corridors that seem to lead nowhere. The cavernous space of the chapel recalls that of a vast theater, an impression intensified by the peripheral placement of figures seated along the walls in pews. Drawing attention to large, open surfaces that bear the inscription of a precise line, Rivette captures the abstract, primitive dimension of a Matisse painting. The sparse lighting afforded by the flickering flames of candles accentuates the cold blue interiors of the convent, while the wind whistles beyond its thick walls. Dialogue is gradually reduced to confidences whispered in the corridors, sung prayers in the chapel, and the ritualistic coda of "Ave Maria," "Deo Gratias" exchanged before bed. The cloistered atmosphere of Longchamp is intensified by the omnipresence of witnesses and the moral codes that these witnesses bring to bear. The punitive Mother Superior's accusation, "There is something wrong in your mind.

You have schemes" is answered by Suzanne's anguished confession, "My body is here, but my heart is not."

The architectural and ideological center of Longchamp is the chapel, which reproduces the dimensions of a theater set that opens out into the audience. Similarly, Suzanne's apartment at Longchamp assumes the dimensions of a dressing room, where she is repetitively robed and disrobed: first, she is dressed in the bridal gown when she assents to her role as the bride of Christ; then, she is undressed when she is forced to wear a hair-shirt beneath her habit; again, she is re-dressed as a reward following her sung performance at Matins; she is completely stripped of her habit and veil following the discovery of her legal petition; finally, order is restored, and she is dressed once again before her departure from Longchamp. Suzanne's sung performance at Holy Week Matins, where she admits to playing her role like "an actress in a theater," reproduces the temporal dimensions of an *entr'acte,* which is a performance occurring between the acts of a play that often includes music or dancing. If Suzanne's concert establishes a momentary respite, an intermission of sorts, between the routine performances required of her at Longchamp, it also marks a decisive interval in the progression of the film narrative.

Suzanne's departure is accompanied by the dramatic shift from Longchamp's dark blue interiors to light, extravagantly lush settings of the secularized convent, where transgressive passion is soon aroused. Rivette's mise-en-scène bears resemblance to the rococo seductions of eighteenth-century painter Jean-Honoré Fragonard that disclose the turbulent passions existing just beneath the smooth veneer of family and institutional manners.[5] The vertiginous ensemble of foliage, fountain, and cloud in Fragonard's *Blind Man's Buff* (1775) may have inspired Rivette's rendering of the initial rendezvous between Suzanne and Mme. de Chelles within the convent garden. The film scene is suffused with an almost dreamlike atmosphere that, like Fragonard's tableau, associates states of reverie with the experience of nature. Such allusions to paintings in the film are motivated not only by the novel's setting but also by Diderot's extensive writings on pictorial composition in *Essais sur la peinture* and *Salon de 1767*. In this instance, Rivette's scenic rendering provides a visual illustration of the painting's title, for Suzanne is literally blindfolded in the scene, spinning at the center of the band of nuns who flutter around her. Suzanne's blindness to darker forces, coupled with the blithe oblivion of those who surround her, serves as an ominous portent. The disquieting intensity of her conversation with Mme. de Chelles intrudes on the unperturbed ambiance of the convent garden, a tension marked by the flickering contrast of light and shadow. The hushed intimacy of the nuns' inaugural tête-à-tête intensifies to the point of madness and erotic delirium in the scenes that follow.

The film's closing sequence makes explicit the implicit connection Rivette draws between theatrical staging and the ideological staging of institutions. As Suzanne prepares for her final performance as a salon prostitute, she gazes into the mirror, her countenance hidden behind her mask that announces her new social role. She then drifts into the sparkling space of the salon, where she becomes indistinguishable from the other prostitutes who, like the nuns of Longchamp, are all uniformly dressed. In this final scene, Suzanne joins the secular world where she is forced to recognize her own image, an ideological construction determined by yet another institutional apparatus, which mirrors the apparatus of oppression and sadistic power prevailing within the dark corridors of Longchamp. Differences between inside and outside, sacred and secular, chaste and unchaste collapse within this final scene, as the nun is momentarily caught and held within an institutional hall of mirrors that conspire to perpetually reflect her image as the crystallized creation of theatrical and ideological staging. As though refusing her role one final time, Suzanne moves stealthily toward an open window. She suddenly jumps, offering a chilling parody of a theatrical exit. The spectator is required to read this final tableau as a crucifixion and solemn requiem for the martyred body of the nun.[6]

In his first film adaptation, Rivette explores the parameters of the tableau—moving from novel, to the theatrical scene, to the pictorial tableau—in full circle to redefine the theatricality of Diderot's novel in his film. In its capacity to mix art forms, *La religieuse* respects what Rivette has described as the "impure nature" of cinema itself: "It [Cinema] is an impure art, complex, between the novel, the theater, painting, music, dance, etc., and it is understandable that in this indeterminate place from within the middle of the traditional arts, that we would want to look sometimes in this direction, or in that direction . . ." (qtd. in Conférence de presse 34). Rivette's exploration of theatricality through the tableau in *La religieuse* lays the foundation for his later films, *Hurlevent* (Wuthering

Heights; 1985), an adaptation of Emily Brontë's novel modeled on the tableaux of Balthus (Balthasar Klossowski), *La belle noiseuse* (1991), an adaptation of Balzac's novel that features painting in its plot, and the late work, *Ne touchez pas la hache* (Do Not Touch the Axe; 2007), another Balzac adaptation structured as a series of tableaux.

| | |

Rivette returns to the tableau in *La belle noiseuse* (1991), as does the Balzacian painter Edouard Frenhofer, after having abandoned it for a certain period of time to explore alternative modes of theatricality and their relation to the process of artistic production. His observation that "There are two kinds of filmmakers, those for whom painting serves as a departure point, and those who arrive there following their journey" reveals his own relation to the tableau, which serves him both as a departure point and as a point of return (qtd. in Aumont, "Patron" 217). Awarded the Grand Prix at the 1991 Cannes Film Festival, *La belle noiseuse* is an adaptation of Balzac's nineteenth-century novella *Le chef d'oeuvre inconnu* (The Unknown Masterpiece; 1831). Rivette had contemplated this Balzac adaptation since the completion of *Hurlevent*. There, he had transposed Brontë's nineteenth-century novel *Wuthering Heights* (1847) by modeling certain scenes on French painter Balthus's india ink illustrations, analyzing and transforming them to form his own unique portraits.[7] Balthus's tableaux provided Rivette with an important point of reference in recounting the tragic story of Catherine Earnshaw (Fabienne Babe), a woman not unlike Suzanne Simonin, whose passionate love for the gypsy waif Heathcliff (Lucas Belvaux) is curtailed because of the demands of social norms and conventional morality. At times, there is no dialogue, only the plaintive voices of a Bulgarian choir whose beautiful, dissonant chant laments their unrequited love. The configuration of pictorial and theatrical tableaux found in *La religieuse* and *Hurlevent* crystallizes in *La belle noiseuse,* which is, deservedly in my view, the most critically acclaimed of Rivette's adaptations. In it, painting provides the crucial point of commonality between the novel and Rivette's adaptation of it.

*Le chef d'oeuvre inconnu* begins in 1612 on a cold winter morning in Paris. An aspiring painter named Nicolas Poussin paces fretfully before the door of the celebrated court painter Porbus. The arrival of another mysterious visitor, Frenhofer, allows Poussin to enter the studio virtually unnoticed. There, he gazes admiringly at Porbus's portrait of Saint Mary of Egypt, but Frenhofer points out that it requires more than mere mastery of artistic style to render a lifeless form into a living, breathing woman. To illustrate his point, Frenhofer seizes the palette and brush and transforms the tableau into a masterpiece. Poussin and Porbus, rapt with admiration, hear about his unfinished work, "Belle noiseuse," which he has been working on for ten years but has been unable to finish because of the lack of a flawless model. Poussin becomes possessed by an overwhelming desire to see "La belle noiseuse," and so convinces his young mistress Gillette to sit for Frenhofer. Porbus later approaches Frenhofer with a proposition: Poussin will lend Frenhofer his beautiful lover Gillette in exchange for the right to view "La belle noiseuse." When the moment of unveiling finally arrives, the two men, who have been waiting just beyond the door, hurry into the studio and look around for the much anticipated "Belle noiseuse." The two are incredulous at first, for they are only able to discern emerging from the corner of the tableau a bare foot whose delicate beauty captivates them. "La belle noiseuse" has been buried, they claim, beneath the coats of paint that the artist has applied in his quest for perfection. Betrayed by his viewers, Frenhofer weeps in despair and dies that night after burning his canvases.

Rivette shifts the novel's opening from seventeenth-century Paris to contemporary France, from a dark, midwinter morning to a warm, windy, midsummer afternoon at château d'Assas in Provence. The film opens in the garden of the hotel, where Marianne (Emmanuelle Béart) and Nicolas (David Bursztein), assuming the respective roles of Gillette and Poussin, engage in a flirtatious frolic, which scandalizes two British tourists enjoying afternoon tea. The romantic repartee of the couple unravels around the photograph that Marianne has just snapped of the unwitting Nicolas scribbling in the garden. Marianne refuses to let Nicolas see it, nor is the spectator privy to it; she provokes further debate by demanding money for it, which he disputes. When Nicolas proposes to Marianne that she visit his hotel room to "talk business" concerning ownership of the photograph, a mysterious female voiceover narration suddenly intervenes, querying, "Why was she suddenly so uneasy? Because of the visit to the Frenhofers?" The intervention of a female narrator at this point signals the shift in focus from novel to film.

In *Le chef d'oeuvre inconnu,* Poussin plays a central role in the story as the apprentice artist, whereas in the film, Marianne is introduced to us as the apprentice artist, a freelance photographer who is both the creator and owner of images. The voice of narration intervenes once again in the couple's dialogue to introduce the character Balthazar Porbus (Gilles Arbona), who arrives at their hotel to accompany them to the artist's château. Rather than the painter of Balzac's story, Balthazar Porbus is an alchemist, who collects paintings as well as houses and women. Like one of the three kings from the Orient paying homage to the king, Balthazar Porbus, driving "like crazy," arrives from the east by way of Geneva—not to pay tribute to the artist but to purchase art. He too brings a precious gift to Frenhofer as an offering—the ravishing beauty Marianne—destined to become the artist's model. Rivette's referencing of the name "Balthazar" does not merely evoke the notion of spiritual pilgrimage but also pays homage to the painter Balthus (Balthasar Klossowski).

*La belle noiseuse* introduces the aging artist Frenhofer (Michel Piccoli) as preoccupied and oblivious to time; he wanders into the courtyard, where he joins Liz (Jane Birkin) and the guests, who are anticipating his arrival. The back-and-forth shifting in the film between the dark, hushed interiors of the château and light, lush garden settings forecloses the manner in which disturbing passions threaten to destabilize the sanctity of family and community. An ominous portent disrupts the group's soirée when the invited guests, engaged in casual conversation with Liz and Frenhofer during dinner, become privy to Porbus's epileptic seizure. Without warning, Porbus dramatically collapses. As his head hits the table, Liz, and then Marianne, turn to look as his body falls onto the floor. The traumatic moment erupts unexpectedly, shattering the tranquility of the idyllic gathering. This dramatic shift in tone associated with the transition from daylight to night, from the harmonious vistas experienced within nature to the haunting specter of death encountered within the walls of the château, invokes filmmaker Alain Resnais's *Providence* (1977), in which an aging British novelist Clive Langham (John Gielgud) makes peace with members of his family during a late afternoon gathering at his country estate. Resnais uses the story of an artist, as does Rivette, to reflect on the creative process; *Providence* probes Clive's inner experience as he agonizes over his coming novel. As Clive's children gather around him, a 180-degree circular pan reflects on the vastness of the surrounding vista as the day fades away. Rivette not only recirculates Resnais's themes in his film but also reinvents his signature shot, adopting a semicircular pan or alternatively a semicircular cutting pattern, not simply to show the natural environs but to provide transitional moments of reflection between the confined space of the artist's château and the terrifying freedom offered in the cinematic panoramas of the Provençal landscape.

Leaving their dinner unfinished following Porbus's unexpected illness, the three men retire to Frenhofer's cavelike studio. Nicolas, still eager to see the mysterious tableau "La belle noiseuse" that Frenhofer had alluded to earlier, allies himself with Porbus, who proposes to Frenhofer that he complete the painting using Marianne as his model. As Nicolas and Porbus solidify the deal with Frenhofer, they become allies in their quest to advance their respective ambitions—art and finance. Both men seek access to the finished tableau, as *objet d'art* and as merchandise, through Marianne's body. Yet it is the signifier "noiseuse" that establishes the initial connection between Frenhofer and Marianne. She surprises him when she recognizes the word, which she claims to have heard in Quebec, defining it as "nuts" like "going nuts." Frenhofer elaborates further, defining it as "the beautiful pain in the ass." The signifier reoccurs in translation later that evening, when Marianne reproaches Nicolas for having "sold her *ass*." The next day, however, she changes her mind and decides to assume the role of "La belle noiseuse," thereby wreaking revenge on the men by becoming a "pain in the ass" for both of them.

These initial sequences of the film retell the entirety of Balzac's novella with the exception of three key moments—the physical act of painting, the unveiling of the masterpiece, and its immolation. The substantial portion of Balzac's story is disclosed during the film's prologue. The remainder of Rivette's adaptation then proceeds to chronicle the act of creation that finds closure in the act of internment. Like Balzac's characters Poussin and Porbus, the film spectator must also wait attentively for the final unveiling of Frenhofer's tableau. Could it be that the hours that the two characters in the novel spend waiting anxiously at the door of Frenhofer's studio determine the film's four-hour duration? Yet the film spectator, unlike Balzac's characters, is also invited to share in the process of painting *itself*. Rivette explains his method: "We tried truly to make a film not that talked about painting, but that approached it. We were creating a path towards painting" (qtd. in Conférence de presse 34). By refusing to make a "film of a painting," where the filmmaker uses an already completed work sufficient unto itself, Rivette avoids the mistake that Bazin points to in "Painting and Cinema" where not only "is the film a betrayal of the painter, it is also a betrayal of the painting and for this reason: the viewer, believing that he is seeing the picture as painted, is actually looking at it through the instrumentality of an art form that profoundly changes its nature" (165).

Bazin is responding directly in this passage to the popularity of postwar feature films about famous artists that offer the spectator "an anecdote instead of a painting," whereas he praises art documentaries, such as Alain Resnais's *Van Gogh* (1948), which arise from "the histology of this newborn aesthetic creature, fruit of the union of painting and cinema" (169, 168). Bazin would applaud *La belle noiseuse,* in which the story of a painter precipitates a profound exploration of painting and cinema as parallel temporal processes. Rivette's study of duration in *La belle noiseuse* may, in fact, have been inspired by Bazin's writings on film and painting. Bazin maintains that the two art forms present two modes of temporality, noting that a film sequence confers a temporal unity that is "horizontal . . . and geographical," whereas painting "develops geologically and in depth" (165). Frenhofer explains painting as a geological expedition in which the artist returns to "the sound of the origins. The forest and the sea mixed together. That's what painting is." Similar to geological science that studies the earth's origins, Rivette's film forces us to contemplate the excavation of a tableau buried by time and its restoration. Frenhofer's will to deny time in the creation of a "timeless" work of art is mirrored in Liz's will to arrest time by producing the replicas of animals in her studio, where she carries on the analogous activity of taxidermy.

Rivette conceptualizes the structure of *La belle noiseuse* as a series of tableaux, similar to a triptych comprised of three key moments—the physical act of painting, the unveiling of the painting, and its interment—which are framed by a prologue and an epilogue. Such Diderotian tableaux that provide the film's structure occasionally overlap with those of theater, offering the semblance of a classical five-act play. Through its rigid adherence to a unity of time and place, the film establishes an emblematic affinity with theater, which is accentuated by the implicit comparison Rivette constructs between the artist's studio and a theater set. Rivette refuses to adhere to Balzac's novelistic description of a cluttered atelier and instead returns to the sparse decor of theatrical staging used in *La religieuse*. Indeed, Marianne entering Frenhofer's studio for the first time remarks that it "looks like a church."

The atelier is not the architectural center of the château, as it is segregated from the center by a labyrinthine outdoor walkway, yet it is where the three key moments that structure the film's story unfold. The first panel of the filmic triptych places the act of painting on display. Time is marked during the modeling session not only by the gradual shift from daylight to darkness, but also by the jump cuts that Rivette inserts as a reflexive reworking of the profilmic code for the passage of time. Typically, such cuts would be used to condense time, demarcating a temporal ellipsis followed by a perceptible change in the artist's drawing to show the work accomplished. Multiple jump cuts during this spatially static scene force our attention to the means by which cinema shows temporal development. During the second modeling session, the focus shifts from the artist's creative process to the relation between artist and model. As Frenhofer twists Marianne's limbs into the unendurable positions he desires, in a sense, he takes her captive in order to realize his vision. As Marianne extends her arms outward horizontally across the bench where Frenhofer has positioned her, her pose momentarily resembles a crucifixion, recalling the Passion of Suzanne Simonin. During the third day, however, Marianne's determined nature seeks expression through her poses. The balance of power established during the first two sessions shifts radically from the will of the artist to that of the model. She insists, "Let me find my place, my movement, my timing." It is only when Marianne learns to rely on her own inner impulses, which provide her with motivating power, that the process of creation can proceed. It is only when Frenhofer learns to work in a relation of reciprocity with her that he is able to create.

It is evident that the painter Frenhofer prioritizes the visual image, and in this respect, his method resembles that of a film director; does Rivette conversely work like a painter? Indeed, Rivette borrows Frenhofer's palette of red, white, and blue in *La belle noiseuse*. Rivette's use of primary colors in *La belle noiseuse* may be read, in part, as an homage

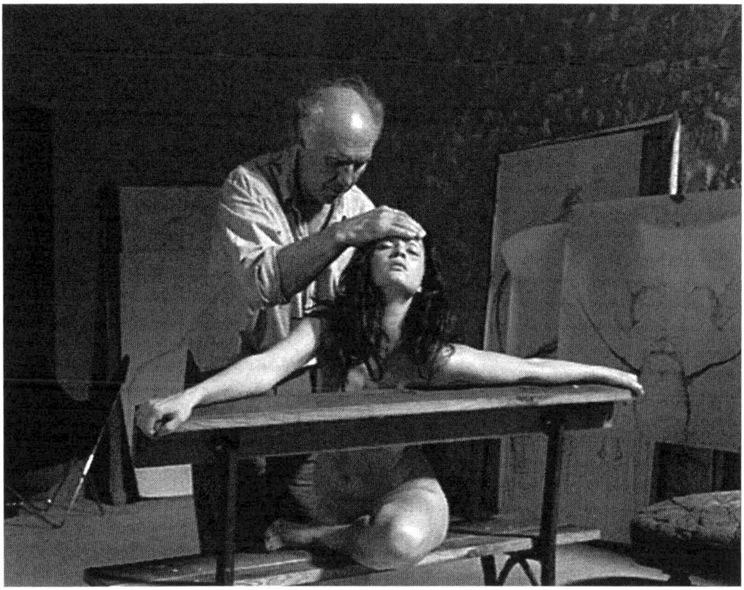

Figure 3. Frenhofer takes Marianne captive in *La belle noiseuse.*

to Godard, whose use of red, white, and blue in such films as *Une femme est une femme* (A Woman Is a Woman; 1961), *Le mépris* (Contempt; 1963), and *Pierrot le fou* (1965) is well known (Shafto 60–65). Yet the red, white, and blue tri-colors never acquire abstract dimensions in *La belle noiseuse,* as they do in Godard's films, nor do they define dissociated shapes within the environment (Shafto 65). Rivette makes use of the blinding whiteness of the Mediterranean light, as did Matisse, and the intensity of the blue sky, if only to accentuate the dark, hollow space of the atelier, which, like a cinema theater, offers both the film's audience and its characters a respite from the brilliance of "natural" light for a certain duration of time.

The color white designates place and time in *La belle noiseuse*; it also connotes creation and decay. The blank, white canvases lining the studio walls seem to extend the white stone walls surrounding the château. Whereas the white of the tableaux invites the painter's brush stroke and the possibility of creation, the labyrinthine walls recall an endless maze, threatening to enclose the painter within a sterile void.

Red is used less frequently in the film but holds an especially intense emotional and symbolic resonance. From the film's first moments, red connotes an indeterminate danger and an erotic anticipation; Marianne wears a red blouse to greet Porbus, who first arrives at the hotel in a bright red car that completely dominates the frame. When Nicolas first senses the perils implicit in Marianne's modeling engagement with the painter and feels jealous, his nose unaccountably begins to bleed; the red blood threatens to stain his shirt and invade the chalky environment of Liz's studio lined with chemical-filled replicas. From the outset, Frenhofer advances the notion that blood represents the true test of authenticity, declaring that a true work of art can be identified by "blood on the canvas." Much later, a large red cross marks the original painting, "La belle noiseuse," serving as the signifier identifying the authentic work from its copy. A final flash of red and white is what we see when Magali accidentally lifts up the tarpaulin to reveal a small portion of the original painting before its final interment within the château walls. The mock tableau that is unveiled the following day before the public is a white nude posed within a blue background, betraying the traces of the Manichean battle between blue and red waged in the war of reworking the original.

The unveiling of Rivette's film *La belle noiseuse* occurred at the Cannes Film Festival, where it received critical accolades. Immediately following the film's warm reception, the shorter, two-hour version *La belle noiseuse: Divertimento* (1991) was released. Rivette's second film was completed, in part, to fulfill a contractual obligation with his television coproducer FR 3, who had agreed to finance a two-hour film, not a four-hour opus. His use of different takes from the original *La belle noiseuse* to construct a phantom film *Divertimento* mirrors Frenhofer's reduplication of his original unfinished work. The title of Rivette's "mock" film "Divertimento" provides a reflexive commentary on its "minor" status. Rivette confided in a taped 2002 interview with Frédéric Bonnaud that the title was a private nod to one of his favorite composers, Igor Stravinsky, who drew a four-movement concert-hall suite, which he called the Divertimento, from the complete ballet, *The Fairy's Kiss* (1928). A musical term, "Divertimento" is defined historically as an "eighteenth-century suite of movements of light, recreational music, sometimes for open-air performances for a small number of players," whereas its meaning in the twentieth century shifts to "a not-too-serious work" (*Oxford Dictionary* 241). We might ask whether *Divertimento* is, in fact, a "not-too-serious" work in comparison to its predecessor.

In *Divertimento,* the focus on the process of artistic creation is substantially reduced. In the long version, duration allows intimate sounds to surface, like measured breathing, the sipping of coffee, the scratching of pen on paper, and the high-pitched drone of the cicada. While the abbreviated duration of *Divertimento* affects its tone and texture, Rivette's decision to omit the prologue and its female narrator affects the meaning of the film. In electing to elide the female voice that frames the story, he shifts its focus from Marianne's evolution in *La belle noiseuse* to the unchanging contractual concerns between the men and the subsequent exchange of money. Marianne's development is disclosed at the close of *La belle noiseuse* by the female voiceover, who intervenes to interpret the character's actions for the audience: "Marianne put on her old mask again, or maybe a new one," establishing an implicit comparison between the film's epilogue and the end of a play. The voice informs the spectator, "the story is coming to an end soon" and at last, reveals its identity to us, "Marianne is me, it was me." By framing the film's story as a subjective flashback, the narrator Marianne reclaims the story as her own. She openly taunts the spectator with the prospect of her mystifying departure, saying "You won't learn what becomes of Marianne tonight," refusing to be ruled by the inevitability of a conventional happy ending. Marianne's evolution from innocence to self-awareness in *La belle noiseuse* mirrors Rivette's own mysterious trajectory. In the absent presence of the camera's gaze that innocently celebrates the grand masterpieces lining the salons and corridors of the château, Rivette revisits the grand transcendental orders of Platonic forms, individual genius, and authorship (Foster 62–63); he rediscovers them in close compositions that encourage the contemplation of the artist's hands at work and the images he creates; and he finally relinquishes them, for in staging Marianne's final departure from château d'Assas, the institutional domain of paternal artistic genius, Rivette envisions his own exodus from the old transcendental orders that painting invokes. His return to the realm of cinema is presaged in the release of his double film *Divertimento*, a work whose uncanny reflexivity throws the status of transcendental orders into question.

Scenes are shifted in *Divertimento* so that the film's closing scene focuses on Porbus discussing monetary figures with Frenhofer for the purchase of "La belle noiseuse." By switching the final scene, Rivette radically changes the film's focus from the process of artistic creation to the final product defined in terms of its market value, thus providing an ironic metacommentary on the film's relation with its coproducer. *Divertimento* thus illustrates the adage: "When you paint a picture for the court, you do not put your whole soul into it; to courtiers you sell lay figures duly colored" (*Chef d'oeuvre* 38). Yet the citation also invites the spectator to speculate: is the original *La belle noiseuse* truly a *chef d'oeuvre* or lay images edited for the courtiers at Cannes?

A fascination with possession drives the final scenes of both films, apparent in Porbus's penchant for monetary possession, in Nicolas's frustrated desire to possess Marianne, and in Marianne's acquisition of self-possession as she assumes her masked persona. It also preoccupies Rivette as metteur en scène, who asserts that the notion of "possession" is at the core of theatrical, pictorial, and literary representations: "'*Possession, possession . . . La possession est impossible.*' Of course, a painter, a writer, a metteur en scène fantasizes about the idea of possession, all the while knowing that it doesn't exist . . ." (qtd. in Conférence de presse 34). As a metteur en scène, Rivette realizes from the outset that it will be impossible to fully possess and, thereby, reproduce the literary text, be it by Balzac, Brontë, or Diderot, yet he is nonetheless fascinated by the possibility. It may be more than coincidence that the pictorial tableau figures centrally in each film adaptation, for it embodies the seductive possibility of possession, of delimiting the spatial infinity that might be the provenance of cinema. Yet Rivette also recognizes that his illusion of possession, which propels the adaptation, must remain unattainable, as it is premised on a denial of cinema's domain that extends to that "diffuse space without shape or frontiers that surrounds the screen" (Bazin 107). Rivette confesses at last: "Painting is among the greatest temptations of the cinema, yet at the same time, it is only a temptation, since everyone already knows that cinema is also the contrary of painting" (qtd. in Conférence de presse 34).

### A Revolution in Realism, Reflexivity, and Oneiric Reverie: *Jean Renoir le patron*, *L'amour fou*, *Out 1: Noli me tangere*, and *Out 1: Spectre*

It was during the filming of the documentary *Jean Renoir le patron* (1966), which consisted of three programs for the fledgling television series "Cinéastes de notre temps" (cofounded in 1964 by the late Bazin's wife, Janine Bazin, and *Cahiers* critic and filmmaker André S. Labarthe), that Rivette discovered a new vision of filmmaking based on that of the aging director. Rivette had felt compelled to completely alter his course following the experience of *La religieuse*, when he found himself hemmed in by his own scripted adaptation of Diderot's text. He found inspiration for a stylistic revolution in Renoir, who, in his estimation, had created "a cinema which does not impose anything, where one tries to suggest things, to let them happen, where it is mainly a dialogue at every level, with the actors, with the situation, with the people you meet, where the act of filming is part of the film itself" (qtd. in Aumont et al. 11). The two weeks that he spent with Renoir, listening to him talk about the cinema and his relationship with his actors, renewed his desire to pursue completely different avenues in his own work. Rivette also was inspired by the work of documentary filmmaker Jean Rouch, whose films, he insists, uphold the tradition of realism established in Renoir (qtd. in Aumont et al. 34). Rivette's relationship with his actors would shift significantly following his encounter with Renoir and would become central to the experimental style of *L'amour fou* (Mad Love; 1969), *Out 1: Noli me tangere* (Out 1: Touch Me Not; 1970), and *Out 1: Spectre* (1971; released 1974).

Rivette's stylistic revolution coincides not only with the completion of his documentary on Renoir but also with the cultural revolution in France following the events of May 1968. Testifying to the radical moment of cultural change, the nearly thirteen-hour *Out 1: Noli me tangere,* and the reedited four-hour version, *Out 1: Spectre,* represent the culmination of Rivette's effort, which began with *L'amour fou*, to break from the strictures of narrative form, from the inflexibility imposed by a script, and from the acting style required by rigid adherence to the script. The four-hour experimental *L'amour fou* (the title pays tribute to André Breton's 1937 surrealist text) initiates Rivette's exploration of temporal duration. At the request of the film's distributor, Cocinor-Marceau, a reedited two-hour version was also produced and released in tandem with the original; however, Rivette did not sanction the release of this reedited film, and so disowned it. This unauthorized version was subsequently refused commercial distribution and thus remains unavailable for commentary. The full-length film edited by Nicole Lubtchansky uses duration in a mise en abyme construction where Rivette's 35 mm black-and-white film records a television crew directed by André S. Labarthe, which uses 16 mm black-and-white film stock to document a stage production of Jean Racine's seventeenth-century play *Andromaque* (1667). Rivette uses reflexive theatricality in the film to explore the boundaries of classical theater and the Italian Renaissance stage, which had largely determined the mise-en-scène of both *Paris nous appartient* and *La religieuse*. In *L'amour fou*, Rivette pushes beyond the boundaries imposed by narrative, script, and acting style, which he felt had constrained him during the filming of *La religieuse*, to enter into a new dimension in filmmaking, which is disclosed in this Pirandello citation used to introduce the story outline: "I have thought about it and we are all mad" (qtd. in Aumont et al. 24).

| | |

Forced to work within the severe budgetary restrictions imposed by the film's producer Beauregard, Rivette was compelled to shoot *L'amour fou* in Paris with a limited production team, few decors, and in just five weeks. The film reworks the story and structure of *Paris nous appartient*, moving back and forth between the world of the theater and the world backstage, between the work of a theater director, Sébastien Gracq (Jean-Pierre Kalfon), who oversees his troupe's rehearsals of a production of *Andromaque*, and the life he shares with his partner Claire (Bulle Ogier), an actress involved in the production. While *L'amour fou* shares with *Paris nous appartient* its focus on theater, each film provides a singular response within its respective era. Whereas *Paris nous appartient* can be viewed as a prescient, political response to the menacing rise of Gaullisme in the late 1950s, *L'amour fou* does not openly address politics but rather evolves from within, and thereby reflects the pervasive atmosphere of revolt, unrest, and uncertainty in the years immediately preceding the events of May '68. Dismissive of the film directly based on political themes, Rivette describes *L'amour fou* as "a deeply political film," as his "Prima della rivoluzione," because of its moral stance on human relationships, affirming that the moral choices made by those involved with the production, during the filming and editing, are finally political choices (qtd. in Aumont et al. 36; qtd. in Baby 1968, 19). Rivette did not believe that film was the medium for sermonizing: *L'amour fou* instead offers a serious inquiry into film's complex means of production, which is why it remains one of the most powerful and political of films to have come out of the New Wave.

Rivette confided to me at Café de la Bastille in 1999 that, of all his films, *Paris nous appartient* and *L'amour fou* were the two that he viewed as autobiographical, to a certain extent. The figure of the director takes center stage in both. It is not difficult to see elements of the young, idealistic filmmaker Rivette in the beleaguered theater director Gérard Lenz, who confides to Anne that he would be willing to do almost anything to put on his play. It is well known that Rivette similarly encountered financial difficulties during the filming of *Paris nous appartient,* which was among the first of the New Wave films to go into production but the last to be released, in late 1961. We can surmise that Rivette encountered the moral dilemmas borne by Gérard in the course of the film's protracted production process and, perhaps, was even fearful of losing his actors and crew to well-subsidized television productions. He must have felt himself to be—far more so than his *Cahiers* colleagues—a chartered member of the "order of exiles" that Gérard insists he has been inducted into. Whereas Gérard encounters the difficulties of directing a play not well known to French audiences, Sébastien stages a canonical classic in a highly experimental style in *L'amour fou*. Unlike Gérard, Sébastien appears to be oblivious to financial considerations, expressing his disdain for public perception: "I don't think that the work can reach the public or please them." Rivette may have similarly suspected that the experimental textual strategies of *L'amour fou* and also its duration would preclude its commercial viability; if so, his suspicions have proven correct, because the film remains currently unavailable in any format. Unlike the solitary, tormented director who in *Paris nous appartient* confronts existential choices, the figure of the director in *L'amour fou* is bisected into theater director Sébastien and television director Labarthe. The threat that had been implicitly posed by the media to the theater director in *Paris nous appartient* invades the stage in *L'amour fou* and is even reflexively incorporated into the play's production. We can surmise that Rivette would have identified easily with either role, for each, at times, mirrors the other.

At this point in his film career, Rivette was eager to examine theater from a completely different perspective, that of documentary reportage (qtd. in Cohn 29). Labarthe was the obvious choice to direct the 16 mm film of the theater troupe. Rivette's admiration for the televised series, "Cinéastes de notre temps," that Labarthe had cofounded, and his work with him on *Jean Renoir le patron,* which had also been shot in 16 mm black-and-white film, motivated his choice. Rivette allowed Labarthe and cameraman Étienne Becker complete freedom on the set. Labarthe adopts a mock–cinema verité style, zooming in at crucial moments to capture an actor's expression in close-up, yet he does not intentionally interfere with the dramatic progression of the play. Offstage, he played a pivotal role in the interviews he conducted with members of the troupe.

While Labarthe and Becker were shooting their 16 mm footage, Rivette and his cameraman Alain Levent were simultaneously filming the troupe from a greater distance with a 35 mm Mitchell camera. Rivette maintains that the 35 mm camera was there to merely record the events as neutrally as possible, maintaining the same invisibility and proximity to the stage as that of a theater spectator (qtd. in Aumont et al. 19). He characterizes the diminutive role of the 35 mm camera in the theater as akin to "the intruder who doesn't come too close because he'll get yelled at if he comes any closer, who watches from the corners, who looks down from the balcony, always hiding a bit. It has its oppressed voyeur side to it, like someone who can never come up as close as he would like to, who doesn't even hear everything" (qtd. in Aumont et al. 18). The scenes in the theater testify to the disparity between the Mitchell and the Coutant, which Rivette describes as "two opposite forms of indiscretion, a passive one and an active one, one sly and one bossy," respectively, while pointing to the inalterable presence of the reality that preexists both (qtd. in Aumont et al. 18). Rivette was well aware that the grainy, unpolished look of the 16 mm footage would come to represent the "cinema" vis-à-vis the seeming transparency of the 35 mm film. Yet its role in *L'amour fou* was not entirely predetermined, and Rivette was surprised to discover that "the

16 mm brought in suspense, . . ." not simply in terms of the fiction that at times seemed closer to a conception of the cinema associated with Hitchcock than Renoir, but also in terms of the very nature of the 16 mm that when intercut into the 35 mm film recharged it, plastically and dynamically, making "it possible to give the shots back the power they had in the rushes and which they lost in the end-to-end; . . ." (qtd. in Aumont et al. 21).

The actors' work and that of Kalfon in the role of metteur en scène Sébastien take center stage in theater scenes; however, the film spectator is never permitted to remain pleasurably immersed in theatrical spectacle. Passive identification with Rivette's 35 mm camera is virtually impossible because of the frequent, intermittent jumps to Labarthe's 16 mm images, which are complemented by the periodic appearances of Labarthe and his TV crew filmed in 35 mm. The white, box-shaped stage, literally housed within the Palais des Sports in Neuilly, is surrounded on all four sides by several rows of empty seats, thus resembling, as Hélène Deschamps observes in her important study of the film in *Jacques Rivette: Théâtre, amour, cinéma*, "a boxing ring," "a circus ring," or even "a blank cinema screen" (22). Freed of all decor that would serve to demarcate space and time, actors resemble astronauts cast adrift within the vacant white chambers of a spaceship, similar to those in Stanley Kubrick's *2001: A Space Odyssey* (1968). Onstage, these performers rehearse scenes from Racine's five-act play that reworks Greek myth to present three interwoven stories of unrequited love set in the thick of the Trojan War. The play is never performed in its entirety, however. Rehearsed scenes recur in piecemeal and are scattered throughout the film. What *L'amour fou* retains of Racine's canonical classicist tragedy is the residual "savagery" of its alexandrine verse in which, Rivette maintains, the words have "the same violence as the actions of the Living Theatre's plays: words that hurt, that torture" (qtd. in Aumont et al. 23).

It was, in fact, the physicality of Ogier's and Kalfon's performances in the experimental productions of fringe director Marc'O that, Rivette notes, had initially inspired him to make a film chronicling three weeks in the lives of a couple (qtd. in Cohn 28). Well-known to the artistic community that frequented La Coupole in St. Germain, members of Marc'O's company were practiced in the techniques of improvisation and psychodrama, having performed in such theatrical productions as

*Les bargasses* and the 1968 film *Les idoles*. Rivette was impressed by these young actors, whose "performance style had not been deformed by a certain tradition associated with *Le Conservatoire*," which was heavily reliant on the conventional interpretation of character psychology and sentiment (qtd. in Cohn 28). Rivette hand-picked Ogier, whose physical demeanor defines the role of the apprehensive actress Claire, initially cast in the role of Hermione in *Andromaque*. Having already worked as both a professional actor and also a metteur en scène of various theater productions, Kalfon embraced the role of Sébastien, the director of *Andromaque* and an actor playing the key role of Pyrrhus in his own production. Once filming began, Rivette allowed Kalfon the latitude to stage the play according to his own conception, and also welcomed those actors from Marc'O's troupe that Kalfon brought to the set with him, Michèle Moretti in particular, who in the role of Michèle acts as Sébastien's assistant, and also Josée Destoop who, in the role of Marta, fills in as Claire's replacement in *Andromaque*.

Structured self-consciously as a flashback, the film begins at the story's end, completing a circular narration that opens and closes with Claire's departure by train to an undisclosed destination, as Sébastien remains behind, listening to an audio recording of her voice from the solitude of their apartment while his anxious troupe anticipates his belated arrival at the theater. A cut from Sébastien's pensive expression to the subsequent scene in the theater where Claire is rehearsing her lines invites us to read this scene and, indeed, the remainder of the film, from his point of view as his recollection of the past. Yet rather than providing an immediately comprehensible visual image of the past as would the traditional flashback, *L'amour fou*'s reflexive presentation of both film and theatrical performance raises theoretical issues concerning the problem of vision. As the rehearsal of *Andromaque* progresses, a conspicuous oscillation between 16 and 35 mm representations of Claire's performance places in question the film's visual presentation of memory. Recalling the use of the flashback in modernist films like Alain Resnais's *L'année dernière à Marienbad* (Last Year in Marienbad; 1961) or Chris Marker's *La jetée* (1962), its appearance at the outset of *L'amour fou* raises comparable questions about the status of the image, memory, and daydream, which demand, as Maureen Turim affirms, "an investigation into the means of narration, voice, and 'vision' in films" (220).

Claire's subsequent refusal of the role of Hermione precipitates her departure from the set, where Sébastien remains with Labarthe and his TV crew. Sébastien phones his ex-girlfriend Marta, who agrees to replace her. An experienced performer, Marta assumes Claire's role gracefully and welcomes the presence of the TV crew, even granting Labarthe an interview, during which he assumes the self-appointed role of "psychoanalyst." Indeed, Marta's rise from the stage to the stature of televised celebrity is made possible by Labarthe and his TV crew. Meanwhile, Rivette's 35 mm camera impassively records Claire, who sequesters herself in her apartment, where she is beset by suspicions that a conspiracy has formed among the theatrical players expressly to exclude her, foremost among them Sébastien, who she believes is unfaithful to her. Claire's jealous obsession recalls that of Racine's "proud" Spartan heroine Hermione, who is driven to seek revenge against her betrothed, the king, Pyrrhus, because of his perceived betrayal of her with his Trojan captive Andromaque. When Claire airs her suspicions to Sébastien, she taunts him with flattering portraits of the other women, Célia (Célia-Andromaque), Maddly (Maddly-Céphise), and Michèle, who work with him on the set of *Andromaque*. A 16 mm image of each woman taken from Labarthe's rushes shot in the theater accompanies each description and illustrates it, thus throwing the film's visual presentation of imagination into question.

As Marta recites Hermione's lines in the theater, addressing an audience of stage and screen spectators, Claire reinvents the role at home, repeating identical lines while recording them onto the audiotape that she replays to herself. Marta's dark onstage persona mirrors that of the fair-haired Claire, whose solar, translucent presence, as Deschamps points out, is underscored by her association with the name "White Queen," inscribed on a brasserie marquis (53). This epithet could as well refer to her blond American counterpart, Jeannie (Gena Rowlands), a high-class hooker who is caught up in a frenetic whirlwind of desire and the desperation of a couple in John Cassavetes's 16 mm independent production, *Faces* (1968). Unlike Cassavetes's camera that relentlessly moves forward to frame Jeannie's face in illuminating close-up, Rivette's

35 mm camera keeps its distance to reveal Claire's evanescent bodily appearance that seems at times to vanish within the overexposed shots of the sun-drenched apartment she inhabits, or the passageways connecting those Paris stores she frequents. As Claire's connection to the darker world of theater becomes increasingly tenuous, she refuses its scripted verse and instead chooses to play with sheer sound. Crouched beneath the window of her apartment, she records various sound effects, such as a sonorous choir on the radio, an airplane roaring overhead, a high-pitched flute, and even her own breathing, and then numbers them in sequence as would a sound editor planning to retrieve them for a future film production. At one point, she even tunes in to Arthuys's haunting musical score from *Paris nous appartient* playing on her radio and rerecords it as if to resurrect the past.

As Claire's isolation deepens, Marta's shady seduction of Sébastien becomes visibly evident, represented in silhouette as the two leave the theater together at dusk. Marta clearly inhabits the lunar realm of the theater; however, black actress Célia in the role of Andromaque is the literal "Black Queen," Hermione-Claire's scripted rival for the love of Pyrrhus-Sébastien. When her jealous fixation reaches a pinnacle of intensity, Claire approaches Sébastien as he sleeps and attempts to pierce his eye with a hat pin. This peculiar episode, Rivette confides, represented "a crisis, a bad patch, as everyone has" and adds that he based it on an actual incident that occurred in the life of dramatist Luigi Pirandello, whose wife Antoinetta was not only truly mad but also prone to paroxysms of jealous rage (qtd. in Aumont et al. 24).[8] Alone in her apartment, Claire not only relives the role of Racine's jealous heroine Hermione but also that of Pirandello's mad wife in contradistinction to her double Marta, who discloses to Labarthe that she assumed the name of Pirandello's mistress, Italian actress Marta-Abba, to pay tribute to the playwright. Marta's stage name that foregrounds her professional stature as a theater performer also places her within a double-tiered Pirandellian scenario, which determines her relation to Claire, with whom she must compete—not only for the love of the director Sébastien-Pyrrhus but also that of dramatist Sébastien-Pirandello. Such multilayered scenarios continue to open up in *L'amour fou* that both intrigue and frustrate the film spectator, in the same way that the Russian doll that Claire purchases to amuse herself ultimately ensnares her within a seemingly endless process of opening and reopening, ad infinitum.

Rivette confides that *L'amour fou* was ultimately "a film entirely about rehearsals/repetitions: the rehearsals of *Andromaque,* which are only repetitions of the same words and the same scenes; his [Sébastien] life with Claire that unfolds repetitively, in the same places, with the same heads, at the same bistrots where the two go twice or three times, . . ." (qtd. in Simsolo 88). Indeed, the metaphor of the mirror determines the relation of repetition and difference that exists between film formats (16 mm and 35 mm), spaces (inside and outside the theater), characters (scripted and nonscripted), directors (TV and theater/theater and film/film and TV), and stories (*Andromaque* and *L'amour fou*). Sébastien's role as director at times mirrors that of Labarthe, for he remarks to Labarthe after having seen the rushes that he finds the production to be "too directed, too manipulated" (which could refer either to his perception of his own role as a theater director or to the role played by Labarthe, who is also directing a production). Moreover, Rivette's role is likewise mirrored in that of his alter ego Sébastien, who claims in the course of the same conversation with Labarthe that he finds himself to be "too manipulating," later confiding to his assistant Michèle that he rejects the role of the "metteur en scène papa" who feeds actors their ideas (without doubt a veiled reference to Rivette's newfound willingness to allow actors the freedom to improvise during the shoot). Even the intermission that begins and ends with a dissolve of two empty chairs on the theater set divides the film into two halves that mirror each other.

Finally, the couple's separate psyches come to reduplicate each other when, in the second half of the film, the madness that invades Claire and that silences her finally overtakes Sébastien. This transmutation commences in the scene where Claire rediscovers her voice when she witnesses her own self-abnegation mirrored in his. After an evening out at a familiar bistro, Claire expresses to Sébastien her intention to leave him. Voiceless, Sébastien simply stands before her and begins to lacerate the shirt he is wearing with a razor blade. As it becomes apparent that he is out of control and means to cut all the clothes in his wardrobe into shreds, Claire, perceptibly troubled, repeats in quiet desperation,

"Stop, Sébastien, stop!" and thus assumes the therapeutic role toward him that he had previously played with her. Their shifting interaction recalls the character dynamic in Ingmar Bergman's *Persona* (1966) in which a famous stage actress starring in *Electra*, Elizabeth Vogler (Liv Ullmann), is struck dumb following a psychosomatic illness, and her caretaker, Nurse Alma (Bibi Andersson), then speaks for both of them while she cares for her companion during her convalescence.

Sébastien and Claire, formerly sequestered in separate spaces of work and play, respectively, finally reunite in the apartment where they enclose themselves for two days. Laughing hysterically, they huddle in bed and phone the theater, making up the entirely believable story that Sébastien has decided to take time off to rethink the play. Like truant children, they both don matching black bowler hats and draw larger-than-life–sized portraits of Claire on the wall above their bed. Claire impulsively decides to cut these out and then declares triumphantly, "Each has his own work to do, in his own time!" As the two cradle each other, rocking back and forth, boundaries between their psyches begin to blur. Bit by bit, Sébastien's mock-historical description of *Andromaque* is reduced to gibberish as prerecorded sounds of the surf and waves crashing around them obliterate his words. Claire's elegiac voiceover narration retrieved from audiotape supersedes his discussion of the play, when it inaugurates a montage sequence in which black intervals punctuate successive still images of the lovers' intertwined bodies framed from diverse angles. She affirms, "We're like fishes. We pass each other and meet. Then, we sleep. Early morning, late morning. We're there." In this voiceover recitation, Claire and Sébastien's struggle acquires an aural dimension by which each attempts to appropriate narrative agency, each with a measure of success. Through the voice, Claire is able to imaginatively reenvision her relation with Sébastien in a panoply of illustrative, oneiric images. Yet, her elusive narration simultaneously serves as the extension of the audio recording that in the film's opening sequence prompted Sébastien's flashback, and so, sutures the successive, descriptive images into the film's visual presentation of his memory. In either instance, regardless of which aural perspective predominates to determine a reading, the sequence remains, as Deschamps points out, "the only representation possible of emotional truth" (85–86).

Figure 4. Sébastien and Claire in *L'amour fou*
Photographer Pierre Zucca. Courtesy
of Cocinor and BFI Collections.

Dressed as deranged mountaineers, Claire and Sébastien join forces during the latter part of the episode when they proceed in the frenzied spirit of *folie à deux* to chop down a wall in the apartment with an axe. Totally improvised and unplanned, the event stands apart within a film based on rehearsals, repetitions, and reduplications. No retakes were possible, as the space and the decor were literally in tatters afterward. Ogier insists that she and Kalfon were waiting for Rivette to stop them and say, "Cut!" but he refused to intervene, as he was eager to see where the actors would go on their own (qtd. in Frappat, *Secret* 140). In a final crazed gesture, Sébastien tosses his axe directly into the television screen, which implodes, emitting a brief flash of light and puff of smoke. This visceral attempt to destroy a medium omnipresent throughout the production of the play is as inane as it is exhilarating. Rivette has suggested that Claire and Sébastien's zany antics in this sequence recall those of Barnaby Fulton (Cary Grant) and his wife Edwina (Ginger Rogers), who in Hawks's *Monkey Business* (1952) ingest a potion that induces regression and psychically reshapes them as troublesome teens (qtd. in Aumont et al. 22). In the lull that follows the exhilaration of autodestructive acts, Sébastien and Claire come together in an exhausted embrace on the balcony above Rue de Turbigo. This fated moment on top of the world echoes that of émigré gangster Tony Camonte and his sibling moll Cesca, who in the final stand-off scene in Hawks's *Scarface* (1932) similarly reunite in an incestuous embrace, throwing themselves into a last-ditch effort to fend off the police force that closes in around their sequestered apartment, as Cesca proclaims, "You're me and I'm you, and it's always been that way."

Face to face with her lover, Claire at last understands that they have "played too much" and that she no longer wishes to see Sébastien. He phones the theater to schedule a rehearsal and subsequently returns to work, where the television crew rejoins him. *Andromaque* is soon ready to be performed in full. A slow pan follows Sébastien as he paces from room to room through an apartment in shambles. The phone rings, and it is Françoise at the other end who is calling to let him know that Claire has left him. As Claire waits at the station for her train to depart, the costumed actors at the theater touch up their makeup and anxiously await Sébastien's arrival. Claire confides to Françoise, "I feel that I've just woken up." With this final admission, Claire's eyes metaphorically open, as she retrospectively reenvisions the film's story from within her perspective as her daydream. At that very moment, Sébastien's eyes metaphorically shut, as his recollection of the past initiated by her audio recording has just commenced back at the flat, reframing the film's narrative from within his perspective as a flashback. In situating the originating moment of Sébastien's flashback at the film's opening rather than at its end, Rivette invites the spectator to fill in this temporal gap, and in so doing exposes the film's duplicitous narrative logic, which implodes, at last, to offer not a conclusive ending, but rather an interrogation of personal identity that occurs when memories and daydreams are cut loose and dispersed. *L'amour fou* ultimately calls for the murder of conventional vision and, in this way, aligns itself with Breton's surrealist poetics of love, expressed in his own *ars poetica*: "Reciprocal love, such as I envisage it, is a system of mirrors which reflects for me, under the thousand angles that the unknown can take for me, the faithful image of the one I love, always more surprising in her divining of my own desire and more gilded with life" (93). A final image of the vacant, white stage seems to wipe away Sébastien and Claire's shared past and uncertain future, circling back to the film's opening, where the impatient audience, like the fussy, crying child recorded in synch, awaits the recommencement of the play's performance. Rivette wryly concedes, "It is a film that won't stop ending. That's why it lasts so long." (qtd. in Aumont et al. 26)

| | |

Lasting twelve hours and forty minutes, *Out 1: Noli me tangere* (Out 1: Touch Me Not; 1970) premiered on September 9–10, 1971, at the Maison de la Culture in Le Havre. Attended by a small group of roughly three hundred spectators who had completed the trek from Paris to the provinces, this exceptional weekend event resembled a religious pilgrimage, rather than a conventional screening experience. Characterized by Martin Even, a reviewer for *Le Monde,* as a "Voyage Beyond Cinema," it would be the film's only public projection of the 16 mm unprocessed color work print (13). There have been quite a few screenings of the finished print since then, the first of which was at the Rotterdam Film Festival in February 1989.[9] More recently and for the first time in the United States, the restored, 750-minute version of *Out 1: Noli me tangere* was screened in its entirety at a complete Rivette retrospective at the Museum of the Moving Image in New York in December 2006. At the museum's *Encore* presentation that I attended, the film was shown to an appreciative, sold-out audience over a two-day weekend in eight distinctive episodes, with brief breaks between each one. The obvious care that the museum staff took in their programming of the event reflected their concern to remain true to Rivette's initial conception of the film that was to have been broadcast on French national television as an eight-part serial. Sadly, the film was not shown on television at the time it was made because the ORTF (Office de Radiodiffusion-Télévision Française) refused to purchase it. *Out 1: Noli me tangere* was finally shown as a serial on the Paris Première cable channel in the early 1990s after it had been restored.

Rivette's interest in serial form is reflected in his choice of the film's title, which is inspired by an ancient tableau by Giotto entitled *The Resurrection* (*Noli me tangere,* 1303–1306); the tableau that depicts the resurrected Christ between parallel worlds of the living and the dead forms one part in a cycle of twenty-three scenes from the Life of Christ displayed in

Padua's Scrovegni Chapel. While Giotto's fresco cycle provides a touchstone for the film's structure, the initial impetus for Rivette's experiments with seriality, as Jean-André Fieschi has suggested, may have come from avant-garde composer Pierre Boulez, whose system of "total serialization" in *Structures* for two pianos (book one: 1951–1952; book two: 1961) had revolutionized the sound world (875). In 1964, Rivette conducted an interview with Boulez to explore the possible parallels between the composer's method of "guided chance" and that of the metteur en scène, who similarly wishes to reconcile chance and composition in the invention of "a kind of labyrinth," or maze, "with a number of paths" ("Alea" 31, 29). In "'Sonate, que me veux-tu?'" (1960), Boulez had elaborated at length on the idea of the maze in the modern work of art, characterizing it as "certainly one of the most considerable advances in Western thought, . . ." while opposing it to the classical conception of the work as "*one*, a single object of contemplation or delectation, which the listener finds in front of him and in relation to which he takes up his position" (145). In the subsequent *Cahiers* interview with Rivette, Boulez confessed that he saw the evolution of film form as comparable with that of contemporary music, which had moved beyond a closed Copernican conception of the universe to "a universe of relative forms" where it was perceived to be in "'permanent revolution'" (24, 26). In contradistinction to Western classical music that is opposed to active participation, Boulez viewed aleatory music as a multiple phenomenon, which permits its listener to "understand a work only by passing through it and following its course with total, active, constructive attention; . . ." ("Where Are We" 462). Indeed, Boulez's creation of a labyrinthine network of different versions of works may have provided Rivette with the inspiration to reedit *Out 1: Noli me tangere* to create *Out 1: Spectre* (1971; released 1974), a substantially different work that he describes as "a different film having its own logic; closer to a jigsaw or crossword puzzle than was the other, playing less on affectivity, more on rhymes and contrasts, ruptures and connections, caesurae and censorship" (qtd. in Baby 13). Boulez's radical enterprise of total serialism no doubt appealed to Rivette, whose films *Noli me tangere* and *Spectre* provide a distinctive alternative to classical continuity style in much the same manner that Boulez's complex, serialist compositions represent an alternative to classical tonality.

The prologue of Honoré de Balzac's suite of three novellas, *Histoire des treize* (The Thirteen; 1833–1835), in which the myth of the nineteenth-century criminal conspiracy takes shape, provides a point of departure for the film's serial structure comprised of thirteen main characters. Balzac describes *The Thirteen* in his prologue: "Criminals they doubtless were, yet none the less were they all remarkable for some one of the virtues which go to the making of great men, and their numbers were filled up only from among picked recruits. Finally, that nothing should be lacking to complete the dark, mysterious romance of their history, nobody to this day knows who they were" (11). While Balzac's prologue provided Rivette with the historical backcloth and formal parameters for his almost thirteen-hour film, the novelist's own use of serial form may have also served as a source of inspiration. Balzac's celebrated novel, *Le père goriot,* first appeared in serial form in 1834, and little more than a decade later, Balzac articulated his ambitious plan for a collection of 144 novels that together were to comprise *La comédie humaine*. Not considered a series, per se, *La comédie humaine* may, nonetheless, have provided the impetus for *Noli me tangere* in its combination of multitudes of diverse characters drawn from every stratum of society and in its attempt to reflect the dramatic shift in cultural values in the wake of the French Revolution. More than a century later, *Noli me tangere* chronicles Paris in April 1970, two years after the cultural revolution of May '68. Indeed, Rivette subsequently explained that he had hoped the audience would interpret the film as a post–May '68 reunion of sorts where it would be evident that "the group of thirteen individuals had probably met and talked for some time until May 1968 when everything changed and they probably disbanded" (Rosenbaum, Sedofsky, and Adair 22). In *Noli me tangere,* Rivette relinquishes Balzac's authorial autonomy, however, which is evident in the novelist's ability to draw a realistic psychological portrait of those characters who inhabit the city. Instead, Rivette introduces the element of chance into his film, allowing each actor to invent the social context for his/her own character and, while filming, develop this character as he/she wished. In addition, the actors were kept in the dark during the shoot as to what the others were doing. In inflicting such an unorthodox method on his actors, Rivette follows the precepts of Boulez, who had insisted that the aleatory work, like a railway station, must keep "a certain number of passageways open by means of precise dispositions in which chance represents the 'points,' which can be switched at the last moment" ("Sonate" 146). Like a pointsman in the midst of a mazelike assemblage, Rivette allowed "chance" meetings to proceed between characters, often at unanticipated moments, which would thereby produce unexpected outcomes. In this manner, the film, like the aleatory work, permitted the element of surprise.

An exemplary illustration of Boulez's method of "guided chance," the film's labyrinthine evolution ultimately would present all its participants—the actor, the director, and the spectator alike—with different pathways to follow. *Noli me tangere* opens with the dual stories of rival theater troupes (Michèle Moretti in the role of Lili, who is performing Aeschylus's *Seven Against Thebes* with her collective, and Michael Lonsdale as the director Thomas, who is rehearsing Aeschylus's *Prometheus Bound*). Aeschylus's plays staged in the film originally required a chorus: the Chorus of Oceanides orchestrates the action of *Prometheus Bound,* as the Chorus of the Theban Women reflects the dramatic action in *Seven Against Thebes*. In classical Greek dramaturgy, members of the chorus encircle the principal characters of the drama; their ritual recitations build gradually to a feverish, bacchic frenzy, where movement and gesture become integral to the drama (Matheson 143–55). The sonority of Aeschylean poetry, which the chorus accentuates in a succession of long and short intonations, is at least as important as the words themselves. French playwright Paul Claudel, who translated Aeschylus's *Oresteia,* compared the Aeschylean chorus with a "living harp" (410). In *Noli me tangere,* however, filmed rehearsals present delicate slivers of Aeschylus's plays in piecemeal. In this manner, Rivette strips Aeschylean verse of its dramatic signification and divests the actors' gestures and movements of significance. What remains in the film are empty signs—words, gestures, movements—removed from their Aeschylean context, that stand in the present tense of the film as the signs of residual theatricality, a theatrical remainder with meaning factored out.

It is through Aeschylus that Rivette rejoins dramaturge Antonin Artaud, who was an adaptor of the Greek dramatists. Artaud prefaces his adaptation of Seneca's Thyestes, claiming, "All the Great Myths of the Past dissimulate pure forces" and affirms that he "wants to attempt, by means of an adaptation of a Mythic tragedy, to express their natural forces

Figure 5. Lili and her collective in *Out 1: Noli me tangere.* Photographer Pierre Zucca. Courtesy of Cocinor and BFI Collections.

on the stage and to deliver the theatre to its true goal and calling" (qtd. in Sellin 36). Artaud used Greek drama to restore to the theater its ritual dimension and so liberate it from its servitude to psychology. Pointing to the connection between Artaud and Rivette, Lauren Sedofsky observes: "Like Artaud, Rivette has created a 'nontheological space' (Derrida), which admits the tyranny of neither text nor auteur. It is a space in which the actor's grammar of gesture and voice may play creatively without impediment" (Rosenbaum, Sedofsky, and Adair 19). Artaudian theatricality informs the first three hours or so of *Noli me tangere,* in which Rivette moves back and forth between long rehearsal sequences, while the spectator, like the members of each troupe, experiences the sonority and incantatory qualities of language, and thus must question the status of the meaningful, spoken word. The filmed rehearsals of Aeschylus accomplish a fusion of sound and sense, of theatrical and profilmic space, and thus may be understood, in Boulez's terms, as "no more and no less than an attempt to organize delirium" ("Sound, Word, Synthesis" 182).

The protracted temporal dimension of the thirteen-hour version is associated from the outset with its intensive focus on theater. This "feeling of time" created in the first three hours in which "almost nothing happens," Rivette affirms, distinguishes the experience of *Noli me tangere* from that of *Spectre,* which was treated "much more as a fiction about certain characters" (qtd. in Rosenbaum, Sedofsky, and Adair 22). To condense time, Rivette relinquishes episodic form in *Spectre.* Thus, black-and-white outtakes do not introduce the successive episodes, as in *Noli me tangere,* but instead are scattered throughout the four-hour version. Moreover, Rivette adds sound to black-and-white stills in *Spectre,* so that they generate what he describes as a "meaningless frequency," as though transmitted by a machine, sometimes in relation to what has already been seen or what will be seen, "and sometimes with no relation at all" (qtd. in Rosenbaum, Sedofsky, and Adair 23). Assailing the audience with seemingly random images and automated sounds, Rivette sought to "interrupt[s] the general dream of the characters in *Spectre*" (qtd. in Hughes). Rivette does retain the long version's fictional core, however, to produce a shorter film, which he describes as "much tighter" and "much more compelling" than he had initially anticipated (qtd. in Eisenschitz, Fieschi, and Gregorio 47).

In *Spectre,* it is the characters Colin (Jean-Pierre Léaud) and Frédérique (Juliet Berto) and their escalating involvement with the machinations of the Thirteen that take precedence from the outset. Colin makes his initial appearance in both versions careening through sidewalk cafés, while attempting to pass himself off as a deaf-mute. The modulations of his harmonica replace words, as he moves from table to table passing out greeting cards marked "Message of Destiny" to solicit donations from the clientele. Colin becomes implicated in the intrigues of the Thirteen almost immediately when a cryptic message is passed to him in a café by Marie (Hermine Karagheuz), a member of Lili's collective. To crack the code of the conspiratorial web at work around him, he rummages through his collection of novels and falls upon *The Thirteen*. He scrawls the number "13" on the blackboard alongside the author's name, "Balzac." Jean-Pierre Léaud/Colin's position as a student at the blackboard and his obsessive engagement with Balzac recall the actor's earlier role as the preoccupied adolescent Antoine Doinel, who in Truffaut's *Les quatre cent coups* (The Four Hundred Blows) sets his bedroom on fire with a candle-lit shrine to Balzac. The character's name "Colin" opens up yet another field of references, invoking Balzac's mutable character Jacques Collin (a.k.a. Vautrin, Trompe-la-Mort, Abbé Carlos Herrera) who in *Splendeurs et misères des courtisanes* is also a thief, of sorts. While filching from Balzac to create his own character and story, Colin often uses words to achieve a "dislocation" of reality—rather than the illusion of reality constructed in the classic readerly nineteenth-century novel (Ionesco 26). The spectator is forced to use the film text as the character Colin uses Balzac—as a pretext for the purposes of discovery.

As the mystery deepens, Colin and Frédérique both find their way to the elusive Pauline-Émilie's (Bulle Ogier) hippie boutique. Posing as a journalist from *Paris Jour*, Colin first gains access to the out-of-the-way boutique, *L'angle du hasard* (The Crossroads of Chance), which serves as a front for an underground newspaper that could be allied with the Thirteen. He suspects as much and begins to frequent the boutique, where he falls under the spell of the charismatic Pauline-Émilie. At the point where Colin's inquiry virtually derails because of the exigencies of courtship, Frédérique takes up the baton. She discovers the Thirteen, their plans for a new city, and their cover provided by the Crossroads of Chance from personal correspondence filched from the desk of an unsuspecting chess player, Étienne (Jacques Doniol-Valcroze), whom she has playfully hoodwinked. When her subsequent attempts to blackmail this chess player and the lawyer Lucie (Françoise Fabian) using the letters fail, she makes her way to the Crossroads of Chance where, disguised as a dapper young hustler, she attempts to shake down Pauline-Émilie and later succeeds, exchanging the stolen letters for cash.

Whereas the fictional center remains very similar in the short and long versions, the final hours of *Noli me tangere* are largely given over to long sequences, which place on display the disintegration and, in certain instances, the demise of a character, as in the case of Frédérique, who in the long version is gunned down in the street.[10] A dreamlike logic would seem to determine the conclusion of the thirteen-hour version when the locus of action inexplicably shifts from the city to the beach. Like sleepwalkers, the Paris denizens migrate in succession, one after the next, to the haunted seaside villa of Aubade, as if in search of a "dawn serenade" (the translation of "aubade"), a sanctuary in the wake of an apocalyptic misadventure.[11] Perhaps the most disquieting moment on the beach occurs when Thomas and several members of his troupe retreat to the shoreline where they commence a chant, the residue of a theatrical rehearsal gone awry. Dazed, Thomas collapses, crying at first but then laughing, until he at last falls silent. The prominence of the beach in the closing moments of *Noli me tangere* recalls its import within the final iconic shot of Antoine Doinel/Léaud in *Les quatre cents coups,* where, as Fiona Handyside points out, the seascape marks the "very final edge of the nation" and so intensifies the characters' "aimlessness and lack of direction" (148).

Left behind in the deserted industrial wasteland of Paris, Colin must reconcile himself to the apparent dissolution of the Thirteen and his failed romance with Pauline-Émilie. In a lengthy improvised sequence in *Noli me tangere,* the camera records Colin as he confides his woes to the writer Sarah (Bernadette Lafont), who before she returns to Aubade gives him a magic charm, an Eiffel Tower key chain, to console him. Colin slowly walks away, murmuring, "Pauline, Pauline . . ." and later tries to conjure up her love, flicking the charm so that it swings around above his hand, as he counts to see whether it rotates thirteen times. When this fails, he drops the trinket and directly addresses the camera, muttering, "It didn't work." In *Spectre,* the decontextualized close-up of Colin flicking the Eiffel Tower trinket is all that remains. It is repositioned at the close of the four-hour film where it might be understood as a wry allusion to the inadequacy of utopian political groups and their mantras to inspire revolution. Yet such an allegorical interpretation could be seen to offer a seductively patent conclusion. The final image is designed to tempt the spectator who, like Colin, may feel compelled to solve this textual "jigsaw or crossword puzzle," for as Morrey and Smith have observed in their discussion of games and play in Rivette's films, "*Spectre* plays with the audience, . . . in the sense that one plays with a toy, or a cat with a mouse. Authorial control and superiority is established and constant" (128). Given this, we might revisit the final emblematic image of *Spectre* and read it, alternatively, as a reflexive authorial commentary on the inability of the reedited four-hour version to reproduce the more profound moral stance of *Noli me tangere,* a film that in its respect for durations rejoins the tradition of realism found in the cinema of Renoir and Rouch insofar as it refuses to impose meaning but instead allows for the element of chance.

An "orderly anarchist" in the tradition of Boulez, Rivette desires to confront the audience and transport it from its habitual notion of a film where characters and events are readily comprehensible and actions are governed by a deterministic causality (Jameux 270). Taken together, *Noli me tangere* and *Spectre* contribute equally to the kind of cinema Rivette had called for in the aftermath of May '68, a cinema that would provide "at least an experience, something which makes the film transform the viewer, who has undergone something through the film, who is no longer the same after having seen the film" (qtd. in Aumont et al. 37). For Rivette, this experience is at times incantatory and violent, associated with Artaudian theatrical aesthetics and Greek dramaturgy. At other times, this experience is silent and dreamlike, an effect accentuated by uncanny duplications and multiplications (doubled scenes, doubled theater and theater/film directors, doubled theatrical spaces and scripts) that are endlessly mirrored in (and by) *Spectre*.[12] In "permanent revolution," the serial films *Noli me tangere* and *Spectre* draw the audience into their imaginative sphere, while providing the final trace of a transitional decade.

### Sounding Out the Operatic: *Les filles du feu* (*Duelle* and *Noroît*), *Merry-Go-Round*, and *Le Pont du Nord*

Rivette reconceptualized the notion of the film serial in the mid-1970s, when he conceived of *Les filles du feu* (Girls of Fire), a cycle of four films. He borrowed his film tetralogy's title from Gérard de Nerval's publication *Les filles du feu* in which the celebrated poem *El Desdichado* (The Disinherited) appeared in 1854. That Rivette borrows his title from this nineteenth-century poet is highly significant, as Nervalian verse resonates with the musicality of magic formulas, their power of suggestion surpassing their intelligible content. The everyday world and memory are transfigured through dream in Nerval; the poet's memory is thus able to move beyond temporal boundaries, and his individual past merges with that of all humanity to proclaim a mystical future. Such preoccupations clearly provide the impetus for the cycle of films whose official title submitted to C.N.C. (Centre national de la cinématographie), *Scènes de la vie parallèle* (Scenes from a Parallel Life), reflects Rivette's intent to look beyond "those things linked, either closely or distantly, to what was going on in France at the time" (qtd. in Daney and Narboni 327: 13). In recasting the chimerical Nervalian dreamscape in *Les filles du feu,* Rivette turns his glance from the conservative backlash of the 1970s, which had been put into place with the election of Giscard d'Estaing, whose politics provided the French citizenry with a modern and moderate alternative to Gaullism. Rather than focusing on contemporary history, Rivette constructs a mythological universe in *Les filles du feu,* a musical landscape inhabited by ghosts and goddesses.

Clearly, the cycle represents the culmination of Rivette's dream of a cinema showing continuous programs, which was initiated in *Out 1: Noli me tangere,* and in some sense can be viewed as a supplement to the unfinished serial, *Out* 1, 2, 3 . . . Rivette confirms that each of the four films in the cycle was to have represented a different genre—a love story, a film of the fantastic, a western, a musical comedy—and that certain characters were to appear from film to film in different guises (Daney and Narboni 323–24: 48). Unfortunately, the four films that Rivette envisioned were never completed; however, he did finish filming the fantastic thriller *Duelle* (Duel; 1976) and *Noroît* (Northwest Wind; 1976), which were to serve as the second and third parts, respectively, of the four-part film series. *Duelle* is a fantastic tale in which phantom goddesses move freely through Paris locales that are transformed into magical spaces—from modern hotel to metro station, from an aquarium to a dance studio, from a deserted park at dawn to a spectacular nightclub. Sun and moon goddesses Viva (Bulle Ogier) and Leni (Juliet Berto), respectively, launch an investigation into the whereabouts of a missing Lord Christie, and their quest results in double murders and mysterious duels. Though originally conceptualized as a western, *Noroît* returns to an uncanny terrain of medieval myth and island piracy where Celtic goddess of the sun Giulia (Bernadette Lafont) and goddess of the moon Morag (Géraldine Chaplin) enter into treacherous intrigues that end in a macabre duel to the death.

The fourth and final film of the cycle never went into production. Eduardo de Gregorio, the co-scenarist of *Duelle* and *Noroît,* recalls it as a comedy set in a palace featuring Anna Karina, the Italian Walter Chiari, and Jean Marais in the role of a Catholic cardinal (qtd. in Frappat, *Secret* 152). The film that was to have formed the first part of the cycle, *Marie et Julien* (Marie and Julien; 1975), remained unfinished. Rivette had only shot several scenes of it before he was forced to abandon the set and the shoot altogether, succumbing to a state of nervous exhaustion. The film scripted by Gregorio, Marilù Parolini, and Claire Denis was to have featured Albert Finney in the role of a solitary man who is haunted by the memory of a woman whose identical double, played by Leslie Caron, seduces him. The recent release of *Histoire de Marie et Julien* (The Story of Marie and Julien; 2003) is a retooling of this old project from the 1970s.

In a 1981 interview with critics Serge Daney and Jean Narboni, Rivette revealed that he conceived of uniting his cycle of films through a "progression of complication linked to the intervention of music on action" (qtd. in *Cahiers* 323–24: 48). Rivette has never elaborated on the precise type of musical rapport he envisioned, yet he insisted that "this experience of real sound and improvised music is something I would have liked to pursue; we commenced this practice with a certain reticence in *Duelle* and *Noroît*; we will go further in the fourth" (qtd. in Daney and Narboni 327: 18). Although *Merry-Go-Round* (1977–1978; release 1983) is not considered part of the unfinished tetralogy, the film takes shape through its relationship to the music of Barre Phillips and John Surman. The film relies on musicians' improvisation, as do *Duelle* and *Noroît*, yet in *Merry-Go-Round* the musicians' recital occurs in a different time and space (and thus in different shots) from the time and space of the actors' performance, thereby creating a unique perceptual experience unlike that of the other two films. While this formal feature sets it apart from those in the cycle, *Merry-Go-Round* is informed by the genre conventions that shaped Rivette's overall conception of the tetralogy. Its story primarily relies on the codes of the detective film and the road movie. The film opens as two young drifters, Léo (Maria Schneider) and Ben (Joe Dallessandro), turn up at Charles de Gaulle airport to await the arrival of a third party known to both of them, Élisabeth (Danièle Gégauff), who is not only Léo's sister but also Ben's girlfriend. They exchange notes and discover that Élisabeth has arranged a rendezvous with both of them, and so are concerned when she fails to appear. The two commence the search for the missing Élisabeth, which takes the form of a rambling odyssey through the environs of Paris. *Merry-Go-Round* closes, as do the other two films in the cycle, with a duel that occurs within a magnetic field. In each of the three films, the improvisation of musicians—Jean Wiener on piano in *Duelle,* the Cohen-Solal brothers on drums and flute in *Noroît,* and Barre Phillips and John Surman on bass and clarinet in *Merry-Go-Round*—complement the actors' improvisational style. A fraught attempt to reinvent multiple genres within an experimental form, *Merry-Go-Round* was not released until 1983 and received sparse attention from critics. The film's innovative use of improvised music, however, provided the impetus for Rivette's subsequent work in such landmark films as *Le Pont du Nord* (1982).

| | |

Throughout the decade of the 1970s, Rivette is concerned to accord a certain import to music in the production of meaning and, in this way, he moves his art into the realm of operatic dramaturgy. Of the films that comprise the cycle, *Noroît* is perhaps the most straightforwardly operatic, the most indebted to opera in its conception. *Noroît* represents Rivette's attempt to bring together the three arts—music, dance, and poetry—and in this respect the film bears resemblance to the composite work of art, the *Gesamtkunstwerk,* which in Richard Wagner's terms becomes "the mutual compact of the egoism of the three related arts" (5). Rivette achieves an effective interplay between the three arts in his film; yet music does not underscore the words in the manner of Wagnerian opera but follows a parallel path, creating an independent adjacent atmosphere that makes its own comment on the actions. Film music has more often followed the Wagnerian concept, underscoring the script to create atmosphere and build emotional climaxes (Kernodle 17). Rather than using music to establish a linear, oriented dramatic time, Rivette uses music in *Noroît* to instate the predominance of lyrical time—that of an impressionist opera. Rivette uses music to frustrate meaning, creating a film that slips from the reality principle associated with the temporal progression of narrative events into the pleasure principle elicited through music.

It is through opera—specifically, Claude Debussy's impressionist work *Pelléas et Mélisande*—that Rivette remembers his friend and mentor Jean Cocteau. In 1962 poet and cinéaste Cocteau designed the decor and costumes for the Marseille production of *Pelléas,* which went on to Metz and Strasbourg, and then in 1963 replaced the centenary production at the Opéra-Comique (Nichols 162). Cocteau's designs were modeled on the original Jusseaume and Ronsin designs produced for the opera's première performance in 1902. Shortly before his death in 1963, Cocteau disclosed plans for a filmed version of Debussy's opera that was, unfortunately, never produced (Touzot 403). During this time, Rivette enjoyed a particularly close, even filial, relationship with Cocteau. Indeed, Rivette disclosed in a personal interview in 1999 that Cocteau was "the guilty one" whose concern and camaraderie brought him to a career in filmmaking. In this context, we may be tempted to characterize Rivette's film as the posthumous completion of Cocteau's final project—the opera-film of *Pelléas et Mélisande*. At the least, *Noroît* discloses the legacy of a theatrical and operatic style passed on to Rivette from Cocteau and, ultimately, from Maeterlinck and Debussy.

The story of *Noroît* is not based solely on the opera *Pelléas et Mélisande*. The film also announces itself as an adaptation of Elizabethan dramatist Cyril Tourneur's play, *The Revenger's Tragedy* (1607), and as such, must be considered as a central work within any discussion of theatricality in the films of Rivette.[13] Black title screens divide the film into five acts, underscoring its source in Tourneur's play. Rivette's choice of Tourneur is highly significant, for it is through this revenge tragedy that Rivette pays tribute to Artaud. *The Revenger's Tragedy* was among the plays Artaud most admired, and he had specifically planned a production of it at Théâtre Alfred Jarry in the 1927–1928 season. Rivette rejoins Artaud through Tourneur, whose themes of revenge and betrayal are especially well suited to his engagement with conspiracy narrative and with theatrical or filmic fictions as forms of conspiracy. From this perspective, the spectator is invited to read *Noroît* as the realization of both Cocteau's and Artaud's unfinished film and theater productions, respectively. While the story of *Noroît* is prismatic, as it is informed by the multiple intertextual sources, it does conform to classical Aristotelian form when viewed from a singular perspective of theatrical style. Beyond its contribution of character motivation, decor, and script, *The Revenger's Tragedy* provides *Noroît* with an Aristotelian dramatic form, thus determining a beginning, a climax, and a conclusion. Although the film adheres to Aristotelian tripartite form, it is not driven by the dynamics of Aristotelian dramaturgy found in Tourneur's play. Rather than the arrow of teleology of the Aristotelian drama, in *Noroît* we have a field of intertextual forces where the intersection of theater and opera styles disturbs stable signification, leaving moments of incoherence in the construction of meaning. The synopsis of the film that follows will show the manner in which the film story adheres to the singular stylistic register of Tourneur's play, focusing on those moments where film and play overlap.

The film begins on a deserted beach set on "A small island in the Atlantic, off the coast of a larger one." Like a compass, the film's title *Noroît,* which translates *Northwest Wind,* points to the film's geographical coordinates vis-à-vis the central locale of Paris. Sounds of the ocean surf blend with those of a woman's voice mourning the death of her brother Shane (a respectful nod to George Steven's 1953 western, *Shane*). In this opening scene, we first meet Morag (Géraldine Chaplin), who is lying prostrate on the beach, bent over Shane's body. Framed against an unforgiving horizon, a disconsolate Morag declares her desire for revenge and then proceeds to recite a passage from the opening of Tourneur's play that mirrors the revenge theme proclaimed in her opening monologue: "O thou goddess of the palace, mistress of mistresses/to whom the costly-perfum'd people pray" (I.iii, lines 6–7). As she speaks these lines, she assumes the theatrical role of the Revenger Vindice, who at this point in the play dons a disguise that will enable him to seek revenge in secret for his mistress' death. Like Vindice, Morag will engage in complex schemes of revenge to avenge Shane's murder.

Tourneur's play motivates Morag's movements in *Noroît*. Like Vindice, Morag seeks revenge, and so attempts to infiltrate the court presided over by Giulia (Bernadette Lafont), the female counterpart to Tourneur's philandering Duke. Giulia not only governs the court but the coastline as well. Along with her lieutenant Arno (Anne-Marie Reynaud), she leads her band of pirates who carry on occasional looting and raids. Thus, Giulia understands the potential for disloyalty and fears imminent betrayal from her lovers Ludovico (Larrio Ekson) and Jacob (Humbert Balsan), who are trying to discover where her treasure is hidden. She confesses this fear to her confidante at court Erika (Kika Markham), who later will betray Giulia and serve as Morag's accomplice. Facilitating Morag's efforts to infiltrate the court, Erika encourages Giulia to hire a bodyguard and suggests Morag. Morag and Erika then conspire, attempting to sabotage a pirate attack led by Giulia, which succeeds in spite of their efforts. Consequently, they seek their own bizarre brand of revenge, secretly staging rehearsals for a performance of the play, *The Revenger's Tragedy*. Morag and Erika's scheming activities culminate in an apocalyptic duel between Morag and Giulia on the ramparts.

If Tourneur's revenge drama motivates Morag's actions, the cinema, specifically Fritz Lang's *Moonfleet* (1955), motivates Giulia's and provides the impetus behind the pirate subplot. The film's opening images of the Dorsetshire seacoast mirror those of *Noroît*. Waves crashing over austere cliffs greet an orphaned boy who has arrived in Moonfleet in search of his mother's lost love Jeremy Fox (Stewart Granger), a jaded roué who has since become the leader of a local smuggling ring. The dark world of intrigues that Fox inhabits provides the backdrop for the construction of Giulia's character, a ruler who, like Fox, oversees smugglers' stratagems and colludes in schemes of high seas piracy. While Giulia's militant role and the associated images of swashbuckling piracy are largely derived from those of *Moonfleet,* Lang's depiction of smugglers as a grizzly group of hardened thugs diverges from Rivette's portrayal of the pirates, who in *Noroît* more closely resemble trapeze artists or acrobats, moving with grace and agility, swinging and spinning from hanging ropes that could be mistaken for circus slacklines. The Cohen-Solal brothers' dissonant rhythms enhance the macabre carnivalesque ambiance. In *Noroît,* as Morrey and Smith observe, "[t]he state of being a pirate is a kind of dance . . ." (161). In *Moonfleet,* piracy represents the state of the soul, the final temptation to abandon all scruples for easy rewards. At the core of pirate lore is the discovery of lost treasure. In each film, this discovery precipitates a turning point: in *Moonfleet,* the retrieval of the missing diamond of local legend affords Fox a final moment of moral redemption that ends in his death alone, adrift on a quiet sea, whereas in *Noroît,* the discovery of Giulia's treasure is the prelude to a final dancelike duel to the death between the deities.

This decisive duel between Giulia and Morag marks the end of a murderous masque on the ramparts, which is most obviously an adaptation of the corresponding scene from *The Revenger's Tragedy*. In the masque sequence that includes spectacle, instrumental music, and dance, Rivette clearly transposes Tourneur's drama, creating a far more Artaudian scene. Yet at the same time, the mise-en-scène of the masque draws on Celtic symbolism. Maurice Maeterlinck, author of the play *Pelléas et Mélisande,* had been inspired by Celtic legend. The masque is infused with Celtic imagery and myth, opening with an image of black clouds passing over a full moon, an image demarcating the close of the forty-day festival period during which goddesses can appear on earth and converse with mortals. The magical temporal zone of the masque is based on the mythic Celtic battle Samhain, which Miranda Green has described as "a liminal, dangerous occasion when time and space are suspended, and the barriers between the supernatural and earthly worlds are temporarily dissolved" (44). Thus, the final duel sequence of *Noroît* does not simply demarcate narrative closure within the register of theatrical style, for the rules governing cinematic time and space are suspended, as montage series are periodically replicated and later replayed as red or black-and-white duplications. The uncanny, mirroring effect produced by the repetition of images creates the highly fantastic dimension of the masque, which entails the collapse of boundaries between supernatural and earthly worlds. Shifting into their respective roles as Celtic goddesses of sun and moon, Giulia and Morag remain poised throughout the masque between two worlds—that of humans and that of the spirits.

Maeterlinck's fascination with Celtic myth is evident in the composition and appearance of characters in *Pelléas et Mélisande*. Opera historian Richard Langham Smith observes that Celtic imagery had

Figure 6. The final duel between Giulia and Morag in *Noroît*.

provided the inspiration for Maeterlinck's character Mélisande, adding that even the spelling of the other characters' names—Yniold, Arkël, and Golaud—added Celtic color (4–5, 15). According to Smith, Maeterlinck had been especially taken by the visual art of second-generation pre-Raphaelites Sir Edward Burne-Jones (1833–1898) and Walter Crane (1845–1915), drawing this comparison: "The haunting figures of Burne-Jones's pallid damsels, their dilated eyes on the verge of tears, distilling the world's sorrow, were clearly implicated in the genesis of Mélisande" (4). Rivette's representation of Morag draws heavily on Maeterlinck's pre-Raphaelite figure Mélisande. Both the mise-en-scène of *Noroît*'s opening sequence and composition of the character Morag bear striking similarity to the corresponding scene from *Pelléas et Mélisande*. As the opera opens, we meet Golaud, prince of Allemonde, who hears sobbing and turns to discover the mysterious Mélisande crying by the water's edge. Mélisande's origins remain unknown both to herself as well as to the spectator; like Morag's inexplicable appearance on the shoreline, both characters are enigmas by design. Mélisande's musical motif is soft, calm, and slightly sad, as is the melancholy flute refrain that defines Morag in this scene. On the surface, the capacity of Rivette's characters to seek revenge and persist in diabolical schemes places them closer to those of Tourneur and Lang; however, their underlying power resides in their capacity to convey the atmosphere of dreamlike incertitude that pervades Debussy's opera.

It seems useful briefly to review the plot of *Pelléas* before examining the similarities between it and Rivette's film. The opera opens with Golaud's discovery of Mélisande weeping. Unable to discover who she is or where she is from, Golaud convinces her to follow him. Sometime after her marriage to Golaud, Mélisande seeks relief from the gloomy, dark environs of the castle and retreats to its seaward side in search of light. She is joined there by Pelléas, Golaud's younger half-brother. Pelléas later brings Mélisande to the well where he comes to escape the midday heat. Mélisande begins to play with Golaud's wedding ring, throwing it into the air, but suddenly, the ring falls into the well and is lost. Terrified of Golaud's wrath, Mélisande lies to him, telling him that her ring fell off in a grotto by the sea. Pelléas accompanies her to the sea cove, where they pretend to search for the ring, which, of course, is lost forever. We later find Mélisande seated at the tower window of the castle, singing a simple lament. Pelléas passes beneath her window and becomes enmeshed in her hair. Golaud sees them flirting and becomes jealous. He wanders through the castle's cavernous vaults, encouraging Pelléas to smell the stench of death from the underground lake. Anguished, Pelléas makes plans to leave the castle forever, yet before his departure, he decides to meet Mélisande for a final rendezvous at the well. Hidden in the forest, Golaud sees them together and strikes Pelléas down by the well's edge. Later, we find Mélisande, who lies dying. Golaud questions her, but she dies quietly, a tranquil, mysterious creature.

The decor of *Noroît* is unmistakably indebted to Cocteau's decor from the centenary production of *Pelléas et Mélisande* that gives expression to the poet's earnest wish to re-create the original Jusseaume/Ronsin designs. Indeed, *Noroît* represents the culmination of a chain of homage, for it is with this film that Rivette pays homage to Cocteau's *Pelléas,* who, in turn, pays tribute to Debussy's production. From the film's scenes of dark forest, grotto, garden, and coast to the interiors of the castle, resemblances to those of Debussy's opera are striking.

While the dreamlike atmosphere of Debussy's opera was captured by the dark and light elements of its mise-en-scène, shadow and light define two poles of dramatic action in *Noroît* as well. In both film and opera, landscape elements such as the sun and the moon presage the forces of destiny. The moonlit grotto is a magic landscape in both film and opera, which determines the fate of the characters. Like Pelléas and Mélisande in search of Golaud's lost ring, Elisa and Ludovico approach the sea cave in search of Giulia's lost treasure. Elisa's approach to the grotto seems to draw on Pelléas's description of the cave's entrance: "Let's wait for the moonlight to break through that big cloud; it will illuminate the entire grotto and then, we can enter without danger. There are treacherous spots, and the path is very narrow, between two deep lakes" (II, iii, line 179). The film's mise-en-scène resembles the opera's decor in which the grotto is draped in blue shadows from moonbeams. The dark and light symbolism that is so striking in the film is significant for Maeterlinck. In his essay on "Mystic Morality," Maeterlinck uses imagery strikingly reminiscent of that of *Pelléas* and of *Noroît*: "We believe we have discovered a grotto that is stored with bewildering treasure; we come back to the light of day, and the gems we have brought are false—mere pieces of glass—and yet does the treasure shine on, unceasingly in the darkness" (qtd. in R. L. Smith 110). Indeed, in *Noroît* the treasure discovered by Ludovico and Elisa illuminates the dark grotto with its red radiant light. The sea cave scenes from both *Noroît* and *Pelléas* profit from a dream-like atmosphere in which a poetic moment is grafted onto the dramatic, producing in both an instantaneous translucence.

Rivette clearly borrows his symbolism not only from Maeterlinck but also from Lang, for whom the sea is similarly associated with past and future journeys toward and away from the destiny of a patriarchal fiefdom. In both films and in the opera, the sea is viewed as a source of mystery, an agent of destiny that brought the innocent child to Moonfleet, Mélisande to Allemonde, and Morag to the island kingdom. Whereas the sea is a dark portent in all these texts, the space and light of the sea on a clear day can alternately serve as a source of deliverance. Many scenes from *Noroît* are structured around elements of space, light, and sea. Several scenes from the film stand out in this regard, but perhaps the most visually stunning is the sword duel scene between Ludovico and Jacob on the castle ramparts. Sea, sky, and sun are transformed there into a symbolic force field brought to life by the instrumental music of the Cohen-Solal brothers (flute, bass, and percussion), who improvised the entire scene with utter spontaneity and freedom. The sonic persona of the ocean surf contributes an additional dimension to the instrumentalists' music; in this manner, the sea itself plays a participatory role in the total musical performance. Rivette allowed the musicians' improvised performance to provide his actors with inspiration for their stylized movements and gestures. He found inspiration for music and mise-en-scène in the choreography of American dancer Carolyn Carlson, whose rehearsals he had attended at the Paris Opéra. Rivette describes his experience at the Opéra: "Carolyn Carlson and her dancers were doing their exercises, while at the same time, two musicians, a pianist and a flutist, were there off to one side: there was the body work, the gymnastics of the dancers, while these two musicians continued to play, without the least concern for synchronization, from either group. This rapport pleased me, and I wanted to achieve it, in a certain way in my four films" (qtd. in Daney and Narboni 327: 18). The asynchronous relation between dramatic action and music that Rivette had admired in Carlson inspires the staging of music and musicians in the film.

The sword duel scene stands out for its experimental use of direct sound, music, and dance. It also contributes to the serial dimension of the cycle, serving as a segue to *Duelle,* the second film in the tetralogy. In this film, a cosmic duel between sun goddess Viva and moon goddess Leni takes place within a labyrinthine maze of mirrors lining the walls of a contemporary Pigalle dance club, "The Rumba." This duel is precipitated by the seemingly artless gesture of a mortal Pierrot, a role created for the celebrated dancer Jean Babilée, who is, perhaps, best known for his performance in Roland Petit and Cocteau's ballet in one act, *Le jeune homme et la mort* (The Young Man and Death; 1946), a mimodrama to which Cocteau contributed the libretto. When Pierrot deftly touches a mirror, it shatters instantly, as do all existing boundaries between earthly and supernatural worlds. The scene pays homage not only to Cocteau's ballet but also his surrealist film, *Le sang d'un poète* (Blood of a Poet; 1930), precisely the moment when the poet moves through the mirror to an oneiric realm. Rivette does not restrict himself to film citations from the Coctelian oeuvre, however; indeed, Cocteau's legacy of theatrical style is everywhere apparent in *Duelle,* which takes its inspiration directly from his three-act play, *Les chevaliers de la table ronde* (The Knights of the Round Table; 1937).

In the aftermath of his opium cure, Cocteau dreamed the enchanted universe of *Les chevaliers* where the parallel realities of the human and the supernatural struggle for dominance within King Arthur's court, whose members are possessed by evil doubles governed by the magician Merlin. Perhaps it was in the series of mirror images structuring the narrative universe of *Les chevaliers* that Rivette found inspiration for the mise-en-scène of *Duelle,* and also the conceptual impetus for *Scènes de la vie parallèle*. In *Duelle,* the sun and moon goddesses occupy a magical temporal zone, *une quarantaine* (forty-day period), as they search for the ring that will enable them to remain on the earth; whereas in *Les chevaliers,* Queen Guinevere and those at the court dwell in "a dim twilight where there is no difference between night and day," as they search for "this inexplicable phenomenon," that is the Grail, which "left us" (261). *Duelle* not only reflects the symbolism and structure of Cocteau's play but also directly cites characters' lines from it. Perhaps the most powerful instance of this occurs at the film's close, when Pierrot's sister Lucie (Hermine Karagheuz), who has come into possession of the ring, demonstrates that she has the last word when she recites to the covetous moon goddess Leni the magician Merlin's demented spell, "two plus two no longer equal four/ all the walls can fall away," and then the enchanted numbers, "7. 8. 9. 5. 3. 6. 2." Both mortal and moon goddesses seek deliverance as they subsequently vanish from the twilight world of the *quarantaine* into darkness beneath the roar of the metro, an enigmatic moment that recalls those occasioned by the magician's verses within the enchanted landscape of *Les chevaliers*.

Rivette's invocation of *Les chevaliers de la table ronde* in *Duelle* not only reflects his enduring preoccupation with the relation between theater and cinema but might also be viewed as part of a personal response that culminates in *Noroît,* a tribute to the legacy of poet-cinéaste Cocteau. In this transposition of Debussy's opera, Rivette explores the legacy of operatic style, which determines the parameters of personal and generic recollection in the film. In *Noroît,* he transforms a closed memory associated with operatic ritual into an open memory, the singular experience of the stage into a universal one. Just as opera ensures the spectator's centripetal movement toward interiority and the imaginary of the past, film encourages a concurrent centrifugal, exploratory movement directed toward the world and the present (Moindrot 20). The essence of mystery and ambiguity found in *Pelléas* and captured in *Noroît* remains consistent with Rivette's early theoretical speculations, when he affirmed that an ontological mystery forms the essence of cinema and of all the arts. The tone of *Noroît* that intentionally maintains a sense of mystery is attributable, in part, to Rivette's theoretical convictions; the film's fantastic dimension created through verse and music is inspired by *Pelléas,* Debussy's opera of uncertainty.

| | |

Music and movement inspire the opening scene of *Le Pont du Nord* (1982), in which we encounter a young woman, Baptiste (Pascale Ogier), entering Paris on her motorbike. Following her circular movement through an intersection, the camera frames her point of view to reveal an army of lions appearing before her. Astor Piazzolla's Argentinean tango, which Rivette situates somewhere "between the music of a bordello and that of a church," connects the series of statues with the camera's movement to produce a whirlwind (qtd. in Daney and Narboni 327: 11).

Following the film's release, Marguerite Duras remarked to Rivette, "*Listening* to your film, *this* is how I *see* it" (my italics, 15). A folk song derived from a legend from the Middle Ages inspired the film's title. The legend recounts the dire fate of disobedient children who, having disregarded their mother's wishes, attend a ball on the Pont du Nord. When the bridge collapses into the river, the children all drown, providing justification for the curse, "Such is the fate of obstinate children" (Duras and Rivette 16).

Although Rivette has never confirmed his intent, I personally regard *Le Pont du Nord* as the final film within a trilogy, which includes *Paris nous appartient* in '61, *Noli me tangere* in '71, and the aforementioned in '82, in which each successive film takes the pulse of the city at the close of the preceding decade. Of the three, *Le Pont du Nord* provides not only the most pessimistic but also graphically orchestrated representation of political conspiracy within the city. Rivette returns to the terrors and pleasures of the contemporary cityscape in *Le Pont du Nord,* casting his glance once more over a Paris that was still in the grip of Giscardianism (Rivette regrets that the film was released after the decisive election of May 1981 when François Mitterrand and the Socialist Party assumed power). The film might be read as either a political allegory or hailed as a modern-day ballad, which chronicles the perambulations of its two errant heroines, former prisoner Marie Lafée (Bulle Ogier) and her young cohort, Baptiste. The two appear within a mythic, timeless Paris, each gravitating to the other in a courageous attempt to combat those forces that menace them. Marie, haunted by her recent imprisonment that was the result of her former life as a terrorist, remains claustrophobic. Rivette came up with the idea of the character's claustrophobia to accommodate the shortage of funds available to shoot interiors, as the C.N.C. had refused Rivette funding for *Le Pont du Nord* no less than three times. Indomitable on her motorbike and armed with the dancelike movements of karate, Baptiste battles the menacing armies of "Max," mysterious enemies who can appear at will in the form of lions in the streets and public squares. Baptiste comments, "Max are everywhere. They watch everything that moves." As in *Paris nous appartient,* an ominous conspiratorial force becomes associated with a panoptic gaze that oversees the city. When confronted with it, Baptiste violently rips the eyes out of billboard models appearing in a replicated series, as if attempting to eradicate the look complicit with capitalist commodity culture.

Sleeping rough, Baptiste and Marie huddle together at night, attempting to insulate each other from the chill of late autumn; each day, they must face not only the peril of conspiracies fabricated by the "Max" but also Marie's past that resurfaces in the figure of an old lover, Julien (Pierre Clémenti), whose underworld associations place them in imminent danger. Suspicious of Julien, Baptiste steals his briefcase, uncovering a portfolio of newspaper clippings, accompanied by a map of the city and a peculiar grid that on first glance would seem determined by an occult symbology. Marie grasps the gravity of her situation when the two flip through news headlines that point to the financial scandals, political assassinations, and corruption that had permeated French political life throughout the 1970s. Finally, Marie comes across her own photograph appearing in a news story detailing her participation in a bank robbery. We learn that the heist had been orchestrated by an international terrorist cell whose members had persuaded her to join their ranks. Marie's criminal status, as Morrey and Smith observe, could be said to confirm suspicions about "the ruling class's displacement of its own criminal activities on to a terrorist enemy" and thus, becomes symptomatic of a stratified society where violence has become the preferred mechanism for social change (32).

Eluding the "Max," the two take shelter briefly to inspect the curious map, which Marie identifies as a *jeu de l'oie* (a game of Snakes and Ladders) that she describes as a "children's game," "a game of chance." The numbered squares of the game board would seem to align with the numerical *arrondissements* in Paris; however, certain squares are spatial traps, which constrain the players. Marie identifies one trap as the Prison, and thus can make sense of her own period of detention from within the game's labyrinthine schema, while the other traps known as the Tavern, the Well, the Maze, and the Bridge permit the two women to chart their course within the city. Traversing a city in ruins, in which each terrain becomes a square in the spiral trajectory of the game, the two wage war with the Max, whom they encounter at a construction site where anonymous high-rise apartments are being erected. Later found imprisoned within a synthetic cocoon spun mechanically by a Max, Baptiste is liberated by Marie, who is able to cut away the fibers that threaten to permanently encase her. The heroines' destinies reunite on the rails of the abandoned Petite-Ceinture (Little Belt) line that had encircled and serviced Paris since the mid-nineteenth century. En route, the two trace the circumference of the cityscape where, as Duras observes, "they can no longer stop, they roll along like automobiles, like the news, like New York in Europe, like the cinema, like eternity" (15). It is, perhaps, Agnès Varda's rootless hitchhiker Mona (Sandrine Bonnaire) in *Sans toit ni loi* (Vagabond; 1985) whose aimless wanderings and transient occupation of vacated houses, barren woods, and anonymous train stations preserve the essence of the film and its predecessor, *Merry-Go-Round*.

On the fourth and final day of their journey, Marie and Baptiste arrive at the Bridge, a spatial trap on the game board that within the film overlooks the Canal de l'Ourcq at the Bassin de la Villette in the far northeast corner of Paris. In the early nineteenth century, Napoleon Bonaparte ordered the construction of the Basin of la Villette so that water from the river l'Ourcq running through the woodlands north of

Figure 7. Baptiste battles a Max on the bridge in *Le Pont du Nord*. Photographer William Lubtchansky. Courtesy of Collection Cinémathèque Française.

Paris could be channeled into the city. The Basin thus possesses a two-fold significance, as both a source of life for its city's inhabitants and also as the paradoxical source of their demise having made possible the industrial wastelands of the late twentieth century. The historical import of the Basin of la Villette corresponds with that of the Bridge, which is recounted in the folk song for which the film is named. Both sites offer the citizenry of Paris the possibility of productivity and pleasure. Yet both are traps, not only in the specific sense of the game board but also in the broader sense of their historical and cultural significance. In the song, it is those inattentive, irresponsible citizens whose excesses destroy the Bridge who fall to their Death; whereas in the film, it is the solitary, tragic ex-prisoner Marie, lingering like a melancholy refrain by the canal, where she meets her demise at the hands of a lover whose collusion with conspiratorial forces she could never have anticipated. As she falls, like a pawn from a game board, Baptiste commences a dancelike battle on the Bridge with a Max (Jean-François Stévenin), who seeks to initiate her. In accordance with the rules of the game, in which the square of Death leads to a Recommencement, the two players maneuver across the Bridge, mirroring each other's combative stances. Gridded shots suddenly frame their performance, as if to call attention to the graphic dimensions of the game and its perils—including those of the film itself—from the perspective of the filmmaker. While seeming to impose a fatalistic, predetermined perspective onto the players and the city, Rivette's camera, paradoxically, embraces the immediacy of the theatrical ritual before it, a combative dance in which the movements and gestures of the players and the director alike conspire to "liberate Paris for other films" (qtd. in Duras 16).

## Reenvisioning Genres: *Haut bas fragile*, *Jeanne la pucelle*, *Secret défense*, and *Va savoir*

An intoxicating excursion into genre filmmaking, *Haut bas fragile* (Up Down Fragile; 1995) chronicles the daily lives of three women, Louise, Ninon, and Ida, who live in Paris. Characterized as a "sleepwalker," Louise (Marianne Denicourt) is recovering from an accident that left her in a coma; Ninon (Nathalie Richard) is a delivery girl perpetually traveling from address to address on her mobylette or her roller blades;

the librarian Ida (Laurence Côte), an adopted child, searches continually for the source of a song she thinks she hears or heard before she was born. *Haut bas fragile*'s decor points to the labyrinthine fixity of institutional structures, such as the Paris streets that imprison Ninon in a low-paying job, or the library stacks that reinforce Ida's sense of her own dispossession, or the empty, clinical apartment buildings that encase the upper-middle-class Louise, rendering her infantilized and helpless, a prisoner of her father's overprotectiveness. The occasional intrigues that engage the three women, such as the mysterious "double dealings" of the Backstage gang or the missing documents discrediting Louise's father, become mere pretexts for musical performances that seduce characters who meet briefly and then disperse.

Music in the film provides all three women with the means to oppose those forces that threaten to contain or erase them. A missing melody motivates Ida's search through apartment stairwells and Paris record stores. She alone hears the song "My Lost Love" and its lyrics, "I will do anything to find you again, to see you and hold you again." During these interludes, the lost refrain becomes associated with the adopted Ida's obsessive desire to retrieve her sense of selfhood. Music here presents the possibility of a feminine identity, in absentia. This use of music can be traced to what Gérard Loubinoux describes as "chant within the chant," an operatic form where characters are "inhabited, haunted by some archaic song that awakens strange resonance in them, which exercises a mysterious power of fascination and precipitates peculiar exchanges between them" (86). While observing herself in her bedroom mirror, Ida remarks: "Behind me there is nothing. As if I had no past. A real black hole. As if my legs had no feet." These words of solitary introspection, which Ida begins to sing while observing her mirror image, soon become allied with her obsession with finding the source of the old song, "My Lost Love," that only she hears. Ida's recitative mirrors that of Desdemona during the final act of Verdi's opera in which Desdemona, deceived in love, remembers her mother's maid and the sad song she used to sing. Seated before her bedside mirror, Desdemona sings the "song of the willow": "She wept as she sang on the lonely heath/ the poor girl wept, O willow, willow, willow!" While gazing into the mirror, both Desdemona and Ida seek solace in a melancholic refrain, which recalls the archaic presence/absence of the mother. In both Rivette's film and in the opera, the "chant within the chant" emerges from a primitive, archaic universe, which subtends a superficial world of social conventions and hypocrisy.

Complementing music's role in the lives of the three women, the occasional performances of Backstage singer Anna Karina, feminine icon par excellence of the New Wave, make reference to her appearances within a 1960s cinema "de la jeunesse." At her nightclub Sarah Saloon, Karina reinvents old song and dance routines from Godard's paean to the American musical *Une femme est une femme* (A Woman Is a Woman; 1961) as well as dance numbers from his later films, *Bande à part* (Band of Outsiders; 1964) and *Pierrot le fou* (1965). While Karina's "backstage" performances evoke New Wave locales, Rivette intimated in a personal interview (1999) that the club Backstage was modeled on the New York taxi-dance hall, which became popular following the First World War. In his sociological study of the taxi-dance hall, Paul G. Cressey explains that at the beginning of each musical number, the taxi-girl received a ticket from the patron, which she tore in half, giving one part of it to the ticket collector and storing the other half under the hem of her silk hose (6). At the end of the evening, she redeemed the tickets from the management for a nickel each, and so was often called a "nickel hopper." The commercial and instructional dimensions of the taxi-girl's role is captured in Rogers and Hart's well-known song "Ten Cents a Dance" from the musical *Simple Simon* (1930). Ruth Etting interpreted its lyrics in the show, crooning: "I work at the Palace Ballroom/but gee, that Palace is cheap/ When I get back to my chilly hall room/I'm much too tired to sleep. /I'm one of those lady teachers/a beautiful hostess, you know/ One that the Palace features/at exactly a dime a throw." As the song lyrics suggest, taxi-dance halls were usually located at interstitial areas of mobility, such as tenement districts where small apartments, furnished rooms, and inexpensive residential hotels predominated, thus offering a ready-made clientele. These places of amusement were tinged with an element of social danger, partly because of the inevitable commingling of classes or ethnicities in less expensive venues. Such diversity was the real crux of the anxiety about taxi-dancing.

The taxi-dance hall actually cultivated an alternative countercultural community open to diverse nationalities, races, and age groups. In *Tropic of Capricorn,* Henry Miller describes his hallucinatory encounter with the nymphomaniac taxi-girl Paula, who he recalls had "the loose, jaunty swing and perch of the double-barreled sex, all her movements radiating from the groin, always in equilibrium, always ready to flow, to wind and twist and clutch, the eyes going tic-toc, the toes twitching and twinkling, the flesh rippling like a lake furrowed by a breeze" (107). The anonymity of the taxi-dance hall allowed the bystander to project himself/herself into different roles, keeping his/her real identity a disguise. This capacity to project the self into alternative theatrical roles was not limited to patrons but also included the taxi-girls themselves, who would each adopt a "professional" name that was suggestive of her new self-conception. While the "professionalism" required of the taxi-girl is often associated with prostitution, Rivette's references to this subculture in his film are designed to subvert the sentimental vision of the heterosexual couple offered in the Hollywood musical. Rather than affirming those values associated with a respectable bourgeois culture, Rivette's dance hall aesthetic offers an implicit critique of these values, providing the spectator with a pedagogical dance lesson.

The myth of the American taxi-girl is musically interlaced with French film tradition in *Haut bas fragile,* for Rivette borrows his taxi-dancer's name "Ninon" from the song "Pauvre Petit Coeur de Ninon" at the close of Jean Renoir's *La bête humaine* (The Human Beast; 1938), the Zola adaptation. The song's lyrics tell the story of a fictitious, bewitching girl who breaks men's hearts, referring indirectly to the film's heroine Séverine (Simone Simon), whose sensual allure drives the crazed train engineer Jacques Lantier (Jean Gabin) to commit murder. Although the film aurally invokes Zola's obsessive character Lantier, it is Miller's feverish voyeuristic engagement with the taxi-dancer at the Roseland dance hall that bears marked resemblance to Rivette's mobile camera eye and enlists our entranced participation in Ninon's dance performances at Backstage.

*Haut bas fragile*'s theatrical staging of musical numbers does not simply reflect the New York dance and cinema subculture of the 1920s, but simultaneously refers to the Hollywood "backstage" musical through its incorporation of carefully choreographed dance numbers. The film's opening scene sets up the semantic elements of the taxi-dance hall narrative, introducing Ninon as a taxi-girl who aggressively demands her cut of wages from the management. She definitively decides to seek new employment after she witnesses her boss violently stab a lecherous patron in a back lot. As a delivery girl, presumably of those packages marked "haut bas fragile" (UP/DOWN/FRAGILE), Ninon initiates a romantic interlude with Monsieur Roland, a set designer. As the unsuspecting Roland enters the doorway of the delivery service, Ninon brazenly kisses him, distracting the attention of others and deflecting their suspicion of her following their discovery of a theft from the open cash box.[14] The subsequent dance number at Roland's studio introduces the semantic elements of the 1930s backstage musical, which include the opposition of reality and art. A product of the Depression-era economy, some early 1930s backstage musicals revealed daily life as a constant fight against joblessness and hunger. This lackluster existence is balanced by the joy of production numbers, in which screen characters, as well as the audience, are permitted to temporarily forget their real situation. The characters break out of the normal world into a realm of performance and art, where stylization and rhythm provide a sense of community and beauty absent from the real world.

The Hollywood musical is characterized by the audio dissolve, which, as Rick Altman observes, is a technique that makes possible the seamless passage from the diegetic track of conversation to the music track of orchestral accompaniment (63). In the musical, the audio dissolve transports the spectator from a realm of unrelenting reality (action produces sound) to a magical world (music produces action). In the atelier dance number between Ninon and Roland, Rivette experiments with a variation of the audio dissolve. The scene shifts from diegetic sound without music to nondiegetic music without diegetic sound as Roland and Ninon exchange half-sung lyrics based on metrical repetitions, an interchange that in French plays upon the words "Per-tur-bé" (Dis-turbed) and "Gêné" (Flustered). During this exchange, the linguistic bonds that produce meaning become relaxed, allowing words to return to their primal characteristics of rhythm and rhyme. By melodizing their voice patterns, the couple's movement from diegetic conversation to nondiegetic song is made continuous and imperceptible. Their speech grows more and more rhythmical, thus calling forth and justifying, as it were, the entrance of the musical accompaniment. As Ninon slips naturally from speech to song, she repeats the exercise by subordinating all her movements to the song's rhythm—at an undetermined point we suddenly recognize that the couple is dancing, yet we never saw them begin to dance. Just as their slow slipping from speech to song justifies a further sliding from song to musical accompaniment, so their transition from walking to dancing turns the space around them into a stage. Roland mocks Ninon's semicircular movements, and she, in turn, imitates his.

In *Haut bas fragile,* the intricate interweaving of different dance traditions accentuates rather than diminishes the film's disjointed tone. For instance, the atelier dance number between Roland and Ninon, which relies on codes and conventions of the 1930s backstage musical number, is almost immediately followed by Enzo Enzo's performance of the haunting song "The Willing Castaways" at the dance hall Backstage. The lyrics seem to chart the characters' movement across the dance floor and within the film's diegesis: "Nothing can be done for the castaways who ride the great wave/that rocks them to mysterious islands/ Without a craft, without a raft/without leaving land, the castaways wander." The music that animates "the willing castaways" suspends the flux of narration, yet the dance aesthetic differs from that of the Hollywood musical, where the star couple remains centered and is always facing the camera. Rivette's camera imitates a dancer's movement, as it sweeps past anonymous couples and then spins completely around in a 360-degree circle (Delfour 169). The camera focuses briefly on Ninon as a solo figure, whose pirouettes across the floor seem to replicate those of the camera. A single shot frames her face, which seems to return the camera's look, as though the camera apparatus had become her partner. At this moment, dance movement is suspended as the camera situates the spectator as a participant within the space of the profilmic performance. Within this scene, the camera reproduces the movements of a dancer, thus transforming the passive spectator into an active participant engaged in the profilmic performance. Similar to Miller's New York taxi-dance hall, Backstage's circumscribed performance space preserves the anonymous character of the taxi-dance hall encounter, thus permitting the spectator to project him/herself into different class, gender, or racial roles. This capacity to identify with alternative theatrical roles is preserved through the profilmic performance space of Rivette's taxi-dance hall.

Unlike the nondiegetic music of the Hollywood dance number that provides a release from the causal constraints of the diegesis, the diegetic music at Backstage establishes a causal connection to everyday events within the world. Ninon's easy movement through Paris back streets on rollerblades creates a continuation of the spontaneous dance begun at Backstage the previous night. She arrives at the home address of Louise, to whom she delivers a bouquet of roses, a gift from Roland. Ninon initiates a confrontational conversation with Roland later that night at Backstage, but her revenge on him is not complete until she joins forces with Louise against him. The two dancers perform a viciously liberating duet in which nondiegetic music propels the two up and down the staircase. Once again, the scene's dance choreography mimics that of the Hollywood musical, as Louise and Ninon melodize their voice patterns as the lead-in to the commencement of musical accompaniment and dance movements. The extreme high and low angles that animate their dance number celebrate the reunion of two women—one from the haute bourgeoisie and the other from the lower class—through the everyday ritual of female friendship. The homoerotic power of their dance is enormously powerful and subversive, initiating an alternative space of musical performance, which resembles that of a taxi-dance hall where dancers, as well as sideline profilmic spectators, may indulge in homoerotic fantasies.

Through its intricate interweaving of different dance traditions in consecutive scenes, the film sets up a performance continuum designed to break down the borders between narrative and musical number. The

Figure 8. Ninon and Louise's liberating dance number in *Haut bas fragile*.

film supplants the syntactical logic of the Hollywood musical, which determines the division between narrative and number, with its own idiosyncratic performance style. The borderline that distinguishes the world of the diegetic event from that of the dance number is intentionally blurred. The final scene between Louise and her bodyguard Lucien on the veranda of her apartment exemplifies the conflation of narrative event and musical number. As Louise moves from the apartment onto the veranda, she spins completely around, smoothly integrating her dance step into her stride. Lucien then mimics this movement, spinning around a chair. Louise again reciprocates and rotates around toward the same chair. The give-and-take conversational exchange of the couple remains natural up until this point, but here both characters begin to repeat lines, making their voices conform to a rhythmic pattern. Brushing against a rocking chair, Lucien begins with the remark, "I love you so. I do everything backwards." Louise replies, "Say nothing. Keep quiet. Backwards and forward." The rocking movement of the chair that begins to move back and forth like a metronome mimics that of the characters' bodies and the content of their verbal exchange. At this point, the characters' speech patterns and body movement seem to justify the entrance of musical accompaniment, as would occur in a Hollywood musical number. Yet, this scene frustrates the spectator's expectations. The couple's shift to balletic rotations and metrical voice patterns anticipates the musical accompaniment that never comes. During the scene, Louise and Lucien appear indefinitely suspended between the diegetic event and dance steps. The scene refuses to offer a musical affirmation or conventional closure. Like the characters, the spectator remains transfixed, momentarily suspended between meaning and movement.

This continual oscillation between meaning and motion in the film recalls Ida's search for the source of a song she thinks she hears, or overheard before she was born, and the anxiety of the girl-child's search for the first lost object, the Mother (or her synechdochic stand-in—her maternal voice). Like the rocking movement of objects and characters, Ida's incessant search throughout the film for a missing musical refrain literalizes aurally (and narratively) the backward and forward movement of the *fort/da* game, a child's game of repetition designed to diminish the unpleasure caused by the absence of the mother. This imaginary game, in which the child repeatedly pulls a toy reel back and forth, marks the child's initial attempt to master the drives through entry into language. This game of repetition, premised on the alternation of lack and plentitude, is set into motion in the film's unfolding. In his reformulation of Lacanian theory, Guy Rosolato has characterized the maternal voice as a "lost object," which comes to represent what alone can make good the subject's lack (qtd. in Silverman 85). Rosolato observes that the primordial listening experience is the prototype for the pleasure that derives from music, affirming that it is "the whole drama of separated bodies and their reunion, which supports harmony" (qtd. in Silverman 85).

It is through music that *Haut bas fragile* works to interrogate the relationship of the spectator—above all the female spectator—to the cinema. The camera implicates the film viewer in Ida's attempt to recover the source of the aural "lost object," shadowing her movement from a downtown record store into a vacant hallway or stairwell, or from the dimly lit Sarah Saloon to the open-air hot dog stand frequented by Monsieur Paul, played by Rivette, in pursuit of a haunting refrain. Music gives the film as well as the librarian Ida (whose job at the Cabinet des Estampes in the Bibliothèque nationale is to *oversee* its etchings and photographs) an additional dimension. Music suspends the flux of narration created through linguistic and iconographic sign systems, leaving the spectator momentarily entranced by its hallucinatory rhythms, harmonic resonance, and passion. The final shot of the film frames Ida in Renoirian style, in a deep focus long take that follows her flight down an empty boulevard. Unexpectedly, she refuses singer Anna Karina's offer of a cozy Paris apartment, forfeiting her final opportunity to secure a safe haven and retrieve the source of the mysterious musical refrain. Ida is destined to remain a rootless "castaway," as is the film spectator, continuing to search for the coherent selfhood and sense of mastery that the myth of cinema and its music can no longer provide. Like Rivette's three *flâneuses*, the spectator is generously invited to become an impassioned participant in, as well as observer of, the everyday rituals of the city.

| | |

Art house star Sandrine Bonnaire takes center stage in the two-part historical epic, *Jeanne la pucelle* (Joan the Maid; 1994; 1. The Battles 2. The Prisons), and the *film policier* (translated as French detective film)

*Secret défense* (Secret Defense; 1997). In these films from the 1990s, Rivette transposes disparate genres to fabricate two modern-day feminist parables. Rivette casts Bonnaire in the role of the medieval Christian martyr, "la pucelle," reinventing the Hollywood genre commonly associated with monumental scale, male spectacle, and nationalist themes to create what he describes as an "ébauche" (preliminary draft or sketch) of the work possible on Jeanne (qtd. in Grassin and Médioni). In *Secret défense,* Rivette casts Bonnaire in the role of researcher and criminal investigator Sylvie Rousseau, reworking the popular French genre of the *film policier,* through reference to the Electra myth. Not only do both films construct their central female role around the persona of Bonnaire, they both reveal a deep personal connection to the director.

Rivette's childhood in Rouen, the "Cathedral City" of Normandy where Jeanne was imprisoned and burned at the stake, influenced his decision to make the film. As a child, he was nourished by the work of Charles Péguy, whose three-part dramatic work *Jeanne d'Arc* provides the impetus for the film, particularly the second play entitled "Les Batailles" (The Battles). The epic expanse of Rivette's film distinguishes it from the microscopic study of Jeanne's suffering, sadness, and martyrdom in Carl Dreyer's contemplative silent classic, *La passion de Jeanne d'Arc* (1928). Rivette's film also offers a radical alternative to Robert Bresson's portrait of an unyielding, stoic Jeanne in *Le procès de Jeanne d'Arc* (The Trial of Joan of Arc; 1962). He hand-picked Bonnaire, who he viewed as a corporal performer able to incarnate "the popular side" of Jeanne, rather than her purely poetic side expressed in the earlier films (qtd. in Grassin and Médioni). It was, perhaps, for this reason that Rivette chose the vernacular epithet "la pucelle" (the Maid), for as Jean Collet notes, the name is associated with the Middle Ages, tying Jeanne to a historical trajectory, rather than to a cold, abstract ideal of sainthood ("Histoire" 152). In contrast to an austere judicial ritual, Rivette's intent was to depict Jeanne in motion. Indeed, Rivette decided on the spur of the moment to play the role of Jeanne's confessor at Vaucouleurs, who intercedes for her at a crucial moment in her journey and enables her mission to proceed. Catalan musician Jordi Savall's original score based on Gregorian-based compositions of the epoch sounds out the contemplative, uncertain dimension of Jeanne's journey. As the film progresses, the camera moves continually, not simply recording but researching the historical personage of Jeanne—as enigmatic creature, as seductress, as saint, as madwoman, or as sorceress.

Whereas *Jeanne la pucelle* represents the director's only attempt to produce a historical epic, *Secret défense* remains the sole film considered part of the genre known in France as the *film policier*. As the founding historian of the genre, François Guérif observes, its source is the *roman policier* (French detective novel), a popular literary form that can be traced to the nineteenth-century works of Balzac and Eugène Sue, whose melodramas had formed the basis of *Noli me tangere* (17). For Rivette, the *roman policier* would summon up not only Balzac and Sue but also Gallimard's *série noir,* translations of Raymond Chandler and Dashiell Hammett novels that shaped the evolution of the detective film in the 1950s and inspired numerous film adaptations (Guérif 17–31; Powrie 76). Embracing its literary roots, the *film policier* remains one of the most popular and durable genres in French cinema, serving as the testing ground for young directors who desire a career in filmmaking (Guérif 29; Powrie 75). Curiously, the genre eludes precise definition, for as Guérif observes, it encompasses different categories, such as "the mystery, the thriller, the film noir, the psychological drama, the moral tale, etc." (31). For Rivette, the *policier* would bring to mind American noirs and Alfred Hitchcock's thrillers, summoning up his early years at *Cahiers* when Bazin had fondly dubbed him and his New Wave cohorts, the "Hitchcocko-Hawksians." It would without doubt invoke French iconic stars Jean-Paul Belmondo and Alain Delon, and directors Jean-Pierre Melville and Claude Chabrol. Chabrol's own early interest in the genre is reflected in a piece he published in 1955 in *Cahiers,* "Évolution du film policier." In *Secret défense*, Rivette pays homage to his mentors, reinventing the criminal world of the *policier* to create a film where the conventional line between judge and assassin, hunter and hunted, victim and perpetrator is blurred; where the female heroine Sandrine Bonnaire assumes the central male role of the detective and is thereby empowered "to penetrate everywhere and to expose the hidden truths that the world conceals" (Guérif 31).

*Secret défense* chronicles the investigation launched by cancer researcher Sylvie Rousseau and her brother Paul (Grégoire Colin) into the mysterious circumstances surrounding their father's death. Sylvie's father, Pierre André Rousseau, had fallen from a moving train five years earlier and was killed instantly. Although at the time, his death was attributed to his accidental fall, Paul discovers new evidence that throws suspicion on his father's business associate, Walser (Jerzy Radziwilowicz), who is also his mother's lover. A blurry photograph of their father, who was being shadowed by Walser, provides Paul and Sylvie with the main source of hard evidence, and ultimately serves to visually connect his sudden death with their sister's years before, whose absence is also marked by a fuzzy photo. Sylvie decides to take over the investigation herself and, in this respect, recalls the tenacious investigator played by Fanny Ardant in Truffaut's final film, an affectionate pastiche of the *film policier, Vivement Dimanche*! (Finally Sunday!; 1983). Sylvie travels by train to her hometown to confront Walser. When she points a gun at him, his young secretary Véronique (Laure Marsac), in a desperate attempt to protect him, jumps her. During the brief struggle that follows, the gun goes off, and Véronique is killed. Sylvie thus becomes ensnared in the cycle of crime and criminality that ultimately affects the entire family.

Véronique's identical twin sister Ludivine soon appears and begins to inquire as to the whereabouts of her sister. Walser subsequently seduces her and invites her to stay with him at his estate. Traumatized by the sequence of events, Sylvie returns to Paris. Her suspicions about her father's death are later confirmed when Walser visits her and confesses

Figure 9. Sylvie confronts Walser in *Sécret defense.*

to killing him by throwing him from the train. When Sylvie later informs her mother, Geneviève Rousseau (Françoise Fabian), of Walser's confession, she is shocked to learn of her mother's complicity in the murder and the reason behind it. She returns to Walser's estate, where she prevents Paul from killing him by taking away his gun. Yet Sylvie is not entirely successful in averting violence. While there, she inadvertently blurts out that Véronique is dead, inciting in Ludivine an irrepressible rage. Accusing Walser of the crime, Ludivine takes aim at him with her loaded pistol. When Sylvie tries to protect him by throwing herself in harm's way, she is accidentally shot and killed.

Darkness, multiple murders, and the presence of the investigator all place *Secret défense* within the world of the *film policier,* while returning us to Aeschylean dramaturgy through the Electra myth. The film is a loose adaptation of the first two plays of Aeschylus's *Oresteia,* which is composed of three plays in sequence, *Agamemnon, Choephoroi,* and *Eumenides*. Sylvie's story is modeled on that of Electra, the "bright one," who in *Choephoroi* conspires with her brother Orestes to avenge the death of their father Agamemnon by murdering their mother Clytemnestra and her lover Aegisthus. In *Secret défense,* Sylvie becomes the avenger of her father's death—even though her assassination attempt misfires. Her story of revenge is also modeled on Jean Giraudoux's *Electre* (Electra; 1937), an updated version of the Greek legend. In Giraudoux's play, the character Electra is an inspirational, mythic figure, similar to Jeanne la Pucelle, who is destined to serve as the moral scourge of a nation defined by a lack of mission, initiative, and spirituality (Cohen 115). Giraudoux believed that "in every epoch surge forth these pure human beings who don't want the crimes to be absorbed, and who prevent that absorption and call a halt to these means, which only provoke more crimes and new disasters. Electra is one of these beings. She attains her goal, but at the price of horrible catastrophes" (qtd. in Cohen 106). The legacy of Jeanne la Pucelle lends credence to Bonnaire's interpretation of her role as Electra in *Secret défense*.

Paul's role that is modeled on that of Orestes remains peripheral in the film. In one highly significant scene that Rivette retains from *Choephoroi,* Orestes arrives at the estate of Clytemnestra and Aegisthus disguised as a foreign traveler bearing the news that "Orestes is dead." He discovers that his childhood nurse is the sole character who truly mourns him. The nurse is an important figure in *Choephoroi,* for she is an insider who understands the secret motivations of those in the house. In the film, the figure of the nurse appears in a seemingly gratuitous scene. Paul's unexpected disappearance for several days prompts Sylvie's frantic search for him. She finally discovers that he is recovering from a minor motorcycle accident in the Salpetrière hospital and is being cared for by a nurse, played by Hermine Karagheuz, known for her previous role in *Noli me tangere* as a member of Lili's collective performing Aeschylus and the suspected messenger of the Thirteen. Modeled on Orestes's nurse in *Choephoroi,* Karagheuz is an intertextual "insider" who understands the hidden motivations of those cast members (such as Françoise Fabian/Geneviève Rousseau, who reenacts her role as coconspirator in *Noli me tangere*), in Rivette's "house" engaged in another adaptation of Aeschylus.

Rivette refashions the Electra myth in his film by interlacing it with elements of Raymond Chandler's and Billy Wilder's noir thriller *Double Indemnity* (1944), in which Walter Neff (Fred MacMurray) and Phyllis Dietrichson (Barbara Stanwyck) conspire to stage her husband's death as an accidental fall from a train. The blurred image of Walser on the train platform that Paul produces as his key piece of evidence can also be read by the film spectator as Rivette's intertextual referencing of the noir classic and the name of the murder suspect "Walser" as the director's pun on the name of Wilder's character, "Walter." *Double Indemnity* is not the only American film intertext that emerges in the film, however. Walser's seduction of both Véronique and her twin double Ludivine recalls the detective Scottie Ferguson's (Jimmy Stewart) seduction of both the mysterious Madeleine (Kim Novak) and her double, Judy, in Hitchcock's classic *Vertigo* (1958). Just as we participate in Scottie's emotional crisis, identifying with his gaze as he surveys the San Francisco Bay area through his car windshield, in similar fashion, we participate in Sylvie's crisis through her point of view as she contemplates the Paris cityscape from the metro or the verdant countryside from the window of the ultramodern TGV. The train system that Sylvie frequents throughout the film also pays tribute to Hitchcock's thriller *Strangers on a Train* (1951), in which a tennis player, Guy Haines (Farley Granger), meets Bruno Anthony (Robert Walker) on a train, where they talk about swapping murders. In *Secret défense,* Rivette returns to the *policier,* while liberating it from the conventional demands of the genre. *Secret défense* mobilizes film and theatrical styles—the monumentality of Aeschylean drama, the complex crime patterns of the film noir, as well as the darkness and mystery associated with the Hitchcockian crime thriller—in order to align the everyday world and the ceremonial space of the film.

| | |

*Va savoir* (Why Knows?; 2001) is a dazzling romantic comedy that chronicles a week or so in the lives of three men and three women. The story opens as Camille Renard (Jeanne Balibar), a prominent French actress, returns to Paris accompanied by her companion, an Italian theater director named Ugo Basani (Sergio Castellitto). They are costarring in Luigi Pirandello's play *Come tu mi vuoi* (As You Desire Me; 1931). The play is never viewed in its entirety, yet in *Va savoir,* the audience is privy to select scenes from the finished production of the play, rather than mere rehearsals. In a videotaped interview with Frédéric Bonnaud, Rivette acknowledges that *Va savoir* works according to the principle of ellipsis, whereas the original long version of the film, *Va savoir* + (3 hr. 40 min.), is based on temporal continuity. He affirms that the duration of *Va savoir* + allows Pirandello's play to be understood by the audience as yet "another character" that coexists alongside the others. I personally find *Va savoir* + preferable to the short version for its leisurely, nuanced exploration of theater performance; however, the long version was never commercially distributed and played at only a single cinema in Paris, Le cinéma du Panthéon, for seven weeks. Because only a handful of mostly French spectators will have had the opportunity to see this magnificent film, I will confine my discussion here to *Va savoir,* where the theater serves to counterpoint the melodic lines of the actors' lives and their romantic intrigues. The light, humorous tone of the actors' backstage machinations offsets the reflective quality of Pirandello's play, which offers a serious study of madness, feminine identity, and representation.

Rivette pays homage to filmmaker Howard Hawks in *Va savoir,* where the conventions of the screwball comedy are cautiously intertwined with those of Pirandellian drama, accomplishing the "perilous kind of equilibrium" that Rivette argues Hawks achieved in such screwballs as *Monkey Business* (1952) (qtd. in Hillier 126). The institution of marriage can provide the subject matter for Hawks's comedies where wedding plans are thrown into disarray or the couple's reunion resolved through comic high jinks rather than an officious ceremony. In *Va savoir,* Camille and Ugo's questionable commitment to each other becomes the source of screwball scenarios that at times threaten to disrupt the production of Pirandello's play. In *Come tu mi vuoi,* Camille assumes the play's title role of "The Strange Lady," a lost soul whose disreputable life in Berlin with her lover, Salter, following World War One is suddenly transformed by the arrival of a Venetian named Boffi, played by her partner Ugo. Boffi recognizes in her the beloved "Cia," the missing wife of a wealthy Italian landowner, Bruno. Boffi implores her to leave behind her desperate life to return to her husband, who has been awaiting her return for ten years. "The Strange Lady" agrees to play the role of "Cia" in flight from herself, claiming that she is merely "a body, a body without a name, waiting for someone to come and take it!" (67). Haunted by the vision of a woman who might be herself, "The Strange Lady" consents to be his "Cia," so that he "can re-create me," and "give a soul to this body, which is that of his 'Cia,'" thus building "out of his own memories—his own—a beautiful life, a beautiful new life" (67). "The Strange Lady" is subsequently obsessed with the desire to breathe life into an image of the past, which is emblematically displayed in the oil painting of "Cia," which haunts the Villa Pieri. She is simultaneously terrified by the possibility that she is an imposter, as she attempts to conform to the image of "Cia" in all its particularities.

The film's opening scene isolates Camille in a bright spotlight. The lights subsequently fade up to reveal a theater set. Backstage buzz reveals that the troupe is not doing well financially. Here, Rivette intentionally underscores the resemblance between the struggling director Ugo and Gérard in *Paris nous appartient*. Unlike their fictional troupes, however, Pirandello's actual stage production of *As You Desire Me* experienced a phenomenal run in New York theaters and was subsequently picked up by MGM studio. The MGM adaptation *As You Desire Me* (1932) received critical accolades on its release and featured Greta Garbo (The Strange Lady), Melvyn Douglas (Bruno), and Erich von Stroheim (Salter). Given the film's critical reception and its singular cast, it would seem possible that Rivette's first encounter with the Pirandello play was not at a Paris theater, but at the cinémathèque. Rivette refuses, however, Hollywood's fabrication of a happy ending in which the identity of "The Strange Lady" is finally affirmed in a blissful reunion with Bruno. He instead retains the play's tragic, ambiguous ending in which "The Strange Lady" is replaced by her double, "The Demented Lady," and thus remains condemned to her former ruinous existence with Salter in Berlin.

Rivette revisits the 1930s in *Va savoir,* not only in his references to both the Pirandello play and its film adaptation, but also in his return to the screwball comedy. In *Va savoir,* he revisits the genre, invoking its conventions in order to radically transform them. In screwballs such as Hawks's *Bringing Up Baby* (1938) or *His Girl Friday* (Hawks; 1940), the narrative is driven by a sexual confrontation between an initially antagonistic couple whose ideological differences heighten the conflict between them. As in these screwball comedies, *Va savoir* opens with an initial sexual confrontation between Ugo and Camille, following the opening-night performance of *As You Desire Me*. Camille leaves the theater before the final curtain call, and Ugo returns to their adjoining hotel rooms, where he confronts her. Echoing the sentiments of "The Strange Lady" that she performs in the play, Camille is terribly ambivalent about her return to Paris, her reunion with her ex-lover Pierre (Jacques Bonnaffé), and the memories associated with both. Her evident preoccupation and distress during the performance when she blanks out on stage precipitate a lovers' quarrel between the couple. During the hotel scene, the character Camille is doubly motivated through dual

Figure 10. Camille and Ugo perform Pirandello in *Va savoir.*

intertexts: her memory lapse invokes Pirandello's character, "The Strange Lady," while simultaneously initiating the "battle of the sexes," a convention of the screwball comedy. Scenes in the couple's hotel rooms, which are adjoined through a shared doorway, pay tribute to the archetypal screwball comedy, *It Happened One Night* (Frank Capra; 1934), specifically invoking the celebrated scene where Ellen (Claudette Colbert) and Peter (Clark Gable) "sleep together" separated by a blanket partition called the "Walls of Jericho." At the scene's end, the closed hotel door that seals off their separate bedrooms resembles the walls of Jericho in Capra's comedy; however, it serves in this scene to underscore the notion of chastity between a couple that is already sexually intimate, while paradoxically permitting each the privacy to pursue other sexual partners.

While the disputes that characterized screwball comedies during the 1930s focused on a variety of issues, the ideological differences that inflect the relationship between Ugo and Camille are played out reflexively in *Va savoir* in terms of theater and cinema genres. Camille becomes associated with the popular film genre of screwball comedy, Ugo, the stage and the classical form of Italian theater. The morning after their quarrel, Ugo leaves the hotel and Camille behind to inquire into a missing manuscript, *Destino Venetiano* (Venetian Destiny), written by eighteenth-century playwright Carlo Goldoni, a well-known reformer of the commedia dell'arte and an opera librettist. His research leads him to the library of Nicolas Vernet at the home of Madame Desprez (Catherine Rouvel), where he meets her daughter, the young thesis student Dominique (Hélène de Fougerolles), who is known as "Do," and her half-brother Arthur (Bruno Todeschini). Ugo's casual flirtation with the student Do, which unfolds around their shared search for the missing Goldoni manuscript, recalls the obsessive investigation of theater director Gérard and the student Anne into the whereabouts of the missing audiotape in *Paris nous appartient*. In both films, theater directors, accompanied by student protégées and their half-brothers, search for a text—written or aural—that makes a performance possible. A sunlit stroll along the banks of the Seine inspires the aging Italian director Ugo to kiss the young student Do, recasting the darker Paris landscape of *Paris nous appartient* where Gérard and Anne's promenade across the pont des Arts metamorphoses into a mysterious scenario of murder and conspiracy.

As Ugo and Do remain preoccupied with their mutual search for the missing manuscript, Camille initiates her own research into the whereabouts of her ex-partner Pierre, a professor of philosophy in Poitiers. While the playful flirtation between Ugo and Do reinvents the sinister story of *Paris nous appartient,* which unfolds around the Shakespearian stage, the rekindling of romance between Camille and Pierre relies on the conventions of the screwball comedy, in which men often become the object of the woman's gaze, an indication of an increased autonomy and power. At his favorite park, Camille contemplates their reunion reflexively in terms of vision: "I will see you; you won't be there. I won't see you; you will be there. I won't see you; you won't be there." She stops speaking when she catches sight of him through the trees. The camera tracks to follow her gaze, as she tiptoes to position herself directly before him, where she completes her quiet refrain, "Yes, I see him; he's there." Camille wields control over the camera's voyeuristic gaze, as does the screwball heroine, demonstrating that she is a free subject capable of desire and choice.

The playful flirtation between the two increasingly mirrors that of Ugo and Do. Ugo and Do's romance revolves around their shared search for a theatrical text, whereas Camille and Pierre's shared past is associated with a literary text, his unfinished thesis on the German philosopher Heidegger, which he has since renamed "Heidegger, the jealous one." The walls of Pierre's apartment, where he indulges in reminiscences with Camille, are lined with books, and thus mirror the public and private libraries where Ugo and Do are spending their afternoons in their quest for Goldoni's *Venetian Destiny*. While Pierre attends the performance of *As You Desire Me* to see Camille, meeting her afterward outside the theater, Do and her mother visit Ugo backstage following a different performance. As Ugo's emblematic association with the classical form of Italian comedy extends to the epic scale of Greek myth when he recounts for Do the tale of the goddess Andromeda's sacrifice, Camille's relation with Pierre increasingly moves toward the zany antics, comic violence, and visceral energy associated with the screwball comedy. The genteel restraint of their initial reunion in the park is knocked for a loop during their later rendezvous in Pierre's apartment. Camille has come to explain that she loves Ugo and that while "working under his gaze" in the theater, she has grown up. At first, Pierre seems unwilling to accept this, but he abruptly relents and brusquely escorts Camille to the door. Camille objects, but before she can complete her sentence, Pierre grabs her and shoves her into a storage room, locking her in before leaving. Aware that she must perform that evening, Camille takes drastic measures. Crawling though the skylight to the roof, she surveys the cityscape and finds her escape route by climbing down the outside ladder. Camille resembles the screwball women protagonist, sharing her vitality, physical freedom, spontaneity, and vivaciousness.

In the role of screwball heroine, Camille extends the genre conventions to same-sex relations when she establishes the rapport of accomplices between women. Camille and Pierre's partner, Sonia (Marianne Basler), are initially linked through respective performance spaces: Camille, the stage, and Sonia, the ballet studio where she instructs her young pupils. Following a disastrous dinner party attended by both couples, Camille visits Sonia at her studio to apologize for Ugo's contentious behavior, and later, Sonia attends the play. One evening, Camille spots Sonia in a café, where she is embracing Arthur Delamarche, Do's half-brother. The next morning, Sonia awakens in her studio under the watchful eye of Camille. In the course of their conversation, Sonia discovers that Arthur has not only drugged her but also stolen her ring. The two women become accomplices, and together form a secret pact: Camille promises to get the ring back from Arthur on the condition that Sonia never inquires how she did it. Camille arrives at Arthur's flat and makes a proposition: she will offer him one night with her, but on the condition that he never again approach her. Arthur agrees, and the following morning, Camille retrieves the ring from the flour jar. Like the screwball heroine, Camille uses her sexual prowess to achieve her own ends and those of her accomplice, Sonia. The ring and its inscription "Tempus fugit, manet amor" serve as a talisman that safeguards the woman's soul, legitimating a feminine agency that surpasses the heterosexual romance legally sanctified in marriage.

While Camille and Sonia solidify their female friendship, Ugo and Pierre face off in a duel to the death. Pained at the thought of losing Camille to Pierre, Ugo finally visits the professor's flat to challenge him to a mysterious duel, which will take place at the theater. To the offended goes the choice of place and arms; thus, Ugo leads Pierre to the flies, a sort of gangplank above the stage, where they each must down an entire bottle of vodka until one of them falls over. After a half bottle, the men agree that they might have been friends had circumstances been otherwise. After loudly proclaiming a passage from Heidegger, Pierre falls, causing the spectator some cause for concern. The cut that immediately follows, however, reveals Pierre caught in a net, where he is thrashing about in a futile effort to find the exit. At that point, all the players return to the set of *As You Desire Me*. Marie-Pierre arrives with a Black Forest cake that she has baked for the troupe's final night in Paris; Do enters from the side entrance armed with Goldoni's manuscript, aptly entitled *Festino Venetiano* (Venetian Feast), which she discovered by accident shelved among her mother's cookbooks. Camille strides down the center aisle, declaring that she is looking for Pierre, who is in danger. She spots him hanging above her, and subsequently decides to climb up to join him. Before doing so, she rejoins Camille, who has descended the staircase where the portrait of "Cia" is hung. Camille returns Sonia's ring to her, but Sonia refuses it and gives it back to her. Camille then passionately embraces Ugo, who proclaims, "The theater is saved, the troupe is saved, the world is saved," to which Camille responds, "We are saved." Having lost both the girl and the ring, Arthur sits sulking at the table, but rises to the occasion when he invites Do to dance. Camille and Ugo follow suit and form another dance couple, quietly exiting by the staircase. As the stage lights dim, Peggy Lee croons the lyrics of "Senza fine," underscoring the sentiment of the moment: "There's no end to our love, our hearts, our dreams, our sighs./ No end at all, no sad goodbyes./ No fears, no tears, no love that dies./ The sunlit days, the moonlit nights, the sea, the sand, the starry heights are yours and mine forevermore."

It is the figure of the theater director to which Rivette returns in *Va savoir*. In this recent work, the relation between theater and cinema might be characterized as asymptotic, resembling a geometrical figure that measures the distance as a moving point on a curve that travels an infinite distance from its origin on a perpendicular line: Rivette recommences at the point along the curve where profilmic performance is furthest from the *locus dramaticus,* which is defined as the place of the play's performance. Yet as we follow the film's narrative trajectory, the two separate domains of theater and cinema, linked by the intersection of classical and popular comic genres that represent the *auteur* inscriptions of Pirandello and Rivette, respectively, move closer and closer together until in the closing scene, they have reached the point of infinity—seemingly indistinguishable from each other, yet never identical. Indeed, Rivette returns to a point of origin in *Va savoir*—the mysterious moonlit nights of *Paris nous appartient* return to haunt the sunlit days of "Senza Fine." The repetition and circularity of the films' narrative structures, from the relationship between the theater director and the student in *Va savoir* to that in *Paris nous appartient*, reflect Rivette's return to the labyrinthine decor characteristic of his early work and to the semiautobiographical story elements that characterized it.

### An Occult Theatricality: *Céline et Julie vont en bateau—Phantom Ladies Over Paris, L'amour par terre, La bande des quatre, Histoire de Marie et Julien*

An occult theatricality shapes the story of *Céline et Julie vont en bateau—Phantom Ladies Over Paris* (Céline and Julie Go Boating; 1974), a film whose commercial release coincided with the onset of post-'68 feminism. Rivette's most well-known film among international audiences and critics, *Céline et Julie* enjoyed an immediate and far-reaching success that has been unparalleled in the history of the Rivette oeuvre. We could attribute this to the timeliness of the film's feminist story, which explores the dimensions of female friendship in its depiction of a librarian and a magician, who both witness a bizarre melodrama being staged within a haunted house. We might speculate along with Jonathan Rosenbaum that the film's tremendous popular appeal owes to its exploration of the cinema of pleasure, slapstick comedy, cartoons, musicals, childhood fantasy, and thrillers ("Review"). Yet beyond its pleasurable appeal to audiences, *Céline et Julie* remains, in my view, as important to the history of cinema as Jean Renoir's *chef d'oeuvre, La règle du jeu* (Rules of the Game; 1939). Indeed, Renoir's influence is everywhere present in this landmark film in which Rivette revisits notions of theatricality, casting the Phantom Ladies as actresses who magically intervene in the "theatrical" scenes that are being rehearsed in the haunted house.

The opening sequence of *Céline et Julie* draws on a nostalgic ambiance elicited by the codes and conventions of silent cinema, the esoteric conveyed by magic formulas, and the remoteness of a supernatural world that surpasses the everyday. Ornamental titles introduce the film's story, "Most of the time, it began like that . . .," which are accompanied by a piano playing softly while a woman sings, nostalgically recalling the silent film era. We first see Julie, who is enjoying the summer breeze in a Paris park and reading a book about magic. Closing her eyes, Julie (Dominique Labourier) murmurs a magical incantation and, before long, Céline (Juliet Berto) hurries by, dropping her glasses and, later, her scarf. Julie hails her and proceeds to chase after her through the streets, secluded passageways, and finally up the steep ascent of Butte Montmartre. As the chase through Paris commences, the film's mood and tempo shift. Rather than the depiction of a leisurely, dreamy otherworld, Rivette's camera creates an impression of spontaneity and immediacy, as it weaves through crowded streets, swerves around bookstalls in an open-air market, and is amiably jostled by busy shoppers. The manner in which Rivette's portable 16 mm camera appears to seize improvised events on the streets of Paris, capturing Berto and Labourier's comic antics that are staged there, may reflect Rivette's involvement with the documentary film movement cinema verité (cinema truth), which was launched with the release of Jean Rouch and sociologist Edgar Morin's *Chronique d'un été* (Chronicle of a Summer; 1960). Rouch and Morin's film is presented as an inquiry into the daily lives of a group of Parisians in the summer of 1960. Rivette makes an uncredited and elliptical appearance in it as the boyfriend of one of the interviewees, Marilù Parolini, who has continued to work with him as a still photographer and co-scenarist on numerous productions.

*Chronique d'un été* combines the techniques of reflexivity, theatricality, improvisation, and provocation that Rouch had developed from his previous documentary work in Africa. It was not only Rouch's method of improvisation but also his ethnographic research into West African ritual that had, in all likelihood, inspired Rivette's exploration of the occult in *Céline et Julie*. In "On the Vicissitudes of the Self," Rouch elaborates on the phenomenon of the *bia,* the double, which underlies theories of the self in sub-Saharan Africa. Rouch explains that each mortal being possesses a *bia,* or double, "who lives in a parallel world, that is, a world of doubles" (96). The relevance of this notion to the magical connection established between Céline and Julie in their initial encounter becomes increasingly clear in subsequent scenes where the two form a telepathic rapport and alternately revisit a mysterious house that, while located on 7 bis rue du Nadir aux Pommes, could easily be situated within the "parallel world" that Rouch describes. As the film's story unfolds, the spectator will repeatedly accompany Céline and Julie to this "parallel world," which as Rouch explains, is not only the home of the *bia,* or doubles, but also the home of the imagination, which includes dreams, reveries, and reflections, as well as the abode of transient magicians and sorcerers (96).

Rivette's work rejoins African ritual not only through Rouch but also through avant-garde theater director Peter Brook, who in 1972 led his entourage of actors to Africa, where they played improvised carpet shows in isolated villages. Brook saw in the parallel world that Africans inhabit the basis of theatrical experience, which is associated with a childhood state of oneness: "The African who has been brought up in the traditions of the African way of life has a very highly developed understanding of the double nature of reality. The visible and the invisible, and the free passage between the two, are for him, in a very concrete way, two modes of the same thing. Something which is the basis of the theatre experience—what we call make-believe—is simply a passing from the visible to the invisible and back again. In Africa, this is understood not as fantasy but as two aspects of the same reality" (128).

Brook's deep interest in Africa, which was shared by Rouch and Rivette, is connected to modernism's fascination with the so-called primitive. The paradoxical aspect of modern primitivism became evident during the interwar period of the 1920s and 1930s, an era that saw, on the one hand, the triumphant consolidation of European colonialism and, on the other, the dispersal of artists and poets across the globe in search of a primitive world that offered the contrary of Europe (Shelton 326). Pablo Picasso, Jean Palhaun, Blaise Cendrars, Tristan Tzara, and Georges Bataille, as Marie-Denise Shelton observes, were among those who found a source of inspiration in "the so-called primitive world" (326). Indeed, the revolutionary experiments of the Dadaists and the surrealists were predicated on a return to the "primitive" structures of affective experience (Shelton 326). While economic exploitation and violent political oppression were undeniably responsible for Europe's initial exposure to African art and cultural history, as cultural theorist Sieglinde Lemke points out, the fact that European writers and artists found in African experience a source of inspiration cannot be completely written off as cultural imperialism (412). Modern primitivism provided a means to rethink the relation between black and white cultures as a "vital hybrid," which would destabilize the opposition that the colonialist enterprise was founded on (Lemke 409). This trend in modernism, which Lemke defines as the "primitivist modernist aesthetic," is composed of art works in which the influence of African expression manifests itself not in terms of thematic content but in a blend of forms (410).

Rivette's film reflects the primitivist modernist aesthetic in its understanding of parallel realities associated with the African experience. The mythic "parallel world" of *Céline et Julie* forms the formal and conceptual foundation of Rivette's work throughout the decade, particularly *Scènes de la vie parallèle* (Scenes from a Parallel Life). Yet *Céline et Julie* holds a unique place in the director's oeuvre, for it is his first comedy. In the key 1974 interview with Rosenbaum, Sedofsky, and Adair, "Phantom Interviewers over Rivette," Rivette insists that he had "the desire from the very beginning to do something close to comedy, and even frankly commedia dell'arte" (21). Rivette may have found inspiration in the work of early film comedians, whose comic routines relied on strategies of the commedia, such as Charlie Chaplin, the Marx Brothers, Laurel and Hardy, and W. C. Fields. He might also have watched the performances of Rouch's African actors, who Enrico Fulchignoni compares with those of the commedia, as they are types, wear masks, and thus are able to "facilitate the elaboration of plots, of canvases that can be infinitely multiplied" (180). Aware of Rouch's methods, Rivette similarly allowed Berto and Labourier latitude to invent their scenes but reasserted control over the film's complex structure, producing a final product that, as Berto exclaims, was "Calculated to the millimeter!" (qtd. in Jordan 23).

Rivette relies on comic devices of the commedia in *Céline et Julie,* particularly its word play *lazzi*. Generally, one could describe *lazzi* as comic routines, planned or unplanned, that relied on broad physical gestures, improvised dialogue, and clowning. The interactions between the two women characters often resemble comic routines that rely on word play *lazzi,* which can include the strange use of language, constant repetition, misunderstood words, puns, insults, and storytelling (Gordon 56). The first word play *lazzo* that occurs in the film stands out in sharp contrast to the virtually silent opening chase sequence. Following the intertitles denoting the passage of time, "But the following morning . . .," Céline proceeds to lure Julie into the "parallel world" that she inhabits, appearing out of the blue at the library where Julie works and later that afternoon at the door of her flat. Bemused, Julie invites Céline in to take a shower and listens while her new acquaintance recounts a bizarre, intricate tale about her African safari. In view of Rivette's engagement with the work of Rouch and Brook, it is perhaps no coincidence that Africa serves as the linguistic thread that begins to unravel into a fantastic *lazzo*. Céline begins: "We were dying of heat, every day in the savannah chasing animals. I had a boa conquistador." Here, Céline replaces the term appropriate to her discussion, "boa constrictor," with her own combination "boa conquistador," which not only shifts the cultural context from Africa to Spain, but also the species, from animal to man. Either man or animal could potentially work within the context of her subsequent description: "I had a boa conquistador that quite adored me. He wasn't dangerous. I'd put him around my neck." In the next room, Julie enters into the play with meaning, as she fondles Céline's feather "boa" and wraps it around her neck. Next, Julie tries on her clownish mask of mustache and glasses, becoming a Groucho Marx look-alike, while Céline describes her traumatic escape from the jealous "Zouba, the giantess," who had wanted to skin her alive. Céline borrows the name "Zouba" from a delirious Jerry Lewis monologue in Frank Tashlin's musical comedy, *Artists and Models* (1955), which served as a direct source of inspiration for the sequence. After her shower, Céline finishes her tall tale, disclosing that in the wake of her trauma she had seen a Japanese acupuncturist in Hong Kong and that following her treatment, her hair that had fallen out grew back in—all red—like Julie's, only afterward returning to normal. The entire scene might be read as a tribute either to Jerry Lewis's inspired performance or the Marx Brothers' wacky use of *lazzi*; it could also be understood as directly participating in the comic lineage of the commedia.

The following morning, Céline pretends to be Julie when she answers her phone and engages in conversation with the latter's childhood boyfriend, her provincial cousin Grégoire, a.k.a. Guilou. Unbeknownst to Julie, Céline arranges a rendezvous later that afternoon with Guilou (Philippe Clévenot), whose black-and-white photo she spots on Julie's bulletin board. Wearing her femininity with the exaggerated self-awareness of masquerade, Céline arrives at St. Vincent Square sporting a wide-brimmed white hat and lace dress intended to mimic a bridal gown. Taken in by this performance, Guilou solemnly rises from the bench where he is seated and grandly proposes to Céline, offering her a ring. Céline swoons, sweeping her hand across her brow and knocking her hat off. When music and dance commence to fête the occasion, Rivette reframes the couple, who quick-step their way into the realm of musical theater. The romantic illusion is utterly shattered, however, when Guilou's pants drop to the ground, and Céline tells him to go "jack-off among the roses." As the scene unfolds, the spectator becomes complicit in Céline's masquerade and participates alongside her in a manner best described with reference to the film's title, which contains the phrase "vont en bateau" (go boating) that could be understood as "montent un bateau à quelqu'un" (take someone for a ride or to play a practical joke on someone). While Céline mercilessly rejects and humiliates the distraught suitor who she "takes for a ride," we empathize with her and revel in her charade. Rather than confirming the inscription on the back of Guilou's photo, "the child who has become a man," we identify with Rivette's heroines, "girls who have become women."

The manner in which Céline works Julie's fiancé, conning him out of an engagement ring that she subsequently gives to an anonymous woman onlooker, recalls those scenes from Czech filmmaker Vera Chytilová's revolutionary *Daisies* (Sedmikrásky; 1966) in which two beautiful women, the blond Marie 1 (Jitka Cerhová) and the brunette Marie 2 (Ivana Karbanová), entice rich suitors into paying for extravagant meals in exchange for sexual favors that the two girls never deliver. In both films, canny heroines assume alternate or fabricated identities in order to dupe the men, who delude themselves that they are passing as worldly, seductive, and authoritative. The subversive role-playing of Chytilová's heroines finds its parallel in another scene from *Céline et Julie*. This scene shows how Julie substitutes for Céline, mirroring Céline's substitution for Julie in the earlier scene, when she fields a phone call from the latter's boss, M'sieur Dédé, who runs a club in Montmartre. Céline performs there nightly as the magician Mandrakore, reinventing the Depression-era comic strip character Mandrake the Magician. Switching the name of the act from Mandrakore to Kamikaze, Julie enters the spotlight dressed in a top hat, black tights, and tails. At first, she provides the two men in sunglasses seated in the audience with the provocative striptease that they are anticipating, but then on an impulse, challenges them, "And you, what can you do? Here you are ogling every inch of me behind your refrigerated glasses!" As her frustration and anger mount, she yells outrageous insults at them: "Cosmic twilight pimps! Voyeurs, perverts!" The confrontational quality of this cabaret performance, as Robin Wood notes, pays tribute to Maureen O'Hara's performance as the frustrated ballerina Judy, who in Dorothy Arzner's *Dance, Girl, Dance* (1940) turns on her male audience and harshly scolds them for their shameless attempt "to objectify her as a sexual image for the male gaze" (9).

The choreography of the audition scene from *Céline et Julie* undeniably sets the stage for feminine defiance. In their respective films, Rivette and Chytilová's heroines adopt theatrical personas to subvert the predetermined script of patriarchy, moving from ostensible docility to outright defiance. Chytilová's defiance and daring improvisational method enthralled Rivette, propelling him toward his own high-spirited act in *Céline et Julie*. Rivette's film, in turn, inspired a new generation of French directors, such as Érick Zonka, whose film *La vie rêvée des anges* (The Dream Life of Angels; 1998) pays tribute to *Céline et Julie* in a scene in which the two young heroines, Isa (Élodie Bouchez) and Marie (Natacha Régnier), audition for hostess positions in a French club with a Hollywood theme. Rather than openly contest the female starlet stereotype, as Julie had done, the two women conform to it but in such a way as to implicitly critique it. Dressed in scruffy street clothes and with a thick accent, Isa commences a hilarious improvised performance of the pop diva Madonna's hit number "Like a Virgin," while the svelte blond Marie saunters across the stage as a sultry Lauren Bacall. Although neither girl gets the job, their performances succeed in exposing the enormous gap between the real life of working-class girls and the idealized dream life of starlets.

While the heroines of *La vie rêvée des anges* and *Dance, Girl, Dance* explore the alternately tragic and comic import of female role-playing and competition between women, the two heroines of *Céline et Julie* command the double or *bia* not only to form their own reciprocal relation but a reciprocity between double worlds: the everyday world of home and work in relation to the parallel world of the imagination, located within the "Phantom House" on 7 bis rue du Nadir aux Pommes. Residing within the Phantom House, a second pair of women, the brunette Sophie (Marie-France Pisier), who often appears in blue satin, and the blond Camille (Bulle Ogier), typically dressed in red, serves as the double of their Parisian counterparts, Céline and Julie, respectively. The phantom ladies Sophie and Camille not only inhabit a different space from their Parisian counterparts but also a different story, which demands a distinctively melodramatic comportment, speech, and attire. While Rivette has confided that the commedia provided a source of inspiration for certain scenes involving Céline and Julie, he later indicates that the theatricality of scenes in the house was unplanned: "Even when the theatre is not present in a clear way, it appears in a manner that is almost involuntary. In *Céline and Julie Go Boating,* for example, this happened little by little in the house that became a theatrical space. This was predictable, to some extent, and was subsequently accentuated during filming. I was occasionally struck during the editing to see that certain things were more theatrical than I had foreseen" (qtd. in Armel 63).

The phantom ladies Camille and Sophie are characters within a story that is a loose adaptation of Henry James's novel *The Other House* (1896). Rivette's scriptwriter Gregorio came up with the idea of the James story, and it was Gregorio, along with Rivette and the three principal actors Ogier, Pisier, and Barbet Schroeder, who wrote the dialogue for the scenes within the house. In addition to the collaborative work of composition, the literary history of James's novel also affected the process of adaptation, for *The Other House* was in origin dramatic. The novel first appeared as a play scenario under the title of *The Promise,* was then published as a serialized novel in 1895, and later, in 1909, was adapted into a play. James describes the story as that of a young widower who has lost his wife and has a little girl. After several years, the widower meets a young woman, Jean Martle, with whom he falls in love. Jean Martle, who James describes as his "Good Heroine," returns the widower's passionate affection and perhaps, even more important, shares his love for the little girl (viii–ix). Another woman, Rose Armiger, also figures prominently in the story. James describes this woman as the "Bad Heroine," who has loved the widower from the instant she saw him and who has known him from before his wife's death (viii–ix). On the fated day of his daughter's birthday, the Bad Heroine, Rose, wreaks vengeance against the widower, drowning his child in the river and implicating her rival, Jean, in the crime.

In the film, Rivette modifies the characters from *The Other House* and overlays them onto those taken from one of James's short stories, "The Romance of Certain Old Clothes," the writer's first tale of the supernatural. This tale of the occult chronicles a similar story of jealous rivalry between two sisters and their mutual relationship with a man that they both love. Rivette's film mostly relies on the story's climactic close in which the jealous older sister races off to the attic to open a mysterious Pandora's box, a locked trunk containing her dead sister's dresses and finery. When her husband ascends the stairs to the attic to find her, he is shocked to discover the hideous sight of his wife, who has fallen beside the open trunk, her face marked by ten wounds from two revengeful ghostly hands.

The occult element from the James short story blends well with the melodramatic dimensions of *The Other House* in *Céline et Julie*. While the threads of the two James stories are intricately interwoven within the Phantom House, its principal characters, which include the dour widower Olivier (played by the film's producer, Barbet Schroeder), the jealous older sister Camille, and the sinister seductress Sophie, shift in and out of roles, which at times could be derived from either story. The murder of Madlyn in her bed is the pivotal event from the film that draws the threads of the two stories together: the imprint of the red hand that stains her bed sheets not only invokes the occult event at the close of James's short story but also the melodramatic climax of the child's murder in *The Other House*. Logic dictates that either heroine in *Céline et Julie* could potentially be the culprit, for just as the icon of the red hand serves as the formal marker implicating the hemophiliac Camille in her sibling role from "The Romance of Certain Old Clothes," the scene's content equally condemns the child murderer Sophie, playing the part of the Bad Heroine Rose from *The Other House*.

While the nurse is a minor character in both James stories, in the film, it is this pivotal figure, Miss Angèle, a.k.a. Mys-tère-Angè-le (Mystery Angel), who provides Céline and Julie with an entry point into the Phantom House. Julie discovers her own peculiar transformative power through that of the character Miss Angèle on her return from her initial visit there. Propelled from the house as though tossed from a wind tunnel, Julie returns from a voyage that recalls that of the poet in Cocteau's *Orphée* (Orpheus; 1950), who is hurled through the zone that provides a passageway between the land of the living and the dead. Just as she is catching her breath in a cab, a piece of hard candy unexpectedly emerges from her mouth. Pieces of candy continue to allow both heroines the latitude to move back and forth freely between the space of the Phantom House and that of the city. Bonbons make available to them an interior story, which takes place in the manner of the dramatization of *The Other House* from which it is derived, in the halls that interconnect drawing rooms to stairwells. The rigid camera that frames the characters' violent gestures and histrionic responses accentuates the restricted, theatrical space that they inhabit. The theatricality of the Phantom House draws not only on the melodramatic manner of the stage but also silent cinema. As Julie remarks, "It's an entire epoch . . . a school! The Odeon. A tragedy. . . . They smell like mothballs." This parallel world not only holds an irresistible fascination for its heroines Céline and Julie but also for Rivette, who remembers his first encounter with "the Griffiths, the Stillers, the Fairbanks, all the cinema of the 1910s and 1920s," which left him with "the very strong feeling that there had actually been in the great films of Griffith and Stiller and Stroheim, or the first films of Dreyer and Murnau, an innocence, which had been irretrievably lost" (qtd. in Frappat, *Secret* 64). The parallel world, which the heroines revisit, thus evokes not only the innocence of a childhood memory for them but also the innocence of an art form, which is shadowed by its theatrical ancestor.

Céline and Julie command an authoritative use of the double or *bia* to return to the Phantom House, where they revisit the curious female characters of early crime melodrama and uncover an infanticide. Theatricalization opens up the possibility of transformation for Céline and Julie, who self-consciously deploy theatrical conventions to reenvision their roles and thereby liberate themselves and their cohort Madlyn from "scripted" lives. Wearing matching magical dinosaur rings, the heroines arrive together at the Phantom House and quickly retire to a vacated room, where they dress in identical nurses' uniforms. After their arrival at the house, the heroines rapidly transform it, selecting their own dressing room, similar to the one occupied by Suzanne Simonin in *La religieuse*. Before their entrance onto central stage, they click their rings together and recite an esoteric chant: "One, two, three. Eye of a lynx and head of wood!" While this singsong mantra is intended to bring the two heroines good luck, it also magically breaks time and space within the house into three dramatic acts. Céline and Julie recite it three times just prior to their alternating performances as Miss Angèle, imposing an ulterior dramatic logic that had not been previously apparent. They also transform stately salons into theatrical wings where they can meet backstage between acts to relax and have a smoke, clown around, or exchange notes on their criminal investigation. They are unable to adjust their acting style to the manner of stagey melodrama, however, for they arrive late, muff their lines, miss their cues, and even enter the same scene simultaneously to play the same part. We are provided an intermission of sorts when there is a cut to black accompanied by off-screen applause.

When their attempts to recite lines and mimic pictorial gestures within the terms of the tragic melodrama utterly fail, the two re-create the role of Miss Angèle within the terms of the commedia as a stock comic type known as the "servetta." Like Miss Angèle, the servetta also serves two mistresses in a play: the *prima donna* is the "most poetical and lackadaisical," thus closely resembling Camille, and the *seconda donna* is her darker shadow, thus recalling Sophie (W. Smith 5). Rather than the stern countenance and robotic, restrained responses of the nurse, who simply plays her part in the tragic melodrama of the Phantom House, the role of the servetta that both heroines adopt combines the traits of a sixteenth-century Franceschina with those of a seventeenth-century Columbina. Franceschina, who is typically clad in a simple nurselike uniform with mobcap and apron, is described as supple and strong like a circus artist, whereas the younger Columbina is presented as buoyant and vivacious, possessing a keen wit that enables her to emerge effortlessly from the most involved intrigues (Nicoll 96–97). Be it the robust Franceschina or the clever, sprightly Columbina, the servetta remains on the periphery of the action and, consequently, becomes a spectator herself, who observes the plotting of others and colludes with the audience in the sense that she can discern the machinations of those around her. Assuming the role of servetta, Céline and Julie likewise collude with the spectator, who revels in their clownish antics and listens to their chanting, while Olivier, Sophie, and Camille remain impervious. The two heroines improvise openly when they opt for a delectable Argentine tango instead of the subdued, programmed music of the "mélo." Céline and Julie grasp each other and invent their own bravura interpretation, paying tribute to the light-hearted spirit of Columbina and her entr'acte performances embellished by the tambourine. Rather than celebrating the reunion of the heterosexual couple, the heroines' rollicking dance number defines an intense and potentially transgressive relationship between two female characters.

Madlyn's game of "Grandmother's Steps," which is marked by her count, "One, two, three," echoes the heroines' magical mantra that enables them both to appropriate dramatic space within the Phantom House and move freely within it. The child's game demands that the three Phantom characters stop suddenly and assume statuesque poses as though situated within a tableau, a nod to the nineteenth-century pictorialism that serves as the limit point of the actors' performance within their melodramatic scenario. Subject to perpetual regression in

Figure 11. Céline and Julie opt for an Argentine tango in *Céline et Julie vont en bateau.*

time and space, the three characters, Camille, Sophie, and Olivier, are struck dumb and deprived of movement, frozen momentarily within the tableau of domestic melodrama. In an effort to escape from the three "petrified puppets," Madlyn and her cohorts swallow the bonbons while once more repeating the charmed words "One, two, three," a combination that now indicates the formation of an alternative female threesome that possesses the supernatural power necessary to move at will between two worlds. Transported magically back to their Paris flat, the two heroines are enormously relieved to find Madlyn blindfolded and standing in their bathtub, where she is anticipating yet another game. Céline and Julie invite her to go boating with them. An extreme long shot shows the three ladies in a boat rowing leisurely upstream. Their immersion in the sensual pleasures of the summer sunlight is suddenly interrupted, however, when they simultaneously turn to look at something that lies outside the limits of the frame. Insisting once again on the charmed number three, we are shown three consecutive close-ups of Julie, Céline, and Madlyn, who are all looking intently at something that we do not see. A cut reveals only the sun's rays reflected in the motionless water, when suddenly, a second rowboat silently glides into view. We share the point of view of all three ladies, who watch while the ghostly, frozen figures of Camille, Olivier, and Sophie float quietly by. A panoramic perspective subsequently reveals the two boats drifting apart in opposite directions, one moving toward the light, the other into shadow.

This arresting image that depicts parallel worlds in transit might be viewed retrospectively as an emblematic allusion to a crucial point of passage in Rivette's stylistic evolution. Like two vessels moving through uncharted waters that meet at last, the two distinctive trends that inform Rivette's style prior to *Céline et Julie*—the introspective tableaux of *La religieuse* and the improvised performances of *Noli me tangere*—converge in this film, where they finally find their culmination. Much like his heroines who pass into a world of childhood memory, Rivette revisits an earlier phase in his artistic evolution, that of the tableau. He returns to theatrical and pictorial aesthetics, specifically those contemporaneous with James's literary works, thereby consolidating his earlier approach to the adaptation of Diderot. He relies on the codes and conventions of theatrical melodrama and silent cinema to construct the profilmic space of the Phantom House, which becomes progressively associated with the paralyzing theatricality that condemns its soulless inhabitants. Those very boundaries that had constrained Rivette in *La religieuse*—story, script, and acting style—are insisted upon within the Phantom House, where they ultimately accede to the spontaneous, improvised performance style associated not only with his earlier work, *Noli me tangere,* but also the strategies of the commedia.

The film's final scene returns us to where we began. Cloaked in her blue feather boa, Céline appears to be napping on the same park bench where the chase between the two women had begun. She is startled by the sudden appearance of the redhead who, as she races past, drops her magic book. Céline hails her, but to no avail. She then jumps up and runs after her, thus reentering the tale at its point of commencement. This final textual pirouette in which the two heroines exchange roles illustrates the fully reciprocal nature of a relationship in which each forms the *bia* or double of the other, transforming crime melodrama through comedy, silent tableaux through virtuoso *lazzo,* patriarchal domesticity through feminine telepathy. The parallel worlds that the two inhabit, here, become indiscernible; the everyday world mutates with the dreamlike world of imagination to become one with it. Rivette finally rejoins both heroines in their pursuit of a parallel world, for as the taker (recorder) and giver (reproducer) of doubles or souls or reflections, he similarly assumes the role of the magician who entices us with this possibility.

| | |

In certain respects, the theatricality of *L'amour par terre* (Love on the Ground; 1984) and *La bande des quatre* (Gang of Four; 1989) represents a departure from the formal concerns that had preoccupied Rivette during the previous decade. In these two films, theater is no longer associated with improvisational stylistics or an operatic, esoteric mise-en-scène where chants resonate within cosmic force fields. In both films, theatricality becomes equivalent to the work of a dramatic text. In *L'amour par terre,* actresses Emily (Jane Birkin) and Charlotte (Géraldine Chaplin) rehearse dramatist Clément Roquemaure's (Jean-Pierre Kalfon) new play within his isolated, haunted villa located on the outskirts of Paris. In *La bande des quatre,* four actresses and another attend the reputable theater course taught by Constance Dumas (Bulle Ogier), successively taking their places on the proscenium stage to recite the lines of Enlightenment playwright Pierre Carlet de Marivaux's *The Double Inconstancy*. While both films revisit the "exteriorized" theatricality of *Paris nous appartient* and *L'amour fou* in which the metteur en scène, the troupe, and the text are placed on display, they also reinvent the representation of the occult found in *Céline et Julie*. Recalling James's three spectral figures who reside in the Phantom House, ghosts haunt the houses of *L'amour par terre* and *La bande des quatre,* becoming as audible as an ocean from behind a locked door or soft footsteps from within hollow walls, as tangible as an invisible hand extended from a chimney or an unanticipated oneiric vision.

In *L'amour par terre,* an unfinished theater script provides the pretext for the film's story in which metteur en scène Clément Roquemaure introduces himself backstage to the two actresses, Emily and Charlotte, who are appearing in his play and invites them to his villa. The next day, the two actresses arrive at his residence in St. Cloud, where they discover the magnificent villa Gounod, which also appeared in Alain Robbe-Grillet's *La belle captive* (The Beautiful Prisoner; 1983). Its labyrinthine corridors and baroque enormity recall those of the luxurious palace in Robbe-Grillet and Resnais's modernist classic *L'année dernière à Marienbad* (Last Year at Marienbad; 1961), a film whose experimental strategies with time and sensual visual patterning provide Rivette with an important source of inspiration. When Charlotte and Emily arrive at the villa, they come upon Roquemaure encased within the vermilion tiger-striped walls of his lair. They agree to appear with another actor Silvano (Facundo Bo) in a single performance of the author's unfinished play, which is based on a romantic episode from his past. As the two prepare to assume their new roles and names from the play, their own names within the film's fiction, Emily and Charlotte, invoke those of the nineteenth-century Brontë sisters, anticipating Rivette's subsequent film adaptation of *Wuthering Heights*.

While bearing British authors' names, the two characters are also modeled on their French predecessors Céline and Julie, as they adopt theatrical roles to intervene within the story of the haunted villa. Resembling Céline and Julie, who envision themselves as their doubles, Emily and Charlotte also are able to see phantom reflections of themselves in certain rooms in the villa Gounod where, as Charlotte remarks, "It was as if there were a mirror." The two come into contact with a conjurer, Paul (André Dussollier), who resides there and possesses a gift that enables him to bestow visions on Emily and Charlotte, simply by touching them. The spectator is invited to share their visions, which could be interpreted as the reflection of a mood or a premonition. At one moment, we watch as a slow lateral pan redirects our gaze away from Emily, who is embracing Paul, to reveal her vision of an adjacent room, where she suddenly appears to herself as a corpse overseen by a mysterious young woman in red. We initially share her alarm but later realize that this hallucination is the key scene central to the completion of Roquemaure's play. While the phantom reflections of the two actresses haunt certain rooms in the villa, recorded sound occasionally escapes from others, such as the screeching of tropical birds that have migrated from a rainforest, grand orchestral flourishes, or the roar of ocean waves accompanied by the occasional cry of a seagull. When Emily attempts to determine the source of such sounds, she discovers only a single crab crawling across the floor. She later wonders during dinner whether or not the crab that she and the other guests are served had been washed in with the waves crashing behind the closed door, bearing a supernatural significance akin to the signs of the Zodiac that adorn the circular vestibule.

Like the conjurer, the metteur en scène Barbe Bleu (Bluebeard) also commands doubles. He casts Charlotte in the central role of Barbara-Béatrice, the phantom woman in red from his past who has mysteriously disappeared from the villa and from the lives of those who remain. Emily is cast in the male role that corresponds to the conjurer Paul, while Silvano plays the part of Roquemaure. The theatrical and cinematic scripts converge when, one night, Charlotte confesses to Emily that she not only is rehearsing the role but believes herself to *be* Roquemaure's Barbara "in flesh and bone." Rivette once more calls our attention to the relation between the dramatic role and the real, the replica and original, in a subsequent scene in the garden where Charlotte grapples with L'Amour. She initiates a playful flirtation with the statue of L'Amour but subsequently discovers in the course of mounting it that it is not a marble original but a plaster knockoff when it crashes to the ground and breaks into shards. Rivette finds his source of inspiration for this scene and also the film's title in symbolist Paul Verlaine's poem, "L'Amour par terre," which begins with the line, "The wind the other night has cast down Love/ which, in the most mysterious corner of the park,/ was smiling while maliciously tautening its bow," and continues in the second stanza, "It's sad to see the pedestal where the name of the artist/ can be read with difficulty among the shadows of a tree." The fragile replica of L'Amour that lures Charlotte and the audience like a red herring serves as the metaphoric double of the theatrical production in process in the villa. It also anticipates the trite tableau that Frenhofer offers to his audience in lieu of the interred original in *La belle noiseuse*. Roquemaure ultimately demands that the broken statue be replaced with a replica of the replica, a moment that Rivette underscores in the final shot of the film as though to point to the "sutured" aspect of his own story of L'Amour.

While theatrical reflexivity is central to the two-hour version of *L'amour par terre,* Rivette's exploration of duration and visual patterning is more in evidence in the original 170-minute uncut version of the film, which did not receive commercial distribution until the 2002 release of Arte-Vidéo's restored DVD edition. In the videotaped interview with Frédéric Bonnaud available on the Arte edition's Compléments de Programme, Rivette affirms that he had been forced at the time to cut the film to approximately two hours to conform to the demands of its distributor. To explain how the editing process was accomplished, Rivette describes his approach to the original version, which he affirms "was structured similarly to Raymond Roussel's *New Impressions of Africa,* where there is a phrase, and then a parenthesis, which is tied to yet another phrase, and another parenthesis, ad infinitum" (qtd. in Bonnaud). He claims that to go from two hours and fifty minutes to two hours he simply "lifted the parentheses" (qtd. in Bonnaud). Such parentheses permit Birkin's character Emily sufficient time and space in the original film to indulge in random encounters with offbeat characters on the metro, or Chaplin's character Charlotte to converse easily in a bar one night with the elusive woman from Roquemaure's past, Barbara-Béatrice, who in the two-hour version appears only within the parameters of Roquemaure's play and in his villa. While not entirely dissatisfied with the shorter version, Rivette feels that it unfolds "more in one key," while the uncut film is more complex, and its tone, more melancholic (qtd. in Bonnaud).

Rivette's interrogation of the boundaries between theater and cinema that characterizes *L'amour par terre* crystallizes within the opening sequence of *La bande des quatre*. We watch as Anna (Fejria Deliba) finishes her espresso in a Paris café. She leaves and enters a nearby building, where she becomes engaged in conversation with another woman who enters immediately afterward. We do not realize that we are watching two actresses rehearsing the opening scene of Marivaux's *The Double Inconstancy* until the offscreen voice of Constance Dumas (Bulle Ogier) intervenes, instructing Raphaële (Caroline Gasser) not to rely on her pocket notes during a performance. The film thus begins with an exploration of the parameters of theatrical and profilmic space, inviting us to reflect on our implied position as members of an onscreen and offscreen audience.

Theatrical and cinematic scripts converge within the opening scene of *La bande des quatre* but then diverge in scenes that follow. Theater rehearsals take place on a proscenium stage in an old Paris theater where the mysterious actress and metteur en scène Constance Dumas lives and works.[15] Repeated traveling shots of a commuter train transport the apprentice actresses as well as the spectator back and forth between Dumas's Paris theater and the haunted house in the suburbs of Montfermeil where the four theater students, Claude (Laurence Côte), Anna (Fejria Deliba), Joyce (Bernadette Giraud), Lucia (Ines d'Almeida), and another, Cécile (Nathalie Richard), share their scripts, their stories, and their lives. We are introduced to the house and its inhabitants just as a new student from Portugal, Lucia, is moving into her room, and the lithe, blond Cécile is leaving to pursue a romantic liaison. Cécile jokingly warns Anna, who is taking advantage of Lucia's arrival to move into Cécile's old room, that a ghost persists in occupying the chamber. Unlike the Jamesian occult in evidence in the Phantom House of *Céline et Julie*, the ghost of Montfermeil maintains a complicitous relation with its heroines.[16]

In *La bande des quatre*, the words of the author take precedence in the actresses' individuated interpretations of them. Intervening from the audience in the film's opening scene, Constance interrupts Anna and Raphaële's performance of the respective roles of Silvia and Trivelin from Marivaux's *The Double Inconstancy*. The play tells the story of two young lovers, Harlequin and the idealized country girl Silvia, characters who clearly reflect the commedia dell'arte tradition. The Prince, who has fallen in love with Silvia, puts her love for Harlequin to the test when he imprisons her in his palace. Flaminia, a woman of the court, conspires with the Prince and his servant Trivelin to destroy the love of Silvia for Harlequin. The Prince disguises himself as a common guardsman to seduce Silvia, while Flaminia proceeds to lure Harlequin, who has been brought to the castle to appease Silvia's fury. Against his best intentions, Harlequin falls in love with the duplicitous Flaminia, while Silvia is smitten with the guardsman, whom she later realizes is her Prince. Assessing Anna's interpretation, Constance cautions her students: "it's necessary to express the words, and the words aren't your words, they are the words of Marivaux." Here, Rivette invites us, like the students seated in the theater, to contemplate the work of the text, for he believed, "The work is always much more interesting to show than the result. I can watch a coppersmith in a Rouquier film for three hours. A caldron, even if it is the most beautiful in the world, I will have viewed from all angles in three minutes" (qtd. in Skorecki 29).

During other rehearsals, the actresses perform passages from the classic works of seventeenth-century dramatists, such as Pierre Corneille's little-known tragedy *Suréna,* Jean Racine's *Iphigénie* and *Esther,* and Jean-Baptiste Molière's comedy *Les femmes savantes*. The continual shifting between theatrical registers throughout the film forces our attention to the notion of performance. At one point, Constance reproaches Cécile for her overwrought interpretation of a passage from *The Double Inconstancy* and admonishes her for transforming Marivaux's comedy into a tragedy. Claude counters that she knows how the passage should be interpreted, as other students in the class join in to respond with this light ditty: "I don't want a Prince and I want a Baron even less. Tra, la, la . . . I want my friend Pierre, who is now in prison." The lyrics foreshadow the fate of Cécile's romantic involvement with Antoine Lucas, who is later arrested and wrongly convicted of a crime.

In the film, Cécile's boyfriend, Antoine Lucas, appears only as a televised image and voice broadcast over the radio. Rivette bases his characterization on a *fait divers* detailing the infamous trial of French writer Roger Knobelspiess that was taking place in Rouen at the time of the shoot. Knobelspiess had already been convicted and served time for petty theft, a crime that he denied. Following his release, he was again picked up for theft and placed in a high-security prison. Knobelspiess constantly fought against his false imprisonment and became a *cause*

Figure 12. The rehearsal of *Suréna*, where students discuss Antoine Lucas's escape in *La bande des quatre*.

*célèbre* within the French intellectual and artistic community. Michel Foucault even provided the preface of Knobelspiess's book, entitled *Q.H.S.: Quartier de haute sécurité* (1980). After the left gained power in 1981, Knobelspiess received a retrial and was at last liberated. His subsequent arrest and trial, which was concurrent with the filming of *La bande des quatre,* were discursively constructed by the right-wing press as symptomatic of the laxity of the left and the irresponsibility of intellectuals. The tragic dimensions of Knobelspiess, who Rivette viewed as "a modern-day Jean Valjean," inflect his filmic representation of Lucas (qtd. in Boujut 95). Rivette confides, "In this film, I wanted to look at, along with the little predicaments of my actresses, the dramatic aspect of our lives in contemporary France" (qtd. in Boujut 95).

To stage a mock trial of Lucas/Knobelspiess, Claude, Lucia, Anna, and Joyce band together in a room whose strident red, white, and blue decor invokes the symbolic colors of French statehood. Invading the enclosed space of the theater room where the actresses assume their roles as judge, jury, and accused, an occasional gust of wind intrudes on the performance. We might be provoked to ask, "Is this wind westerly that blows," thus reiterating the memorable line from *Pericles,* or we might think of it as a blast of air from the passing train that throughout the film is moving between stations and scenes. Marivaux's play, which derides the decadence of the French throne and the frivolity of its subjects, unfolds in parallel with the actresses' parodic performance, which exposes the corruption of the contemporary French state and the mindless complicity of its citizens. The implicit comparison that the film provides between classical and contemporary periods forces the spectator to ask: To what degree do Marivaux's Enlightenment subjects who allow themselves to be conned in affairs of the heart resemble those contemporary French citizens who permit themselves to be duped in matters of human rights and justice? At the close of their performance, the actresses sing these verses: "There are things hidden behind things, endlessly, it's tiring/There are reasons for things seeming wrong/never miss anything/When things seem wrong, you look for a cause/and the cause is the innocent/Ah, ah, ah, yes indeed! The innocent make the best victims." The phrase "things hidden behind things," on the surface, implicates the media conspiracy that ensnares Lucas and the actual personage Knobelspiess on which the Lucas character is based; it reflexively implicates the royal conspiracy, which entraps the commedia characters Harlequin and Silvia.

In their attempts to aid Cécile and Antoine Lucas, the troupe has most to fear from the false seducer Thomas Santini (Benoît Régent), a.k.a. Lucien, a.k.a. Henri de Marsay. He approaches each actress by turn under a different pseudonym in an attempt to gain access to their house, where keys to a safe containing incriminating documents are hidden. While driving Anna home after her debut at a photography exhibit, he first introduces himself to her as a printer of false identity cards, then as a painter of stolen cars, and finally as a printer of art catalogs. He later seduces Claude, claiming that he is searching for Frenhofer's stolen painting, "La belle noiseuse"; however, his penchant for profit from the spoils of mechanical reproduction anticipates the character Porbus from *Divertimento*. Joyce later describes him: "This kind of guy, he's a Walmart where you can find everything: friendship, trafficking, loyalty, cheating, ballistics, slick, cultured." Were he a perfume, Anna claims, he would be a potpourri. Joyce and Anna take turns speculating on whom he would be were he a famous man, throwing out the names of Casanova, Pasqua, Jekyll, and Hyde. His Machiavellian character might appease Rivette's wish to "show those cold monsters that are unshowable: the State, Money, the Police, the Party. . . . Everything that terrifies me!"

(qtd. in Boujut 95). After Thomas reveals his (false?) identity card to the actresses to prove that he is, in fact, a criminal investigator, he proceeds to stake out their house to entrap Lucas following the latter's escape from the police. When Lucia's attempt to poison Thomas fails, he roughs her up and gets the keys off her. These are not only the keys that open the safe but also the phantom's keys, which can open the magical theater room. As Thomas attempts to flee, the four women rise up against him and slay him in an effort to save their friend Cécile and liberate Lucas. In this manner, they retain control of the keys that unlock their feminine potential and allow them to take control of their lives and their art.

Rivette dedicates his film "to the prisoners, to one among them, to those who await them." The dedication could be addressed to the contemporary personage Knobelspiess and his cinematic surrogate Lucas, the commedia dell'arte figures, Harlequin and Silvia, the missing actress Joyce, who we assume is arrested for Thomas's murder, and the metteur en scène Constance Dumas, who is ultimately detained for her complicity in Lucas's escape. The film's visual and verbal rhetoric that accomplishes an incessant back and forth shifting between arcane past and media-saturated present, comic and tragic theatrical registers, and theatrical and cinematic role playing, invites the spectator to contemplate the moral vacillation between truth and fabrication at the heart of the French state. The actresses for whom "acting is not lying, but searching for truth" continue courageously with their dress rehearsal of the final scene, in which Lucia recites Silvia's parting words to Harlequin, "Console yourself as you can. . . . Then leave me alone, and that's the end of it." While her line could be read as a reflexive, auteurist remark directed at the film audience, Rivette might remind us, "It's a rehearsal, which is still not theater. The theater commences later, when we are no longer there, when the film has ended" (qtd. in Skorecki 29). In the months following the release of *La bande des quatre,* Rivette returned to the theater in the role of metteur en scène for the first time since his 1963 stage production of *La religieuse*. At Théâtre Gérard-Philipe in Saint-Denis, he directed productions of Corneille's *Tite et Bérénice* and Racine's *Bajazet* with the same group that had performed in *La bande des quatre,* including Laurence Côte, Fejria Deliba, and Bernadette Giraud.

| | |

The phantom film, *Marie et Julien* (1975), was to have been the first film in the tetralogy *Scènes de la vie parallèle,* which, until recently, seemed destined to remain unfinished. When Rivette suddenly disappeared from the set after only three days of filming, novelist Marguerite Duras offered to step in and complete the film, but Rivette's team of actors refused to proceed without him. The few shots that Rivette filmed on the set of *Marie et Julien* have never been found; all that remains is a skeleton script, which was written by filmmaker Claire Denis along with scriptwriters Gregorio and Parolini. The new version closely conforms to this original script, although Rivette was forced to reconceptualize the love story to suit the requirements of his contemporary team of actors, which included Emmanuelle Béart (Marie), with whom he had already worked on *La belle noiseuse,* and Jerzy Radziwilowicz (Julien), the equivocal Walser in *Secret défense*. With scriptwriters Pascal Bonitzer and Christine Laurent, Rivette developed the mysterious third figure of Madame X (Anne Brochet), who in the contemporary version becomes almost as important as the other two characters. Although Rivette had acquired an entirely new team of actors and writers, he rejoins cinematographer William Lubtchansky, who had worked with him on almost every film since *Les filles du feu* (with the exception of *Hurlevent, La bande des quatre,* and *Haut bas fragile*). It is the lens of Lubtchansky that in *Histoire de Marie et Julien* (The Story of Marie and Julien; 2003) recaptures the visual magnificence of the *quarantaine,* the magical temporal zone during which goddesses can appear on earth and converse with mortals. Rivette's interest in magic and fantasy as sources of female empowerment resurfaces in the recent film from its source in the supernatural feminine cosmology of *Les filles de feu* and also in the commedia high jinks of *Céline et Julie*.

While thematically and visually tied to the tetralogy, *Histoire de Marie et Julien* lacks the improvised music that provided a formal connection between *Noroît* and *Duelle*. Yet, the chiming and ticking of clocks in the rambling home of the clocksmith Julien could be said to unite the film with the 1970s cycle through a hollow sonority that Rivette intended. It is through Julien's point of view that the film begins. A traveling shot through a grassy, sun-swept park is retrospectively attributed to the reflective bachelor Julien, who is seated alone on a bench. We share his point of view as he looks up at the foliage of a tree above him. His seemingly arbitrary glance upward recalls that of Julie, who seated in a similar park in *Céline et Julie* glances at the rustling leaves above her just before noticing Céline. When Julien looks down, we identify with his gaze as he spots the spectral Marie, dressed in an all-white suit, walking before him. Unlike the distracted Céline, who scurries away, Marie recognizes Julien immediately and stops to chat. They reminisce about their last rendezvous more than a year ago, and each describes to the other intimate details from the recent past. Suddenly, Marie pulls a large knife on Julien. There is an abrupt cut to a café, where Julien, hunched over the table where his unfinished beer remains, is just waking up after having momentarily dozed off. The entire opening park scene must then be read retroactively as his dream. During a videotaped interview with Frappat in 2004, Rivette acknowledged the influence of Luis Buñuel. In my view, the opening dream sequence borrows from the postsurrealist classic *Belle de jour* (Buñuel; 1967), which opens with a sado-masochistic ritual in which the beautiful bourgeoisie Séverine (Catherine Deneuve) is violently whipped in the Bois de Boulogne, an event that is only retrospectively understood as the heroine's dream following an abrupt cut to her husband watching from their bedroom. In both films, the space of the real ultimately becomes increasingly indistinguishable from the space of dream and erotic imaginings.

The rhythmic repartee between Marie and Julien in the opening scene in the park unfolds in a dreamlike manner that recalls that of Resnais's *La dernière année à Marienbad,* specifically the exchanges between its three somnambulist characters, "X" (Giorgio Albertazzi), "M" (Sacha Pitoëff), and M's mistress "A" (Delphine Seyrig). Resembling Resnais's characters, who appear to be enclosed within their own dimension, Marie is trapped between the living and the dead. She is a *revenante* (a spirit who comes back), a phenomenon that, Rivette observes, is applicable to "those persons who for one reason or another did not succeed in crossing—be it the river, path, tree, hill—the frontier that separates our world of the living and the world of the dead, which lies in the direction of *Noroît* (the northwest), and consequently are condemned to passing certain tests that will allow them to leave this state, which is quite uncomfortable, between the two worlds" (qtd. in Frappat, "Entretien"). Marie confides to Julien that she is seeking "deliverance," although he is initially oblivious to the meaning behind these words and unaware of his role as her mortal liaison.

Immediately following this oneiric encounter, Marie meets Julien at night on a vacated Paris boulevard. Streetlamps coat the urban landscape with a shimmering yellowish cast, which creates a transitional space between light and the darkness that sets the stage for Julien's subsequent rendezvous with Madame X. Emerging from a shadowy, lunar landscape that bears traces of urban industrialization, the third character, Madame X, is impatient for Julien to arrive. Dressed in a tailored blue coat and sporting an oval onyx pendant, this poised figure casually surveys Julien. He asks her, "Madame X, who?" to which she responds, "Madame X, too short of funds." A dealer in fake antique silk, Madame X is utterly vulnerable to Julien's attempt to blackmail her. Her dark presence provides a sharp contrast to the bright, warm sensuality of Marie, recalling the dichotomous divide between the lunar and solar goddesses of *Duelle* and *Noroît*. This contrast is repeated once again in another female pair, which is introduced in a black-and-white photograph depicting Madame X and her blond younger sister, Adrienne, who, like Marie, is also a *revenante*. Like Marie, Adrienne (Bettina Kee) desires death as a means of deliverance from the in-between zone where she has been condemned to wander. Only reconciliation with her mortal sister, Madame X, will provide her with an entrée to the realm of the dead.

Marie initially seeks deliverance through her amorous companion Julien, inviting him to dinner. During their evening soirée, she confides to him that her boyfriend Simon was killed in a car crash, and Julien reciprocates with a similar story, revealing that his ex-girlfriend Estelle returned to her home in provincial Montelban (a place name that invokes the suburb of Montfermeil where the students lived in *La bande des quatre*). They make love, but the following morning Marie disappears. Julien traces her to a hotel room on rue des Ecoles, evoking similar secluded hotel locales in *Duelle*. At this point in the film, Julien is interposed between two women who, while not goddesses, are visually and symbolically associated with the moon and the sun, as he alternates between clandestine meetings with Madame X and quixotic interludes with Marie, respectively. Recalling the duplicitous Thomas Santini from *La bande des quatre*, who acts by turns as seducer and sinister culprit, Julien is both a blackmailer who appears to be part of an insidious criminal underworld and an amiable, lonely bachelor whose sole companion is his playful cat, Nevermore. When he invites Marie to move into his house with him, her assent expresses not only her desire for him but also her need for deliverance.

Marie soon becomes unduly jealous of his ex-partner Estelle, "the girl from Montelban." The morning after she moves into his house, Marie descends dressed in Estelle's blue bathrobe and asks, "Why did she leave her things?" She later tries on Estelle's coat, which dwarfs her slight frame, and then her shoes, recalling the scene in Hitchcock's *Vertigo* in which Judy dresses in the identical style of her double Madeleine to appease the fetishistic desires of her suitor. Marie distracts herself from her jealous preoccupations by redecorating a cluttered storage room, which she does not permit Julien to see. In this musty attic room, she inspects the old furniture, knickknacks, and forgotten paintings, finally uncovering a large mirror in an ornate frame. She contemplates her reflection in it, a mirror image that indicates her duplicitous status as a *revenante,* a supernatural being who spans two worlds, whose soul is "split in two." "One is dead, the other is living," Marie remarks when she sees the photograph of the two sisters, Adrienne and Madame X, respectively. Yet this synoptic description is also a covert reflection on her own double status stratified between two worlds, torn between her desire to replicate the living Estelle and her need to achieve deliverance in death.

After cleaning and rearranging furnishings in the blue room, she carefully positions a stepladder in a central spot, then climbs up to the top step, where she sits and gazes directly up at the rafters. She then recites a Gaelic incantation, which Rivette identifies as the *geis,* a magical incantation derived from Celtic druidism (qtd. in Frappat, "Entretien"). Historian Jean Markale explains the significance of Celtic myth for Rivette's work when he asserts, "Societies that are determinedly patriarchal have at all times been suspicious of everything Celtic (official Christianity is a notable example), because Celtic thought is not consistent with the patriarchal ideal" (16). Markale notes that those historical periods in which the role of women blossomed were marked by a certain renaissance of Celtic thought, such as the Courtly Period of the twelfth and thirteenth centuries when Celtic legends reappeared in European literature (16). Its power surpassed divine and human laws, initiating a new order through the wishes of those controlling it. When Marie invokes the supernatural power of the *geis*, she echoes her pagan predecessors, priestesses, witches, and women lawgivers who imposed their will by ritual and magic means.

The literal meaning of Marie's Gaelic chant remains open to interpretation, yet we might conjecture that this *geis* compels her to reenact her own suicide in order to achieve deliverance. Julien ultimately discovers her secret after a curious conversation with Madame X, who reveals Marie's true status as *revenante* to him. Initially in disbelief, Julien contacts her old friend Delphine (Nicole Garcia), a documents researcher whose name recalls Resnais's leading lady, Delphine Seyrig. She confides to Julien that Marie had gone a bit crazy before her suicide and "become someone else," a prisoner to love, perhaps. Julien retraces Marie's steps to her final residence, where a peculiar porter (Mathias Jung) ushers him to her apartment. Julien is shocked to see that it is identical to the refurbished attic room—red curtains, green world globe, blue walls, and mirror—except for a single hook extending from the ceiling. The porter's eyes widen as he recounts the gruesome discovery of her body spinning around accompanied by the telltale sound that could be Edgar Allan Poe's pendulum, "tic toc, tic toc." It becomes clear to Julien that Marie has re-created the site of her suicide in the secret blue room that seems destined to become her tomb.

The film's final section offers a shift in perspective that is marked by the caption "Marie," as the film's oneiric opening is entitled "Julien." The section commences with her decision to return to Julien's home following her sudden disappearance and brief stay at Hôtel l'Aveyron. She curls up in his armchair and soon falls asleep. Upon awakening, she extends her hand to Julien and leads him to the attic room, where a noose hangs ominously from the rafters. She begins to climb the stairs of the stepladder but swoons, falling back into Julien's arms. A sudden cut returns us to Julien contemplating Marie, who is still asleep in his armchair. Upon awakening, Marie confides to Julien that she has had a dream that resembled an order and must be obeyed. Silhouetted in a scene of ritualistic lovemaking that night, Marie begs Julien to stop her from sleeping. Yet, once again, she sees herself leading Julien trancelike through the house to the blue attic room, where she insists that he watch her hang herself. From this, we can conclude that, for Marie, dreams are manifestations of the *geis*.

The following morning, Marie rises early to meet her double Adrienne in a space situated between indoors and outdoors, the world of the living and the dead. Seated on a red park bench, the two could be in an open-air garden or a greenhouse, yet the pastel yellow stained glass recalls the interior of a chapel. In this ambivalent place that serves as the vestibule to another realm, Marie confides to Adrienne, "I no longer want to be delivered." Upon her return home, she discovers Julien in the attic room attempting to hang himself in an effort to rejoin her forever. She angrily warns him: "If you die, you will not come back." He tries to take his life once more, cutting himself with a butcher knife. Marie struggles with him, and as he pulls away, he slashes his hand and also her wrist. Mindful of the gravity of their dilemma, Marie invokes the *geste interdit* (gesture of prohibition) as she covers her face with both hands, her fingers fully extended as though forming a mask. This gesture empowers Marie, rendering her invisible and nonexistent to those who inhabit the temporal zone of the living. It ultimately allows her to wield control over her own destiny, giving expression to her deep desire to remain with Julien.

This extraordinary gesture of prohibition, which like the *geis* is culled from Celtic epic tradition, was salvaged from the margins of the original

Figure 13. Marie performs the *geste interdit* (gesture of prohibition) in *Histoire de Marie et Julien.*

film script. Rivette and his former co-scenarist Denis had completely forgotten its intended meaning, and so he and his new team of writers gave it a new visual form and magical import. Marie's invocation of supernatural forces through gestures and incantations recalls the pagan power of the seductress Grainne, who in the Celtic tale of Grainne and Diarmuid imposes her will upon her lover Diarmuid by the magical means of a *geis*, forcing him to flee with her and thereby transgress an incest prohibition. The *geis* that projects pagan, feminine power not only governs the vast epic tableau of Grainne and Diarmuid but reappears in the Celtic legend of Tristan and Iseult, where it is transformed into a magical aphrodisiac potion to justify the two lovers' disregard of conventional Christian morality (Markale 208–12). In *Histoire de Marie et Julien*, Rivette returns to pagan mythology to restore the exceptional role of the woman who, in the original tale of Grainne and Diarmuid, is the driving force, able to control her future world, manipulate the man effectively, and bring about his psychic and spiritual metamorphosis as well as her own.

Marie is destined to rejoin the world of the living in the fashion of her powerful Celtic predecessor Grainne, while her blond double Adrienne is fated to vanish forever from the world of the living. When Madame X unexpectedly appears at Julien's door that evening, neither she nor Julien are able to see Marie, who is seated in the armchair watching them. Madame X has come to retrieve Adrienne's letter implicating her in her sister's death. Julien hands it over, and she burns it, fondly bidding Adrienne adieu. Still seated in the living room, Marie quietly contemplates Julien seated in the adjacent armchair holding Nevermore, who is oblivious to her presence. She begins to cry, and her tears trickle down her cheek, falling on the open gash on her arm where Julien had cut her earlier. She is incredulous when she suddenly notices blood flowing from her arm. A fade to black is followed by a medium shot of Julien waking from a nap. He automatically asks the time, but then seems perplexed by Marie's presence and continues to question her, "What are you doing here? Who are you?" She responds, "Marie, the one you love." When he expresses his astonishment and adds that she is not really his type, Marie merely replies, "That's what you think. Give me a little time." This singular moment shared between the lovers that surpasses temporal boundaries returns us to their initial somnambulistic encounter and to Rivette's earlier reflection on the nature of cinema, which he claims "is necessarily fascination and rape, that is how it acts on people; it is something pretty unclear, something one sees shrouded in darkness, where you project the same things as in dreams: that is where the cliché becomes true" (qtd. in Aumont et al. 37). In the fashion of solar Celtic goddesses Grainne and Iseult, Marie is destined to share the future with her lover in passionate, unending cyclical love, a feminine destiny that is celebrated in the recommencement of the 1970s cycle. From this perspective, Blossom Dearie's upbeat rendition of "Our Day Will Come" at the close of *Histoire de Marie et Julien* offers a final flash of hope, a resonant melodic line that celebrates feminine possibility.

Cyclical endings are recurrent in Rivette's work. Within the final exchange of glances between Marie and Julien, which retrospectively resituates the film's oneiric opening within a feminine perspective, Rivette returns to the perennial theme that inflects all his films: time. Similar to the clocksmith's desire in *Histoire de Marie et Julien* to repair the works that line the rooms of his house, the director Rivette seeks to repair time through patience, persistence, and passion for his craft. Clockworks that clutter the film's mise-en-scène point to the director's ongoing obsession—a director who now is no longer young and who acutely senses the preciosity of time remaining to complete those projects destined to otherwise remain unfinished. Not unlike the clocksmith whose mastery is measured in the practical, affective relationship he maintains with an artisanal, manual trade, Rivette merits the title of "patron" (boss), the term that Rivette had formulated while filming *Jean Renoir le patron* to describe the stature of the director within the profession.

## Returning, Departing: *Ne touchez pas la hache* and *36 vues du Pic Saint-Loup*

Rivette returns to the historical costume drama in his largely faithful adaptation of the second novella, *La duchesse de Langeais* (between *Ferragus* and *La fille aux yeux d'or*), of Balzac's nineteenth-century trilogy, *Histoire des treize* (The Thirteen). As we recall, the prologue of *The Thirteen* had provided the impetus for the ambling, improvisational serial film *Noli me tangere* decades earlier. In this recent adaptation that strives to remain faithful not only to the spirit but to the letter of the text, Rivette returns to the novella's original title, *Ne touchez pas la hache*

(Don't Touch the Axe; 2007), and to the tableau, revisiting the themes of desire and possession that, to a greater or lesser degree, inspire all his adaptations. As critics have noted, Rivette's theatrical structuring is very much in evidence in the film's prologue, when we first encounter Sister Thérèse, formerly known as the Duchess Antoinette of Langeais (Jeanne Balibar) (Naremore, 31; Romney, 67; Thirion, 10). Her dramatic appearance from behind a closed curtain where she is cloistered behind the grille of a Carmelite nunnery recalls the encrypted theatrical tableaux at the commencement of *La religieuse*. The intensity of this moment is elevated here because of two previous scenes in the Carmelite chapel that define the Duchess as the lost love of General Armand de Montriveau (Guillaume Depardieu), a celebrated French military officer who has been desperately searching for her for the past five years. His search ends where the film begins, at an organ recital in a chapel on the island of Mallorca, where he recognizes the melancholic strains of "River Tage" (lyrics by J. H. Demeun and music by B. Pollet), a ballad that he continues to associate with his former lover, the Duchess, and their ill-fated romance in Paris.

Framed in a flashback, the film's central story begins five years earlier in Restoration Paris. A heavy brocade curtain is drawn to reveal a dimly

Figure 14. A tableau: General de Montriveau discovers Antoinette in a Carmelite nunnery in *Ne touchez pas la hache*.

lit drawing room in the fashionable neighborhood of Saint-Germain. Returning to the structure of his earlier Balzac adaptation, *La belle noiseuse,* Rivette conceptualizes the structure of *La hache* as a series of brilliantly choreographed tableaux that create the impression of a classical five-act play comprised of three key central acts—the Duchess's theatrically orchestrated seduction and humiliation of the General in her boudoir, the General's vengeance on the Duchess in his lair, and their final missed rendezvous—which are framed by the aforementioned prologue and an epilogue that also takes place at the nunnery, where the General finds that Antoinette has died of an unknown malady. While the central moments in the film take place in the couple's private quarters that preserve the intimacy of their exchanges, the social space of the salon remains the architectural and ideological hub of the story. It is where the Duchess first encounters the dashing General, described by some as the "student of Bonaparte," who has recently returned from an expedition to central Africa. The palpable ease and grace with which the Duchess navigates the space of the salons seem to emerge from within a world of aristocratic entitlement oblivious to the obtrusive thump of the General's wooden leg as he marches over to meet her, bowing deeply. While she is presumably entranced by the tale he tells of his voyage across burning desert sands, it is evident that she has already set her sights on him and intends to take him captive, transforming him not into her lover but her prey. Flattered by the Duchess's obvious interest in him, Montriveau agrees to continue his story the next night at her home, but before he retires vows to have her as his mistress. Neither is motivated initially by amorous fervor, as Morrey and Smith have noted, but by a taste for conquest—for possession (247).

The three central tableaux place the act of seduction on display. An accomplished actress, Antoinette feigns illness and devises a convincing mise-en-scène, which she cunningly unleashes upon the unsuspecting General. In preparation for his arrival, she slips out of her ceremonial evening dress into a strapless dressing gown, checking repeatedly in her dressing room mirror to ensure that her décolletage is complemented by a distraught demeanor that will produce its intended effect. When Montriveau arrives, he finds her in a fire-lit boudoir, barely visible, draped across a divan, her hair down but discreetly cloaked in a chiffon scarf. In the second central tableau, Armand demonstrates that he is equal to her measure, for as Jonathan Romney points out, he emerges as the master of melodramatic mise-en-scène and every bit as much an actor as she (67). At ease in his lair, he painstakingly restages their inaugural rendezvous, shifting the balance of power to his advantage. Puffing on a cigar, he calmly complains to her of a headache, as she lies cowering on his sofa. Rather than the warm, romantic fire of the Duchess's hearth that had helped to kindle his amorous feelings, mysterious red flames crackle and masked men mill about in the adjoining antechamber. Inured to her advances, Armand tempestuously threatens to brand her forehead with a hot poker to mark his possession of her permanently, but recants when she proclaims her willingness to submit to his every whim. Montriveau and the Duchess alternately demonstrate their mastery of mise-en-scène in these successive tableaux in which both wear masks, as Rivette observes, not only to conceal the truth of their feelings from each other but from themselves (qtd. in Mérigeau 65). Crucially, however, neither possesses a sense of timing, the capacity to sense at what moment to strip the mask away. A missed rendezvous precipitates the Duchess's final departure, marked by a cut to black and intertitles that reproduce Balzac's text: "From Hell's Boulevard, for the last time, she looked at the noisy, smoky Paris, bathed in the red of the lights."

The story resumes five years later aboard a merchant brig off the Mallorcan coast, where the General, whom Balzac identifies as one of the Thirteen crew, conspires with his shipmates to recapture the Duchess. In a moment recalling *La belle noiseuse,* the hand of an artist is shown sketching the architectural layout of the nunnery, enabling the Thirteen crew members to plan their exploit and mobilize what Balzac describes in the preface to *The Thirteen* as, ". . . an occult power against which the organization of society would be helpless; a power which would push obstacles aside and defeat the will of others; . . ."(16). As seagulls circle, shrieking violently overhead, Montriveau and his men scale the sheer precipice and enter the convent, if only to discover that they have arrived too late, when they find her dead body alone in a candlelit room. There is no magical reprieve for Balzac's nineteenth-century Duchess—as there had been for the child heroine of *Céline et Julie*—whose lifeless body framed in a final tableau testifies to the ossified theatricality associated with the social and cultural codes of the day. Montriveau departs silently with her cadaver, which he throws into the sea to remember her as but "a book read during our childhood," "a poem." As he releases the body into the deep, his gaze turns away from theatrical and ideological staging of institutions and moves toward the ocean's infinitely open horizon, a "space without shape or frontiers" that returns us at last to the origins of cinema (Bazin 107).

| | |

If *Ne touchez pas la hache* can be considered as a return to adaptation and the scenarios of possession and abandon associated with it, *36 vues du Pic Saint-Loup* (Around a Small Mountain; 2009), might be viewed as an unprecedented departure to a new arena: the circus. The film chronicles the journey of a small family circus troupe in and around the Pic Saint-Loup, one of two distinctive peaks that jut out of the Languedoc scrublands in southern France. On the eve of the troupe's departure on summer tour, its manager and founder Peter dies unexpectedly, and so, they call on his daughter Kate (Jane Birkin), who surprisingly agrees to return after an absence of fifteen years to assist them at the box office. The opening sequence finds Kate broken down on the side of the road while en route to join her family. She hails a passing sports coupe seemingly without success, but then the black convertible circles back. A meticulously dressed Italian, Vittorio (Sergio Castellitto), emerges, like a modern-day knight who has materialized from the medieval legend for which the film is named (Mandelbaum).

It seems useful to briefly review the legend that provides the mythic backcloth of the film's story. In it, three noble lords, Loup, Clair, and Guiral, all in love with the same gentle princess, vie for her hand in marriage. Her father, the lord of the fiefdom of Saint-Martin-de-Londres, promises his daughter to the one who is most valorous and virtuous in battle. When the three knights return years later, renowned for their glorious accomplishments, they discover that the princess has died. The three retire sorrowfully from the world, each to a nearby summit overlooking her tomb. Every year to celebrate the princess's birthday, each one lights a fire in honor of her memory. One year, however, only two fires are lit, the next year, one, and finally, none. Impressed by the hermits' devotion, the villagers name each of the summits after them—Saint Loup, Saint Clair, and Saint Guiral.

Like a knight errant, Vittorio escorts Kate into town and insists on attending that evening's performance. His interest in her is piqued when he overhears her sorrowful soliloquy spoken from the side of the circus ring, where she laments the death of the man she had loved, Antoine. Through close observation and cautious inquiry, Vittorio comes to understand that she has been traumatized, and so is unable to reenter the circus ring where her lover was killed before her eyes fifteen years earlier. He finds a quiet moment and approaches her while she is dyeing multihued fabrics by a gentle stream; there, she explains to him that her life is actually in Paris. He responds that he lives his own life on the move, without vocation, in search of chance encounters and novel experiences. Vittorio's unexpected appearance on Kate's deceptively tranquil terrain evokes unpleasant associations for her; however, Vittorio pursues her and forces the issue, asking her whether she is afraid to enter the ring, a circular arena that, in this instance, represents the world. Seated beside him within the cavernous blue tent, she responds that his intrusive questions have deeply upset her and accuses him of interfering blindly in matters that have nothing to do with him. Similar to "the sleepwalker" Louise in *Haut bas fragile* who is convalescing from a coma, Kate finds solace tightrope walking in the shadow of the Cévennes mountains, tenuously suspended in midair as she crosses the yawning void between the two most prominent peaks (Frappat, "Cinémas de Recherche"). Vittorio continues to circle around Kate's emotional arena, as would an itinerant traveler who threatens to cross over forbidden boundaries, between the spectral past and the present, between medieval myth and the modern-day world.

In flight from memories that continue to haunt her, Kate seeks reassurance in the quotidian, utilitarian world of a Paris boutique, where her dyed fabrics acquire an exchange value on the commodity marketplace. As opposed to the circularity that characterizes the performative space of the circus (the ring, the big top, the acrobats and aerialists' dancelike, circular movements both on stage and off), linear lines define the cloistered space of the city. Perpendicular bars of a prominent iron gate enclose the fashionable boutique within a courtyard; white bars of a balustrade line the workspace where Kate's supervisor awaits her; numbered squares of a commercial color chart allow Kate to appraise her fabric's deep vermillion hue, and she is

Figure 15. Kate suspended in space in *36 vues du Pic Saint-Loup.*

surprised to discover that it appears different in artificial light than in the natural daylight beneath the Pic Saint-Loup. Cloth billowing in the summer breeze at the water's edge does not lend itself to commodification, just as Kate ultimately resists captivity within her former existence. Encaged behind an iron grille on the Rue de Rivoli, she receives an unexpected call from Vittorio, who easily springs her, later confiding his stratagem to the troupe: "All the dragons of our life are, perhaps, those of suffering princesses who seek deliverance."

Vittorio steps quietly into Rivette's role of metteur en scène/ psychoanalyst/ conspirator when he devises a carnivalesque ritual of passage intended to liberate Kate from the ghosts of her past. He conspires with Clémence (Julie-Marie Parmentier), Kate's young niece, and together they choreograph a whip routine that restages the once-popular act in which her lover had perished. Similar to Marie's secret blue room in *Histoire de Marie et Julien,* the blue circus tent provides Kate with a phantasmic stage upon which she must reenact her lover's death by proxy to achieve deliverance. From a perilous position in the center of the ring, she waits for the whip to crack. Vittorio's sentiments undoubtedly mirror those of Rivette when he reflects on the parameters of his art, "The ring is the most dangerous place in the world . . . the place where everything is possible."

The thirty-six views to which the French title refers could indicate the 360-degree movement around the circumference of Kate's emotional life that the film accomplishes, recalling the way in which Max Ophüls's camera literally tracks around its heroine in *Lola Montès* (1955) as she reenvisions scenes from her past (Thomson 669). While the ring permits Lola to restage significant moments from her previous life in spectacular *tableaux vivants,* such performances fail to liberate her from the past, instead imprisoning her within it. Unlike the dizzying centripetal force that draws Lola downward into an inescapable abyss within the film's final moments, *36 vues'* circular finale throws all its players centrifugally outward into the world. As each member of the troupe exits from the big top like spokes from a wheel, each addresses the profilmic audience, then circling around again with improvised one-liners and even a salutatory quote from Shakespeare's play, "All's well that ends well."

Kate, however, does not emerge from the tent to bid the profilmic audience adieu. Clémence directs us instead to her red caravan, paying playful tribute to playwright Raymond Roussel's infamous *automobile roulotte*—a spectacularly furnished house on wheels that provided the reclusive writer with the means to insulate himself from the world, "to travel, almost literally, without traveling at all" (Ford 171). While the caravan seemingly serves Kate in similar fashion, she appears to have abandoned it at the film's end, where it appears tossed to one side like an empty shoebox. Vittorio finds her under the shade of the big top, where he announces his departure that coincides with the end of the summer's tour. The film's story leisurely circles around to end where it began, as the two envision an unexpected reunion by the side of another lonely, winding road. Recasting the translucent dreamscapes of *Les filles du feu,* the lens of Irina Lubtchansky (having replaced her father William Lubtchansky, who died in 2010) pauses on the final, quiet image of a full moon suspended between two peaks illuminating the landscape below—the sanctified space of medieval myth where sadness is appeased and serenity restored.

| | |

At the cyclical close of *36 vues,* we encounter parallel worlds in transit that come close enough to touch but then move apart (feminine and masculine; the living and of the dead; myth and the modern-day world).

Similarly, at the close of the director's career, we can trace within his last two films, *La hache* and *36 vues,* the two distinctive trends that have continued to evolve side by side within his work, from the introspective tableau of an aristocratic boudoir to the free-form physicality of an acrobatic performance; from scripted adaptation to ad hoc invention during a shoot, from the inexorability of the tragic denouement to the unanticipated comic improvisation of clowns. In *La hache,* time is relentlessly present; characters are seemingly unmindful of it, their lives forever altered in the wake of its progression. In *36 vues,* time is elsewhere; yet characters are transfixed by it, seemingly held spellbound from within the ulterior dimension of a personal memory or a myth.

In the same way that each film communicates a unique experience of time and different dimension of theatrical performance, each summons up important moments within Rivette's evolution as a filmmaker. A journey into the past, of sorts, *La hache* may evoke for Rivette his inaugural conversations with Rohmer, who in the early 1950s had initially pushed the novice director toward Balzac, advising him to read all of the author's works; it may be regarded as the mature, auteur Rivette's masterful response to the young filmmaker's mixed experience of adaptation in *La religieuse* (Rivette, in fact, confided to me in a 2009 interview that he no longer feels constrained by the process of adaptation but enjoys the difficult challenge it presents); it may express the director's intent to expand upon his earlier experimental work with *The Thirteen,* even as it evokes his other Balzac adaptation, *La belle noiseuse,* a classic that remains a culminating moment in his career. *36 vues* too recalls earlier days, recapturing the mystery and ambiguity of *Les filles du feu,* in which fantasy and theatrical ritual serve as sources of female empowerment. Although, admittedly, gender roles in *36 vues* are based upon codes of Christian chivalry and courtly love, they are reshaped in the film to offer a persuasive alternative to patriarchal constructions of the feminine. Thus, the medieval French chevalier is transformed into a watchful metteur en scène who intercedes on behalf of the tormented circus aerialist, placing her in a position to reassert control over her own past and, thereby, proceed undaunted into the uncertain future.

Rivette now holds a distinctive position in the history of French filmmaking. Inducted into the famed band of "Hitchcocko-Hawksians" who later formed an artistic school, he initially made films that challenged the opposition between theatricality and realism, fabricating a singular aesthetic that was perceived to be at odds with a film movement acclaimed for its spontaneity and freedom from convention. His later films exceeded those of his New Wave contemporaries in their experimentation with reflexive theatricality, serial form, and duration, pushing beyond the boundaries imposed by conventional narrative. Beyond inspiring the New Wave movement and continuing to reflect, and reflect on, its central tenets, Rivette's enduring contribution to the history of film is unquestionably evident in his sensitive treatment of the histories and destinies of women. His capacity to offer radical alternatives to hegemonic constructions of the feminine continues to be articulated through his engagement with theater and theatrical styles. Some time ago, Rivette likened the role of the filmmaker, as Marc Chevrie reminds us, to that of an acrobat on "a high wire above the void, which itself is the very soul of cinema" (21). At the close of the sixth decade of Rivette's career, we watch with anticipation as he strikes a subtle balance between the political and deeply personal obsession, between myth and fiction, between theater and cinema, in his films that continue to redefine the art of cinema around the world.

### *Notes*

1. Walter Benjamin attributes "the loss of aura" to the increased intervention of technical means in the production and reception of art in the twentieth century ("The Work of Art" 222–23).

2. See also D. N. Rodowick's excellent analysis of *Céline et Julie vont en bateau* in *The Difficulty of Difference* (chap. 5) in which he explores the film's parable of spectatorship using Freud's analysis of a case of female paranoia.

3. In 1960 Jean Gruault worked with Rivette on a treatment for a film project, *L'an II*, which was to focus on the guerrilla warfare of peasants (known as the "choannerie"), who had opposed the French Revolution. The treatment for *L'an II* by Gruault and Rivette is published in *Trois films fantômes de Jacques Rivette: Phénix*, suivi de *l'an II* et *Marie et Julien* (Paris: *Cahiers du cinéma*, 2002).

4. See Thierry Jousse's seminal discussion of the interrelation of theater and cinema in *La religieuse* in "Théâtre de la cruauté"; see also Douglas Morrey and Alison Smith's detailed analysis of *La religieuse* in their chapter on adaptation in *Jacques Rivette* (chap. 7).

5. See also Angela Dalle Vacche's close analysis of Éric Rohmer's adaptation of Heinrich von Kleist's novella, *The Marquise of O* (1976), in *Cinema and Painting* (chap. 3).

6. Jay Caplan in *Framed Narratives: Diderot's Genealogy of the Beholder* proposes that the tableaux that constitute Diderot's novel require "the beholder" to witness the successive trials of Suzanne as "part of the much longer trial (or Passion) that constitutes her narration" (49). One of the small but highly significant changes Rivette made in his adaptation of Diderot's novel is his addition of the final suicide scene to complete the Passion story.

7. In *Jacques Rivette, secret compris,* Hélène Frappat shows how Rivette was inspired by Balthus's (Balthasar Klossowski) india ink illustrations of *Wuthering Heights* (165).

8. For a detailed discussion of the presence of Pirandello in Rivette's work, see Alison Smith's "The Author and the Auteur: Jacques Rivette and Luigi Pirandello" in the Rivette Special Issue of the *Australian Journal of French Studies.*

9. Jonathan Rosenbaum discusses the festival showing and the film's subsequent restoration in detail in "*Tih-Minh, Out 1*: On the Nonreception of Two French Serials" in *Movies as Politics.* In brief, he notes that forty minutes of the sound track that had not been located at the time of the showing were subsequently found and restored. Moreover, Rivette reedited the film, altering the order of certain scenes and deleting a few others; thus, its final running time is 750 minutes instead of 760 minutes (304).

10. When *Noli me tangere* was restored, Rivette cut a key sequence, which Rosenbaum describes as a "raw piece of psychodrama" that featured "Jean-Pierre Léaud in the final episode . . . alone in his room, in a state of hysteria, oscillating between despair and (more briefly) exuberance . . ." ("*Tih-Minh, Out 1*" 316–17, n. 3).

11. Rivette undoubtedly intended the word "Aubade" to also be understood as an "Obade," to which Balzac refers in *The Thirteen,* describing it as, "a kind of lodge with a 'Mother' in charge, an old, half gypsy wife" who "is devoted to the interests of the tribe boarded and lodged by her" (14).

12. See Évelyne Jardonnet's extensive discussion of the uncanny in Rivette's work, particularly her perceptive analysis of *Noli me tangere* and *Spectre* in "L'effet d'étrangeté" (Troisième Partie) in *Poétique de la singularité au cinéma: Une lecture croisée de Jacques Rivette et Maurice Pialat.*

13. Rivette's use of Tourneur is noted within varied contexts, such as Jonathan Rosenbaum Gilbert Adair, and Michael Graham's analysis of *Noroît* in "*Les Filles du Feu*: Rivette x 4," *Sight and Sound* (Autumn 1975): 234–39, François Thomas's discussion of direct sound practice in *Noroît* in "Les Films 'parallèles,'" in *Jacques Rivette: La règle du jeu,* ed. Daniela Giuffrida and Sergio Toffeti (Turin: Centre Culturel Français de Turin, c. 1991), 165–69, Morrey and Smith's discussion of "Play, Theatre, and Performance" in *Jacques Rivette* (chap. 5) and Rivette's own commentary in Serge Daney and Jean Narboni's "Entretien avec *Jacques Rivette,*" *Cahiers du cinéma* 327 (September 1981): 8–21.

14. Nathalie Richard's role as the petty thief (Ninon) is an homage to that of Juliet Berto (Frédérique) in *Noli me tangere.* Her theft of documents from the desk in Roland's studio recalls the scene in which Frédérique steals corre-

spondence from the chess player's writing desk. In a personal interview (2009), Véronique Manniez pointed out that this "writing desk," known in French as a "secrétaire," is indeed, "a guardian of secrets." Its reappearance in *Haut bas fragile* betrays the 'secret' of Berto's phantom presence in the film, paying tribute to the actor following her untimely death in 1990.

15. The role was conceived while Rivette was working on the scenario of *Phénix,* a film that was to have followed *Noli me tangere* but was abandoned because of lack of funds. The film was to have told the tale of a reclusive actress, a role intended for Jeanne Moreau, who resides in a grand Paris theater. The film scenario by Suzanne Schiffman, Gregorio, and Rivette is published in *Trois films fantômes de Jacques Rivette*: *Phénix*, suivi de *L'An II* et *Marie et Julien* (Paris: *Cahiers du Cinéma*, 2002).

16. The house is haunted too by memories of Bulle Ogier's daughter Pascale (Baptiste in *Le Pont du Nord*), who died several years prior to the filming of *La bande des quatre*.

# An Interview with Jacques Rivette*

Café de la Bastille, Paris, June 1999 (Translated by Yolanda Broad and Mary Wiles.)

MW: How did you come to make films?

JR: It was Cocteau, *le coupable* [the guilty one].[1] It was while reading Cocteau's *La belle et la bête* [his journal written between 1945–1946 as he was filming *La belle et la bête*/Beauty and the Beast; 1946] that I got into it, wanted to do it, that I wanted to get together with people, not try to work by myself. Cocteau had the status of a well-known writer at that time, having had successes in the theater, having written books like *Les enfants terribles* [1930]. But, even so, movies were something of ill repute at the time; it was regarded as an odd line of work. And now, well, now, it's become a program, not just in universities, but even in lycées, and this is far worse. The films lycée students see, when they see *La règle du jeu* [Renoir; 1939], they're thinking, "Ah, la, la, *La règle du jeu*!" the way we thought, "Ah, la, la, *Bérénice*!" [Racine; 1670] or "Ah, la, la, *Le Cid*!" [Corneille; 1637].

MW: Were there other points of reference for you from postwar Paris theater?

JR: Yes, Peter Brook is, perhaps, the most obvious. In any case, in France, there aren't many great playwrights. In the twentieth century, there are only two.

MW: Who?

JR: Claudel and Genêt. And, in any case, Genêt is very uneven. And Beckett isn't French, you know, you can't say Beckett is a French author, even if he wrote certain plays directly in French. I think that he wrote *Godot* first in French [*En attendant Godot*/Waiting for Godot; 1948, first performed in Paris in 1953], and then he translated it later. He's a very great author, but it's hard to fit him into the history of French theater. He's more Ireland; he's an Irishman from Paris. I only met him once, by chance, in the 70s. He was impressive, you know, his bearing, he was so handsome, so tall, so calm.

MW: If you had to describe one of your films as autobiographic, which one would you choose? And why? All of them?

JR: None of them. Yes. Two of them have some autobiographic aspects. It's obvious. The first one, *Paris nous appartient*, and then, *L'amour fou*, where everything is transposed. I do remember that one of the reasons that I used Jean-Pierre Kalfon in *L'amour fou* was because he didn't resemble me at all. Everything was different, but there were some moments of . . . solicitude, there are always the feelings, the nuances that come into play, but all the rest is mine. Whenever there are contributions by the actors, by the co-scenarists, I'm delighted. The more that ideas get brought to me, the happier I am. I am not the least bit a "Monsieur, Je Regrette" [Mr. I Regret], but I'm not at all Monsieur Ingmar Bergman either. I admire Bergman tremendously, but well, someone who uses his life to write fabulous scenarios, and then film them just as fabulously, this Dr. Jekyll and Mr. Hyde aspect, I don't understand how it works. It's another way of being.

MW: You have mentioned Mizoguchi's influence on your work, especially in *La religieuse*. Were you also influenced by Japanese Nō theater?

JR: I have seen Nō performances once or twice here in Paris but, here, what you can see in France . . . or elsewhere . . . what is shown everywhere in the West . . . is extremely condensed, because if they showed a real Nō play (actually, it doesn't last all that long) but still, a Nō play does go on, so they condense it down to a half-hour, three-quarters of an hour, and the plays last many times that long in Tokyo, you know, in real performances. Yes, I've seen some, but, in any case, Mizoguchi, he isn't anything at all like Nō, he's a lot closer to Kabuki. He did several films on Kabuki actors. [R. is referring here to Mizoguchi's trilogy on the theater of the Meiji era, *Zangiku Monogatari* (The Story of the Last Chrysanthemum; 1939), *Naniwa Onna* (The Women of Osaka; 1940), *Geido Ichidai Otoko* (The Life of an Actor; 1941)]. There is the film where a couple attends a Nō performance, I believe that it's *Uwasa No Onna* [The Woman of the Rumor; 1954]. All I know of Japanese are Mizoguchi's film titles . . .

MW: In your films, you often use *plans prolongés* [long takes]. Could you comment on this?

JR: Ah, yes, continuous shots, because they're more enjoyable to do, the actors like them better. Almost all actors would much rather act, you know, without being interrupted. At the same time it means you can go faster. In France, we go faster because we're poorer. There are people in America, like Cassavetes, he filmed things that way, sometimes . . .

MW: Were you influenced by Cassavetes?

JR: Well, for my generation, Cassavetes is someone we admired a lot when we saw his films, but you can't say we were influenced by him, because we were more or less the same generation, we were contemporaries, each on his own side of the Atlantic. By the time we saw his first *real* film, which was *Faces* [1968], the film that represents what will become his true cinema, we were already well on our way. In France, Cassavetes's first big success was a film I like a lot, but it isn't the film I like the best, it was *Husbands* [1970], which was his first big success here in Paris with the general public. *Faces* was never released here in commercial theaters; we finally saw it at the cinémathèque. The only one that was commercially released was *Minnie and Moskowitz* [1971]. I'm not exactly like Cassavetes, because he's someone who films even faster than I do.

MW: Could you comment on the relation between women and magic in *Céline et Julie*?

JR: It was Juliet [Berto] who wanted to do that bit with the fake magician. I think that it's an idea she came up with, like an enormous number of the film's ideas. It was either Juliet, or it was Dominique [Labourier] who proposed them as we were talking, chatting, like this. It's really hard to remember twenty-five years later, who said this, who said that. There were so many conversations where we were just having a lot of fun. I never had as much. I don't believe I ever laughed as much as during those sequences, excuse me, during the few weeks when we were all talking with each other, when we tossed out a lot of ideas, ten times more ideas than there are in the film, loads of improbable ideas, we were saying whatever went through our heads, so the film is very reasonable, and funny, ah, well, it was thanks to her, so, I think it was Juliet who wanted to do that bit, and later, it definitely influenced the film that I wanted to make. And then I came upon those books on the Carnival. . . . I think that for me, it's easier to believe that a woman could be a magician than a man. But it's purely fictional, you know. It's easier when it's Juliet or Bulle [Ogier] or Géraldine [Chaplin], or, well, you see. They, yes, I can believe that they have magic powers.

MW: Certainly.

JR: Or at least, waves, in any case . . . Géraldine, she's someone who, the powers she has, it's strange. It's been my pleasure to work with gifted actresses, very intelligent, very different, like Bulle, like Juliet, you know, like Nathalie [Richard], but, I have truly never met anyone like Géraldine. She is someone who, at the very moment that you begin a sentence, replies, "Yes, I've got it" and in fact, she does, she understands everything, she's amazing. There's no reason to tell her the scene because she's already understood it. Her mind works at lightning speed. That's how we did *Noroît*, the film was a disaster, but I have good memories of it because filming it was really crazy, in four weeks, at the ends of the earth in Brittany, you can just imagine . . .

MW: How did you discover the play by Tourneur?

JR: I'm not the one who thought of it; it was Eduardo de Gregorio with whom I was working, with whom I had already worked on *Céline* and *Duelle*. He had seen, I don't know whether in Rome or in another city, a staging of the play where gender roles were reversed, where the male roles were played by women and the female roles by men. The play wasn't successful, and neither was the film because people aren't interested in seeing women as killers.

MW: I think that was an excellent idea.

JR: Ah, well, there's one person who liked the film a lot, when it was shown in New York and that was Susan Sontag.

MW: Ah, yes?

JR: Yes, yes, yes. No, I was delighted, I mean, someone intelligent, thoughtful . . .

MW: Yes, she is a highly respected American critic.

JR: Well, I remember having attended a projection of *Noroît* in London; it was arduous. For the British, it was just not at all their thing, so . . . Plus the fact that the film opens with a title that reads, "A small island, off the coast of a larger one." I had never given it any thought, but suddenly, I realize, I'm in London, and I say to myself, "Good lord! They're thinking it's Ireland!"

Ah yes, that was in '76 or '77. Oh, my, did they ever not like it! Tourneur isn't Shakespeare, though. It's hardly ever played . . .

MW: In the United States, either. Even for Americans, the language is incomprehensible because it's archaic . . .

JR: But this language is purposefully medieval, it's fifteenth-century English, essentially, and written at the very beginning of the seventeenth. We had two English-language actresses Géraldine and Kika Markham, whom we'd met because she was in François's film, *Les deux anglaises et le continent* [Two English Girls; 1971]. Kika was the one who helped Géraldine learn her lines. It's the only time that Géraldine made mistakes, with the quotations from Tourneur. Even Géraldine had difficulty with Tourneur's English, which, in all honesty, is extremely difficult because it's medieval English.

MW: Do you believe that it mixes well with Celtic myth?

JR: Ah, yes, yes. This is entirely from [Jean] Markale's book I had read on Celtic myths. I remember the first projection of *Duelle* that we did in Cannes, not as part of the competition, but for the Cannes fortnight, and, generally, people hated it, and one of the rare people who spoke to me when leaving the film was Jean Rouch, who said to me, you know, this film consists entirely of myths that are also African myths. It all relates back to African myths, because that was his reasoning. He asked me that question on the way out, so I told him no, I swiped it all from this book on Celtic myths, and he said to me, well, what do you know. And I know all those stories; I know them from Africa.

MW: Does the music of the Cohen-Solal brothers come from African music?

JR: You'll have to ask them that. No, I don't think so, no. They're still at it; they've always had a group. I don't remember anymore who thought of them; maybe it was Bernadette [Lafont] who knew them, who'd met them at a performance. I hardly knew them at the time and got to know them while filming. They were terrific. There's a lot in their music that's related to Tourneur's text. They try to produce music that's very Celtic, using more or less Irish or Scottish components.

MW: After watching Jean-Luc Godard's *Prénom: Carmen* [1983], I noticed that the placement of the musicians resembles the way musicians intervene in *Merry-Go-Round*.

JR: Yes, but, *Merry-Go-Round*, this was filmed under very difficult circumstances. I was just recovering from more than a year of illness,

Maria [Schneider] was in failing health, that is, there were two people in poor health during filming, and also, there wasn't any money at all, not at all. It was catastrophic. Sometimes it would be me, sometimes Maria, who would say, we're stopping, we're stopping, but then, we'd keep on going anyhow, the crew would say, no, no, we have to keep going, and so, we kept on going. But at a certain moment we ended up with a montage, and I thought it would be good to have some musicians. This is the only time that I wanted music to come in afterwards to give the film a bit of energy. I already knew [Barre] Phillips, since Juliet [Berto] was making a film with him [*Guns,* Robert Kramer; 1980]. It was during the editing a year later, a year after filming, that two films were essentially made in order to get their sound in the film and, obviously, to get them in the image track. It wasn't really much like the musicians in *Duelle* and *Noroît,* who were completely integrated into the filming, and you can see it. In *Merry-Go-Round,* it's montage. While Jean-Luc, he rehearsed the Beethoven quartet sequence, and he also filmed them at the same time, as far as I know, even if they are completely independent from the rest of the film. Perhaps he shot them on the side, afterwards, I wouldn't know about that. You'd have to ask him. In *Merry-Go-Round,* it's an attempt to add a little tension to the film, which heads off in all directions, with some moments I like a lot.

MW: Why did you feel the need to return to the theater after *La bande des quatre?*

JR: After *La bande des quatre,* I was so pleased with the work we did with the actresses that I wanted to continue. And since they also wanted to do some theater, we got together a small group like that to work with each other on some classics; Corneille, Racine, and Marivaux, is what we were working on. And then at the end of a few months, they wanted to do a real performance, and that's when we dropped Marivaux, which was too hard. But we kept—and we should have *just* kept Corneille. Because, it was already too much, Corneille and Racine. It was just that we wanted to continue to work on those classics . . . on Corneille, which was the driving force. And besides, the work that I did with them and with the guys who had joined them was much more interesting to me, the play by Corneille, that is, *Tite et Bérénice* [1670], than working on Racine's plays, on *Bajazet* [1672]. *Bajazet* is fabulous, I can't speak ill of Racine, but you grasp it all in the very first reading. That's it, we said, we understand it all, but then, afterwards, what were we going to do with it? Whereas Corneille is hard, even for the French, he's hard.

MW: You can imagine that for us . . .

JR: It's like Latin for us. It isn't French. All of those authors were fluent readers of Latin and Greek, but Corneille couldn't read Greek, and that's a big difference between them. Racine read Greek, and Corneille read Latin. And he read so much Latin that it's almost Mallarmé, it's so dense. Corneille's *Bérénice,* it's true that it's a hard play, it's overloaded, each verse says three things, and its characters are infinitely rich. Infinitely more things are happening between Titus and Bérénice, infinitely more things are happening in Corneille's play than in Racine's, where nothing happens. *Bérénice* isn't the Corneille play that I like the best though, even if it's got fabulous language. It's fabulous as a poem, but it's like Shakespeare for you. As a matter of fact, I gather it's hard to translate, like Goethe is untranslatable, like Pushkin is untranslatable, like Dante is untranslatable, well, like all the major poets. I don't know, but, in any case, it was difficult to stage.

MW: I've read a few of Corneille's plays but have never seen them performed on stage.

JR: In France, I'm not the only one, once you get hooked on Corneille, you're lost. It's very deep. He's an author I find very dense, so full of history, of thought. He's a very rich author.

MW: You cite him in your film . . .

JR: Yes, in fact, the theatrical passage I prefer in *La bande des quatre* is the passage of Corneille; there's just the one, it's the little scene performed by Laurence [Côte] and Nathalie [Richard], which is the final play by Corneille, it's one of his most beautiful ones, *Suréna* [1674], and it's going to end badly, and they know it right from the start. They are magnificent, both of them, Nathalie and Laurence, Laurence, who plays the male role, always, of Suréna, and Nathalie, Eurydice.[2]

JR: What is the film, if I may ask you, what is the film that made you want to do your work?

MW: *Paris nous appartient.*

JR: Ah, yes. For me, this is a film with a rapport . . .

MW: Yes . . .

JR: Okay. It is very naïve. It is a terminally naïve film that I filmed some forty years ago, and it's the film of a sixteen-year-old child, but maybe its naïveté is where its strength lies.

MW: And I love *Haut bas fragile.*

JR: Ah, yes, well, me too. Well, that's a more recent film. I really like it. It's one of the ones I like a lot. It's a film we did in a very short time, for purely practical reasons, so it is wasn't planned. It is based on the taxi-dance halls in New York from the 1920s.

MW: This works so well . . .

JR: It's a film we did only because *Jeanne* [la pucelle] was such a wreck from the point of view of production costs. Even though we did it for very little money, it was a bit too much, and so my producer [Martine Marignac], who I'd worked with ever since *L'amour par terre,* felt the need for another film, and for it to be very inexpensive, so, I was asked to do it, and was told, "Well, Jacques, we're going to shoot another film very fast and for very little money." I didn't have any ideas, so what I did was to phone Nathalie [Richard] and then I phoned Marianne [Denicourt], who had both had secondary roles, Nathalie, in *La bande des quatre,* Marianne, in *La noiseuse,* and then Laurence [Côte], who came later. Laurence wanted to tell this story, which was her story, so we worked it in.

MW: Was the film's title and its relation to the three girls based on a notion of music, for instance, high, low, fragile, slow . . .

JR: The title came later. Oh, people were opposed. They were very opposed to that title. I liked it a lot.

MW: I still haven't seen *Secret défense* because it hasn't yet been released in the United States.

JR: I'm sorry. And in Paris, it isn't shown a lot. It's really the story of Electra. Electra is the motor that drives the story, if I dare say so. And, in fact, I didn't think of Sophocles, I thought of Giraudoux, who wrote a version of Electra, rather different from the one by Sophocles, to the extent that Aegisthus plays a very important role in the play by Giraudoux. In Giraudoux's play, Aegisthus defends himself by saying that he killed Agamemnon but that he had a good reason to do it! Ah, ha, ha! While in Aeschylus, he hardly appears at all, and in Sophocles, he has almost no lines, the poor guy. In Euripides, he never appears, and the few lines he has are those reported by a messenger. Giraudoux's *Electra* [1937] is not very well known. The part was performed by Renée Devillers, a good actress who we know from the film by Roger Leenhardt, *Les dernières vacances* [The Last Vacation; 1948], which was filmed in 1947. *Ondine* [Giraudoux; 1939] is a good play because the subject is so strong. One can't really put him on the same plane as Claudel though . . . or Genêt. There's Cocteau, too, who did loads of plays. There are two or three very fine ones, but the others, they are . . . worthless. But, maybe these are written for the actors, because let's face it, they are going to ask for plays, so, okay, he consents and writes them. There is a very fine one that is never staged, which he wrote for himself, *Les chevaliers de la table ronde* [The Knights of the Round Table; 1937]. The subject is intoxication. The entire court of King Arthur is intoxicated, and as a result Lancelot falls in love with Guinevere, and so forth. The play is pretty intense. It is entirely on dependency and, for Cocteau, this meant opium.

MW: Would you agree that the difference for the spectator between film and theater is the presence of the actor's body?

JR: But where does the actor's body have more presence, in the theater or in cinema?

MW: That's the question.

JR: It depends, it depends, but, in the theater, what's most important is the voice, because the voice is crucial, too.

MW: I agree.

JR: But I think an actor's presence is crucial, too. Why are there actors who have presence, and others who don't? There are very fine actors, who act well, who are very intelligent . . .

MW: Yes . . .

JR: But finally so what, who cares? Excuse me . . . Who cares—they don't exist because nobody's there, in theater auditoriums, in movie theaters. And then there are others who aren't very clever, who do whatever, and, zoom, there they are.

MW: Some actors are charismatic . . .

JR: If anything is important, it's the voice. That's why the idea of dubbing is so monstrous. And so is synchronization by actors. I think, in any case, that American films are so bad, because almost all the actors are required to synchronize. Everything is redone; the sound is redone. You can see it, and you can hear it, too

MW: It's interesting to me that in *Paris nous appartient* and *Haut bas fragile*, it's music and the absent voice that compel the characters Gérard and Ida to continue searching forever.

JR: Yes, for me, the voice is one of the two things that theater and cinema share and that give presence to the actor. And the other is *le regard* [the look]. In cinema, it's the look that is crucial; however in the theater, it plays no part. The actor's look is inconsequential in the theater. However, what is very important in the theater, and also in the cinema, but less so, and usually, it is the actor who decides, is timing. For me, this is the quality that gives the actor presence on stage; it's a sense of timing. There's no other way to say it. There's no word in French for it. Tempo means something else. In the cinema, the metteur en scène is supposed to be more or less responsible for this. But if I use *plans séquences* [sequence shots], it's so that the actors can share in the control of the timing. So, timing, voice, and the look. In the era of silent film, it was the look that gave presence to the actor, the way the actor moves, and the body. All the major directors of silent films had an extraordinary sense of this; in silent films, the actors' manner is extraordinary, they have such a bearing . . . they *know*. The greats have so much bearing. There aren't any actors left nowadays who know how to address the audience in that way. They don't know how to speak anymore. Ah, no, what has happened in the United States over the last twenty years is disastrous.

MW: I agree.

JR: Everything is done by management. Just look how many coproducers there are in the credits. Just look at how many coproducers an American film has. Generally, there are five or six coproducers, three or four scriptwriters, at least. What are all those producers in the credits for? They're endless. You see five of them, six of them. There are coproducers and associate producers and line producers, who are there on the set, right? Whereas the others, they are in their offices in the process of calling Chicago, New York . . .

MW: Right. It's more of a business than an art.

JR: Yes, that's right, but it's always been a business; it used to be a business that was run by people who loved it, and in the theater, too. I think that this sort of thing has also happened on Broadway, for musicals aren't what they once were.

MW: When I saw *Haut bas fragile*, I thought of [Vincente] Minnelli's *The Band Wagon* [1953].

JR: Yes, yes, but it's been transposed.

MW: Of course.

JR: In any case, *The Band Wagon* is a true musical comedy with Fred Astaire and his sister [Adele Astaire] . . . right at the beginning of the thirties. I think that it's the last musical comedy that Fred Astaire was in on Broadway with his sister [the Astaire team performed on Broadway in *The Band Wagon* in 1931]. Nothing of the story remains in the film, except that several songs come from the musical and other musical comedies of Arthur Schwartz, since he's the composer. Ah, no, I'm not familiar with musical comedies, except from recordings. I collect all the recordings I can find of Broadway musicals.

MW: Ah, yes?

JR: I don't know whether you go see them. Do you live in New York?

MW: No, I live in Florida.

JR: In that case, you don't get to see any more musicals than I do.

MW: Is there any hope for American cinema?

JR: There are directors like [Robert] Altman and [Alan] Rudolph, I really like Altman even if his films are uneven, who seem to be the only ones who have any rapport with the actors, who like them, who shoot them, who do extended shots of them, which occasionally produces very long films and even then, Géraldine [Chaplin] told me that she was among those who viewed the rough cut of *Nashville* [Altman; 1975] and the rough cut of *A Wedding* [Altman; 1978] and that there were extraordinary moments, which were lost.

MW: What do you think of the French cinema now?

JR: Ah, well, there's some of everything. It has its strengths and its weaknesses, there's some of everything, there are films that are worthless, but . . . there's a vitality, a vitality, even if I don't like everything, but you know, it depends entirely on the gentlemen from Canal + and on the advances, but more on the gentlemen from Canal + these days. Doing a film without Canal + is very difficult as soon as it isn't something that can be shot in five weeks in Paris, the way we filmed *Haut bas fragile*. You can shoot hundreds of minutes per day using *plans séquences* [sequence shots] with, let's face it, terrific crews, and unless you can do that, it doesn't get done, and with terrific actors, too.

MW: Yes. In any case, *Haut bas fragile* is a film that truly possesses a sense of timing; I found this to be so, when I saw it.

## *Notes*

* All bracketed remarks are my own explanations or translations.

1. Cocteau was responsible for the dialogue of *Les dames du Bois de Boulogne* (Bresson; 1945), the film that Rivette saw the day of his arrival in Paris in 1949.

2. Act I from *Suréna* is staged in which Suréna, a Parthian general, and Euridyce, daughter of the King of Armenia, declare their tragic love for each other knowing that each has been promised to another. During their recitation, the actresses in Constance Dumas's class discover that Antoine Lucas has escaped on his way to prison.

# Filmography

*Aux quatre coins* (On Four Corners; 1949)
Principal Actors: Two women and two men, including Francis Bouchet.
16 mm
Silent
Approximately 20 minutes

*Le quadrille* (1950)
Producer: Jean-Luc Godard
Principal Actors: Liliane Litvin, Anne-Marie Cazalis, Jean-Luc Godard.
16 mm
Silent
Approximately 40 minutes

*Le divertissement* (1952)
Principal Actors: Olga Waren, Sacha Briquet, Alain Mac Moy.
16 mm
Silent
45 minutes

*Le coup du berger* (A Fool's Mate; 1956)
Production Companies: Claude Chabrol (AJYM), Les Films de la Pléiade (Pierre Braunberger)
Mise-en-scène: Jacques Rivette
Assistant: Jean-Marie Straub
Screenplay: Rivette, Charles Bitsch, Claude Chabrol, François Truffaut
Photography: Charles Bitsch
Editing: Denise de Casabianca
Principal Actors: Virginie Vitry (Claire), Étienne Loinod (pseudonym of Jacques Doniol-Valcroze—Jean, the husband), Jean-Claude Brialy (Claude, the lover), Anne Doat (Solange, the sister), Jean-Luc Godard,

François Truffaut, Claude de Givray, Claude Chabrol, Robert Lachenay (the guests).
Black and white, 35 mm
30 minutes

*Paris nous appartient* (Paris Belongs To Us; 1958–60)
Production Companies: François Truffaut (Les Films du Carrosse), Claude Chabrol (AJYM)
Mise-en-scène: Jacques Rivette
Screenplay: Rivette, Jean Gruault
Photography: Charles Bitsch
Sound: Christian Hackspill
Editing: Denise de Casabianca
Music: Philippe Arthuys
Principal Actors: Betty Schneider (Anne Goupil), Giani Esposito (Gérard Lenz), Françoise Prévost (Terry Yordan), Daniel Croheim (Philip Kauffman), François Maistre (Pierre), Jean-Claude Brialy (Jean-Marc), Jean-Marie Robain (Dr de Georges), Laura Mauri (his pupil), Claude Chabrol, Jean-Luc Godard, Jacques Demy, Jacques Rivette.
Release: December 13, 1961
Black and white, 35 mm
140 minutes

*Suzanne Simonin, la religieuse de Denis Diderot* (The Nun; 1965–1966)
Production Company: Georges de Beauregard (Rome-Paris Films)
Mise-en-scène: Jacques Rivette
Screenplay: Rivette, Jean Gruault, adapted from *The Nun* by Denis Diderot
Photography: Alain Levent
Sound: Guy Villette
Editing: Denise de Casabianca
Music: Jean-Claude Eloy
Principal Actors: Anna Karina (Suzanne Simonin), Micheline Presle (Madame de Moni), Francine Bergé (soeur sainte Christine), Liselotte Pulver (Madame de Chelles), Francisco Rabal (Dom Morel), Christiane Lénier (Madame Simonin), Charles Millot (Monsieur Simonin).
Release: July 26, 1967
Color, 35 mm
135 minutes

*L'amour fou* (Mad Love; 1967–1968)
Production Company: Georges de Beauregard (Sogexportfilm), Cocinor-Marceau

Mise-en-scène: Jacques Rivette
Screenplay: Rivette, Marilù Parolini
Photography: Alain Levent (35 mm), Étienne Becker (16 mm)
Sound: Bernard Aubouy (35mm), Jean-Claude Laureux (16 mm)
Editing: Nicole Lubtchansky
Music: Jean-Claude Eloy
Script Supervisor: Lydie Mahias
Principal Actors: Bulle Ogier (Claire), Jean-Pierre Kalfon (Sébastien/Pyrrhus), Josée Destoop (Marta/Hermione), Michèle Moretti (Michèle).
Release: January 15, 1969
Black and white, 35 mm
250 minutes
In January 1969, a shorter version of approximately two hours was simultaneously released at the request of Cocinor-Marceau. Jacques Rivette disowned this version immediately following its release, and thus, this film is no longer in legal circulation.

*Out 1: Noli me tangere* (Out 1: Touch Me Not; 1970)
Production Company: Sunchild Productions (Stéphane Tchalgadjieff)
Mise-en-scène: Jacques Rivette
Screenplay: Rivette, Suzanne Schiffman, inspired by *The Thirteen* by Honoré de Balzac
Photography: Pierre-William Glenn
Sound: René-Jean Bouyer
Editing: Nicole Lubtchansky
Script Supervisor: Lydie Mahias
Principal Actors: Bulle Ogier (Pauline-Émilie), Juliet Berto (Frédérique), Michael Lonsdale (Thomas), Jean-Pierre Léaud (Colin), Bernadette Lafont (Sarah), Françoise Fabian (Lucie), Hermine Karagheuz (Marie), Michèle Moretti (Lili), Jean Bouise (Warok), Jacques Doniol-Valcroze (Étienne), Pierre Baillot (Quentin), Éric Rohmer (the Balzac scholar), Alain Libolt (Renaud), Marcel Bozonnet (Nicolas/Arsenal/Papa/Théo), Christiane Corthay (Rose), Sylvain Corthay (Achille), Michel Delahaye (an ethnologist), Jean-François Stévenin (Marlon), Michel Berto (Honeymoon), Edwine Moatti (Béatrice).
First Public Projection: Le Havre, Maison de la Culture, September 9–10, 1971
Color, 16 mm
760 minutes (12 hrs. 40 min.); restored version 750 minutes (12 hrs. 30 min.)

*Out 1: Spectre* (Out 1: Spectre; 1971)
Alternate version of *Out 1: Noli me tangere*
Editing: Denise de Casabianca

Sound Mix: Elvire Lerner
Release: March 1974
260 minutes

*Céline et Julie vont en bateau—Phantom Ladies over Paris* (Céline and Julie Go Boating—Phantom Ladies Over Paris; 1973–1974)
Production Companies: Les Films du Losange et Renn Productions (Claude Berri), with six coproducers: Action Films, Les Films Christian Fechner, Les Films 7, Saga, Simar Production, Vincent Malle productions
Executive Producer: Barbet Schroeder
Mise-en-scène: Jacques Rivette
Screenplay: Rivette, Juliet Berto, Dominique Labourier, Bulle Ogier, Marie-France Pisier, Eduardo de Gregorio
The story of the film within the film inspired by *The Other House* and "A Romance of Certain Old Clothes" by Henry James
Photography: Jacques Renard
Sound: Paul Lainé
Editing: Nicole Lubtchansky
Principal Actors: Juliet Berto (Céline), Dominique Labourier (Julie), Bulle Ogier (Camille), Marie-France Pisier (Sophie), Barbet Schroeder (Olivier), Nathalie Asnar (Madlyn), Marie-Thérèse Saussure (Poupie), Philippe Clévenot (Grégoire).
Release: September 20, 1974
Color, 16 mm/ 35 mm
185 minutes

*Duelle* (*Scènes de la vie parallèle*: 2. *Une quarantaine*; 1975–1976)
Duel, released as Twilight (Scenes from a parallel life: 2. The Forty: 1975–1976)
Production Company: Sunchild Productions (Stéphane Tchalgadjieff)
Mise-en-scène: Jacques Rivette
Screenplay: Rivette, Eduardo de Gregorio, Marilù Parolini
Photography: William Lubtchansky
Sound: Pierre Gamet
Editing: Nicole Lubtchansky
Music: Jean Wiener (direct improvised sound)
Principal Actors: Juliet Berto (Leni), Bulle Ogier (Viva), Jean Babilée (Pierrot), Hermine Karagheuz (Lucie), Nicole Garcia (Jeanne/Elsa), Claire Nadeau (Sylvia Stern).
Release: September 15, 1976
Color, 35 mm
120 minutes

*Noroît* (*Scènes de la vie parallèle*: 3. *Une vengeance*; 1975–1976)
Northwest Wind (Scenes from a parallel life: 3. A Vengeance: 1975–1976)
Production Company: Sunchild Productions (Stéphane Tchalgadjieff)
Mise-en-scène: Jacques Rivette
Screenplay: Rivette, Eduardo de Gregorio, Marilù Parolini, adapted from *The Revenger's Tragedy*
Photography: William Lubtchansky
Sound: Pierre Gamet
Editing: Nicole Lubtchansky
Music: Robert and Jean Cohen-Solal, Daniel Ponsard (recorded direct sound)
Principal Actors: Géraldine Chaplin (Morag), Bernadette Lafont (Giulia), Kika Markham (Erika), Humbert Balsan (Jacob), Larrio Ekson (Ludovico), Anne-Marie Reynaud (Arno), Babette Lamy (Régina), Danièle Rosencranz (Celia), Élisabeth Medveczky (Élisa).
Color, 35 mm
130 minutes

*Marie et Julien* (*Scènes de la vie parallèle*: 1; 1975)
Marie and Julien (Scenes from a parallel life: 1; 1975)
Production Company: Sunchild Productions (Stéphane Tchalgadjieff)
Mise-en-scène: Jacques Rivette
Assistant Director: Claire Denis
Screenplay: Rivette, Eduardo de Gregorio, Marilù Parolini, Claire Denis
Photography: William Lubtchansky
Script Supervisor: Lydie Mahias
Principal Actors: Leslie Caron, Albert Finney, Brigitte Rouän.
Filmed in August 1975, interrupted the third day

*Merry-Go-Round* (Merry-Go-Round; 1977–1978)
Production Company: Sunchild Productions (Stéphane Tchalgadjieff)
Mise-en-scène: Jacques Rivette
Screenplay: Rivette, Suzanne Schiffman, Eduardo de Gregorio
Photography: William Lubtchansky
Sound: Pierre Gamet, Bernard Chaumeil
Editing: Nicole Lubtchansky
Music: Barre Phillips, John Surman
Principal Actors: Maria Schneider (Léo), Joe Dallessandro (Ben), Danièle Gégauff (Élisabeth), Françoise Prévost (Renée Novick), Maurice Garrel (Julius Danvers), Sylvie Meyer (Shirley), Michel Berto (Jérôme).
Release: April 6, 1983
Color, 35 mm
155 minutes

*Le Pont du Nord* (Pont du Nord; 1980–1981)
Executive Producer: Martine Marignac
Associate Producer: Barbet Schroeder (Les Films du Losange/Margaret Menegoz)
Mise-en-scène: Jacques Rivette
Screenplay: Rivette, Bulle Ogier, Pascale Ogier, Suzanne Schiffman
Photography: William Lubtchansky
Sound: Georges Prat
Editing: Nicole Lubtchansky
Music: Astor Piazzzolla
Principal Actors: Bulle Ogier (Marie Lafée), Pascale Ogier (Baptiste), Pierre Clémenti (Julien), Jean-François Stévenin (Max).
Release: March 24, 1982
Color, 16 mm/ 35 mm
127 minutes

*L'amour par terre* (Love on the Ground; 1983)
Production Company: Martine Marignac (La Cécilia, in association with the Ministry of Culture)
Mise-en-scène: Jacques Rivette
Screenplay: Rivette, Pascal Bonitzer, Marilù Parolini, Suzanne Schiffman
Photography: William Lubtchansky
Sound: Pierre Gamet, Bernard Chaumeil
Editing: Nicole Lubtchansky
Principal Actors: Géraldine Chaplin (Charlotte), Jane Birkin (Emily), André Dussollier (Paul), Jean-Pierre Kalfon (Clément Roquemaure), Facundo Bo (Silvano), Laszlo Szabo (Virgil), Isabelle Linnartz (Béatrice), Sandra Montaigu (Éléonore).
Release: October 17, 1984
Color, 35 mm
170 minutes
120 minutes, short version edited by J. Rivette and N. Lubtchansky

*Hurlevent* (Wuthering Heights; 1984–1985)
Production Companies: Martine Marignac (La Cécilia with Renn Productions)
Mise-en-scène: Jacques Rivette
Screenplay: Rivette, Pascal Bonitzer, Suzanne Schiffman, adapted from part one of *Wuthering Heights* by Emily Brontë
Photography: Renato Berta
Sound: Alix Comte
Editing: Nicole Lubtchansky

Music: Pilentze Pee, Trati Na Angelika, Polegnala e Pshenitza, "Le mystère des voix bulgares"
Principal Actors: Fabienne Babe (Catherine), Lucas Belvaux (Roch), Olivier Cruveiller (Guillaume), Olivier Torres (Olivier), Alice de Poncheville (Isabelle), Sandra Montaigu (Hélène), Philippe Morier-Genoud (Joseph), Marie Jaoul (Madame Lindon), Louis de Menthon (Monsieur Lindon).
Release: October 9, 1985
Color, 35 mm
130 minutes

*La bande des quatre* (Gang of Four; 1988)
Production Company: Martine Marignac (Pierre Grise Productions)
Mise-en-scène: Jacques Rivette
Screenplay: Rivette, Pascal Bonitzer, Christine Laurent
Photography: Caroline Champetier
Sound: Florian Eidenbenz
Editing: Catherine Quesemand
Principal Actors: Bulle Ogier (Constance Dumas), Benoît Régent (Thomas), Laurence Côte (Claude), Fejria Deliba (Anna), Bernadette Giraud (Joyce), Ines d'Almeida [Ines de Medeiros] (Lucia), Nathalie Richard (Cécile).
Release: February 8, 1989
Color, 35 mm
160 minutes

*La belle noiseuse* (La Belle Noiseuse; 1990–1991)
Production Company: Martine Marignac (Pierre Grise Productions)
Mise-en-scène: Jacques Rivette
Screenplay: Rivette, Pascal Bonitzer, Christine Laurent, loosely adapted from the novella "Le chef d'oeuvre inconnu" by Honoré de Balzac
Photography: William Lubtchansky
Sound: Florian Eidenbenz
Editing: Nicole Lubtchansky
Music: Igor Stravinsky
Principal Actors: Michel Piccoli (Frenhofer), Jane Birkin (Liz), Emmanuelle Béart (Marianne), Marianne Denicourt (Julienne), David Bursztein (Nicolas), Gilles Arbona (Porbus) and the hand of the painter Bernard Dufour.
Prize: Grand Prix du Festival de Cannes, 1991
Release: September 4, 1991
Color, 35 mm
240 minutes

*La belle noiseuse*: *Divertimento* (1991)
Alternate version of *La belle noiseuse.*
Editing : Nicole Lubtchansky
Sound Mix : Bernard Le Roux
120 minutes

*Jeanne la pucelle* (Joan the Maid; 1992–1994)
1. *Les batailles* (The Battles) 2. *Les prisons* (The Prisons)
Production Company: Martine Marignac (Pierre Grise Productions)
Mise-en-scène: Jacques Rivette
Screenplay: Pascal Bonitzer, Christine Laurent
Photography: William Lubtchansky
Sound: Florian Eidenbenz
Editing: Nicole Lubtchansky
Music: Guillaume Dufay/ Jordi Savall
Principal Actors: *Paris 1455*: Tatiana Moukhine (Isabelle Romée). *Vaucouleurs*: Sandrine Bonnaire (Jeanne), Baptiste Roussillon (Baudricourt), Olivier Cruveiller (Jean de Metz), Jean-Luc Petit (Henri Le Royer), Bernadette Giraud (Catherine Le Royer), Jean-Claude Jay (Jacques Alain), Jacques Rivette (the priest). *Chinon*: André Marcon (Charles, the dauphin of France), Marcel Bozonnet (Regnault of Chartres), Jean-Louis Richard (La Trémoille). *Poitiers*: Bernard Sobel (Pierre de Versailles), Wilfred Benaïche (Mathieu Mesnage), Jean-Pierre Becker (Jean d'Aulon). *Orléans*: Bruno Wolkowitch (Gilles de Laval), Lydie Marsan (Hermine), Pierre Baillot (Jacques Boucher), Vincent Solignac (Pierre d'Arc, the brother of Jeanne), Mathias Jung (Jean Pasquerel). *The Environs of Paris*: Florence Darel (Jeanne d'Orléans), Germain Rousseau (the confessor of the Dauphin), François Chattot (Arthur de Richemont), Emmanuel de Chauvigny (Gros-Garrau), Didier Agostini (Montmorency), Nathalie Richard (Catherine de la Rochelle). *Beaurevoir*: Philippe Morier-Genoud (Philippe le Bon), Yann Collette (Jean de Luxembourg), Monique Mélinand (Jeanne de Luxembourg), Édith Scob (Jeanne de Béthune), Hélène de Fougerolles (Jeanne de Bar). *Rouen*: Alain Ollivier (Pierre Cauchon, the bishop of Beauvais), Michel Berto (Guillaume Erard), Jean-Claude Frissung (Nicolas Loiseleur), Frédéric Witta (Jean Massieu).
Release: February 9, 1994
Color, 35 mm
*Les batailles* (The Battles): 160 minutes, *Les prisons* (The Prisons): 175 minutes

*Haut bas fragile* (Up Down Fragile; 1994–1995)
Production Company: Martine Marignac (Pierre Grise Productions)

Mise-en-scène: Jacques Rivette
Screenplay: Rivette, Nathalie Richard, Marianne Denicourt, Laurence Côte, Pascal Bonitzer, Christine Laurent
Photography: Christophe Pollock
Sound: Florian Eidenbenz
Editing: Nicole Lubtchansky
Principal Actors: Nathalie Richard (Ninon), Marianne Denicourt (Louise), Laurence Côte (Ida), André Marcon (Roland), Bruno Todeschini (Lucien), Anna Karina (Sarah), Wilfred Benaïche (Alfredo), Stéphanie Schwartzbrod (Lise), Laslo Szabo (the voice of the father), Jacques Rivette (Monsieur Paul), Enzo Enzo.
Release: April 12, 1995
Color, 35 mm
170 minutes

*Une aventure de Ninon* (*Lumière et compagnie*)
(An Adventure of Ninon: Lumiere & Company, 1995)
Mise-en-scène: Jacques Rivette
Principal Actor: Nathalie Richard.
Release: December 28, 1995
Black and white, 35 mm
52 seconds
To celebrate the centenary of Auguste and Louis Lumière's first film program in 1895, forty directors from all over the world were asked to make a film with the restored hand-cranked camera. Each director, including Rivette, filmed a single sequence lasting fifty-two seconds, with no synch sound or artificial lighting.

*Secret défense* (Secret Defense; 1997)
Production Company: Martine Marignac (Pierre Grise Productions)
Mise-en-scène: Jacques Rivette
Screenplay: Rivette, Pascal Bonitzer, Emmanuelle Cuau
Photography: William Lubtchansky
Sound: Éric Vaucher
Editing: Nicole Lubtchansky
Principal Actors: Sandrine Bonnaire (Sylvie), Jerzy Radziwilowicz (Walser), Grégoire Colin (Paul), Laure Marsac (Véronique/Ludivine), Françoise Fabian (Geneviève), Hermine Karagheuz (the nurse), Berndette Giraud (Marthe).
March 18, 1998
Color, 35 mm
170 minutes

*Va savoir* (Who Knows?; 2000–2001)
Production Company: Martine Marignac (Pierre Grise Productions)
Mise-en-scène: Jacques Rivette
Screenplay: Rivette, Pascal Bonitzer, Christine Laurent
Photography: William Lubtchansky
Sound: Florian Eidenbenz
Editing: Nicole Lubtchansky
Principal Actors: Jeanne Balibar (Camille), Sergio Castellitto (Ugo), Jacques Bonnaffé (Pierre), Marianne Basler (Sonia), Hélène de Fougerolles (Do), Bruno Todeschini (Arthur), Catherine Rouvel (Madame Desprez).
Release: October 10, 2001
Color, 35 mm
150 minutes

*Va savoir* + (Who Knows?; 2000–2001)
The original version of *Va savoir, Va savoir*+ played only seven weeks at a single cinema in Paris, le cinéma du Panthéon, to an audience of 1,734 spectators.
Release: April 24, 2002
220 minutes

*Histoire de Marie et Julien* (The Story of Marie and Julien; 2002–2003)
Production Company: Martine Marignac (Pierre Grise Productions), Cinemaundici, Arte France Cinéma, VM Productions
Mise-en-scène: Jacques Rivette
Screenplay: Rivette, Pascal Bonitzer, Christine Laurent
Photography: William Lubtchansky
Sound: Florian Eidenbenz
Editing: Nicole Lubtchansky
Principal Actors: Emmanuelle Béart (Marie), Jerzy Radziwilowicz (Julien), Anne Brochet (Madame X), Bettina Kee (Adrienne), Olivier Cruveiller (editor), Mathias Jung (porter), Nicole Garcia (Delphine, the friend).
Release: November 12, 2003
Color, 35 mm
151 minutes

*Ne touchez pas la hache* (Don't Touch the Axe; 2006)
Production Company: Martine Marignac and Maurice Tinchant (Pierre Grise Productions), Cinemaundici, Arte France Cinéma
Mise-en-scène: Jacques Rivette
Screenplay: Pascal Bonitzer, Christine Laurent, adapted from "La Duchesse de Langeais" by Honoré de Balzac

Photography: William Lubtchansky
Sound: Florian Eidenbenz
Editing: Nicole Lubtchansky
Music: Pierre Allio
Principal Actors: Jeanne Balibar (Antoinette de Langeais), Guillaume Depardieu (Armand de Montriveau), Anne Cantineau (Clara de Sérizy), Marc Barbé (Marquis de Ronquerolles), Thomas Durand (De Marsay), Nicolas Bouchaud (De Trailles), Mathias Jung (Julien), Julie Judd (Lisette), Victoria Zinny (Mother Superior), Remo Girone (Father Confessor), Bulle Ogier (Princesse de Blamont-Chauvry), Michel Piccoli (Vidame de Pamiers), Paul Chevillard (Duc de Navarreins), Barbet Schroeder (Duc de Grandlieu).
Release: March 28, 2007
Color, 35 mm
137 minutes

*36 vues du Pic Saint-Loup* (Around a Small Mountain; 2008)
Production Company: Martine Marignac and Maurice Tinchant (Pierre Grise Productions), Cinemaundici, France 2 Cinéma, Rai Cinéma, Alien Produzioni
Mise-en-scène: Jacques Rivette
Screenplay: Rivette, Pascal Bonitzer, Christine Laurent, Shirel Amitay, Sergio Castellitto
Photography: Irina Lubtchansky, William Lubtchansky
Sound: Olivier Schwob
Editing: Nicole Lubtchansky
Music: Pierre Allio
Principal Actors: Jane Birkin (Kate), Sergio Castellitto (Vittorio), André Marcon (Alexandre), Jacques Bonnaffé (Marlo), Julie-Marie Parmentier (Clémence), Hélène de Vallombreuse (Margot), Tintin Orsoni (Wilfrid), Vimala Pons (Barbara), Mickaël Gaspar (Tom).
Release: September 9, 2009
Color, 35 mm
84 minutes

## Television

*Jean Renoir parle de son art* (Jean Renoir Discusses His Art; 1957)
Direction: Jean-Marie Coldefy in collaboration with Rivette
"Le cinéma et la parole" (22 minutes), "Les progrès de la technique" (23 minutes), "Le retour au naturel" (15 minutes). Interviews with Jean Renoir by Jean-Marie Coldefy, Janine Bazin, Jacques Rivette.

*Jean Renoir le patron* (1966)
Production Company: ORTF
Mise-en-scène: Jacques Rivette.
Photography: Pierre Mareschal
Sound: Guy Solignac
Editing: Jean Eustache
Principal Actors: Jean Renoir, Michel Simon, Marcel Dalio, Pierre Braunberger, Catherine Rouvel, Charles Blavette, Pierre Gaut.
Three Programs: "La recherche du relatif" (94 minutes), "La direction d'acteurs" (90 minutes), "La règle et l'exception" (70 minutes)
Black and white, 16 mm

## Theater

*La religieuse,* Denis Diderot (The Nun; 1963)
Mise-en-Scène: Jacques Rivette
Adaptation: Jean Gruault
Run: From February 6 to March 5, 1963.
Studio des Champs-Elysées, Paris.

*Bajazet,* Jean Racine, and *Tite et Bérénice,* Pierre Corneille (Bajazet; Titus and Berenice; 1989)
Production: TGP, Le Château de Carte, Capella Films
Mise en scène: Jacques Rivette
Lights: Caroline Champetier
Art Direction: Manu de Chauvigny
Run: From April 18 to May 20, 1989
Théâtre Gérard-Philipe (TGP), Saint-Denis (Seine Saint-Denis)

| | |

Rivette received the Grand Prix National du Cinéma in 1981

# Bibliography


Aeschylus. *The Oresteia by Aeschylus*. Trans. David Grene and Wendy Doniger O'Flaherty. Chicago: University of Chicago Press, 1989.

Altman, Rick. *The American Film Musical*. Bloomington: Indiana University Press, 1987.

Andrew, Dudley. *André Bazin*. New York: Oxford University Press, 1978.

Armel, Aliette. "Jacques Rivette. Autour du cinéma." (Interview with Jacques Rivette) *La nouvelle revue française* 520: Special Issue (May 1996): 60–69.

Armes, Roy. *French Cinema*. New York: Oxford University Press, 1985.

Artaud, Antonin. *The Theater and Its Double*. Trans. Mary Caroline Richards. New York: Grove Press, 1958.

Attali, Jacques. *Noise: The Political Economy of Music*. Trans. Brian Massumi. Theory and History of Literature 16. Minneapolis: University of Minnesota Press, 1985.

Aumont, Jacques. "Renoir le Patron, Rivette le Passeur." In *Le théâtre dans le cinéma*. No. 3 of the *Conférences du college d'histoire de l'art cinématographique*. Ed. Jacques Aumont with the assistance of Alain Philippon. Paris: Cinémathèque française, Musée du Cinéma, Winter 1992–93. 217–36.

Aumont, Jacques, Jean-Louis Comolli, Jean Narboni, and Sylvie Pierre. "Time Overflowing: Interview with Jacques Rivette." Trans. Amy Gateff. In *Rivette, Texts and Interviews*. Ed. Jonathan Rosenbaum. London: British Film Institute, 1977. 9–38. Rpt. of "Le temps déborde: Entretien avec Jacques Rivette." *Cahiers du cinéma* 204 (September 1968): 6–21.

Baby, Yvonne. "Entretien avec Jacques Rivette." *Le Monde*, December 21, 1961. 14.

———. "Entretien avec Jacques Rivette." *Le Monde*, October 2, 1968. 19.

———. "Entretien avec Jacques Rivette." *Le Monde*, October 14, 1971. 13.

Balzac, Honoré de. *The Thirteen*. (*Histoire des treize*) Vol. 12. New York: Peter Fenelon. Collier & Son, 1900.

———. *The Unknown Masterpiece*. (*Le chef d'oeuvre inconnu*) Vol. 22. New York: Peter Fenelon. Collier & Son, 1900.

Barthes, Roland. "Diderot, Brecht, Eisenstein." 1973. In *Image-Music-Text*. Comp. and trans. Stephen Heath. New York: Hill & Wang, 1977. 69–78.

Bazin, André. *What Is Cinema?* Vol. 1. Comp. and trans. Hugh Gray. Berkeley: University of California Press, 1967.

Benjamin, Walter. "The Paris of the Second Empire in Baudelaire." In *Charles Baudelaire. A Lyric Poet in the Era of High Capitalism*. Trans. Harry Zohn. London: Verso, 1983. 9–106.

———. "The Work of Art in the Age of Mechanical Reproduction." In *Illuminations*. Trans. Harry Zohn, ed. Hannah Arendt. New York: Schocken, 1968. 217–51.

Bonnaud, Frédéric. "Entretien Inédit avec Jacques Rivette: Compléments de Programme." In *Jacques Rivette: Six films, versions intégrales*. DVD box edition. Arte-Vidéo, 2002.

Boujut, Michel. "Entretien avec Jacques Rivette." *L'événement du jeudi* 224 (February 16–21, 1989): 94–95.

Boulez, Pierre. "Alea." 1957. In *Stocktakings from an Apprenticeship*. Comp. Paule Thévenin. Trans. Stephen Walsh. Oxford: Clarendon Press, 1991. 26–38.

———. "'Sonate, que me veux tu?': Third Piano Sonata." 1960. In *Orientations: Collected Writings by Pierre Boulez*. Ed. Jean-Jacques Nattiez. Trans. Martin Cooper. Cambridge, Mass.: Harvard University Press, 1986. 143–54.

———. "Sound, Word, Synthesis." 1958. In *Orientations*. 177–182.

———. "Where Are We Now?" 1968. In *Orientations*. 445–463.

Bradby, David. *Modern French Drama 1940–1990*. 2nd ed. Cambridge, U.K.: Cambridge University Press, 1991.

Breton, André. *L'amour fou*. (*Mad Love*) Trans. Mary Ann Caws. Lincoln: University of Nebraska Press, 1987.

Brook, Peter. *The Shifting Point: 1946–1987*. New York: Harper & Row, 1987.

Burton, Richard D. E. "The Unseen Seer, or Proteus in the City: Aspects of a Nineteenth-Century Parisian Myth." *French Studies: A Quarterly Review* 42.1 (January 1988): 50–68.

Caplan, Jay. *Framed Narratives: Diderot's Genealogy of the Beholder.* Theory and History of Literature 19. Minneapolis: University of Minnesota Press, 1985.

Chabrol, Claude. "Évolution du film policier." *Cahiers du cinéma* 54 (Christmas 1955): 27–33.

Chevrie, Marc. "Supplément aux voyages de Jacques Rivette/J.R." *Cahiers du cinéma* 416 (February 1989): 20–25.

Claudel, Paul. *Oeuvres complètes*. Vol. 8. Paris: Gallimard, NRF, 1954. Rpt. of "Un quart d'heure chez M. Claudel, par Charles d'Ydewalle." *La nation Belge*, March 26, 1935.

Cocteau, Jean. *The Knights of the Round Table*. Trans. W. H. Auden. In *The Infernal Machine and Other Plays by Jean Cocteau*. New York: New Directions, 1963. 179–291.

Cohen, Robert. *Giraudoux: Three Faces of Destiny*. Chicago: University of Chicago Press, 1968.

Cohn, Bernard. "Entretien sur l'"amour fou,'" avec Jacques Rivette. *Positif* 104 (April 1969): 27–38.

Collet, Jean. *Le cinéma en question: Rozier, Chabrol, Rivette, Truffaut, Demy, Rohmer.* Paris: Éditions du Cerf (coll. 7ème Art), 1972.

———. "*Jeanne la pucelle*: Histoire et territoire." In *Jacques Rivette: critique et cinéaste*. Ed. Suzanne Liandrat-Guigues. *Études cinématographiques* 63. Paris: Lettres modernes / minard, 1998. 141–61.

"Conférence de presse (extraits): Jacques Rivette, Cannes 1991." *Cahiers du cinéma* 445 (July 1991): 34.

Cressey, Paul G. *The Taxi-Dance Hall: A Sociological Study in Commercialized Recreation and City Life*. Chicago: University of Chicago, 1932.

Dalle Vacche, Angela. *Cinema and Painting: How Art Is Used in Film*. Austin: University of Texas Press, 1996.

Daney, Serge, and Jean Narboni. "Entretien avec Jacques Rivette." Special Issue: "Situation du cinéma français." *Cahiers du cinéma* 323–24 (May–June 1981): 43–49.

———. "Entretien avec Jacques Rivette." *Cahiers du cinéma* 327 (September 1981) : 8–21.

Daussois, Guy. Rev. of *Suzanne Simonin, la religieuse de Diderot*. *Le populaire de Paris*. *Agence France-Presse: Le festival à travers la presse française et étrangère* 2 (May 7, 1966).

Debord, Guy. *The Society of the Spectacle*. Trans. Donald Nicholson-Smith. New York: Zone Books, 1995.

Delfour, Jean-Jacques. "*Haut bas fragile*: de la danse du temps au temps de la danse." In *Jacques Rivette: critique et cinéaste*. Ed. Suzanne Liandrat-Guigues. *Études cinématographiques* 63. Paris: Lettres modernes /minard, 1998. 163–73.

Delvau, Alfred. *Les dessous de Paris*. Paris: Poulet-Malassis, Librairie-Éditeur, 1862.

Denis, Claire, dir. *Jacques Rivette, le veilleur*, interviewed by Serge Daney. "Cinéma de notre temps," 1990. Rpt. in "Le veilleur: Entretien avec Jacques Rivette," *Jacques Rivette: La règle du jeu*. Ed. Daniela Giuffrida and Sergio Toffetti. Turin: Centre Culturel Français de Turin / Museo Nazionale del Cinema di Torino, c. 1991. 29–40.

Deschamps, Hélène. *Jacques Rivette: Théâtre, amour, cinéma*. Paris: L'Harmattan, 2001.

Diderot, Denis. *"The Paradox of Acting" by Denis Diderot and "Masks or Faces?" by William Archer.* Trans. Walter Herries Pollock. New York: Hill and Wang, 1957.

Duras, Marguerite, and Jacques Rivette. "Sur le pont du Nord un bal y est donné: Un Dialogue avec Marguerite Duras et Jacques Rivette." *Le Monde*, March 25, 1982. 15–16.

Eisenschitz, Bernard, Jean-André Fieschi, and Eduardo de Gregorio. "Interview with Jacques Rivette." Trans. Tom Milne. In *Rivette, Texts and Interviews*.

Ed. Jonathan Rosenbaum. London: British Film Institute, 1977. 39–53. Rpt. of "Entretien avec Jacques Rivette," *La nouvelle critique* 244.63 (April 1973).
Even, Martin. "'Out 1': Voyage au-delà du cinéma." *Le Monde*, October 14, 1971.
Fieschi, Jean-André. "Jacques Rivette." In *Cinema, A Critical Dictionary: The Major Filmmakers*. Ed. Richard Roud. Vol. 2. New York: Viking Press, 1980. 871–78.
Ford, Mark. *Raymond Roussel and the Republic of Dreams*. Ithaca, N. Y.: Cornell University Press, 2000.
Foster, Hal. "The Crux of Minimalism." In *The Return of the Real: The Avant-Garde at the End of the Century*. Cambridge, Mass.: MIT Press, 1996. 35–69.
Frappat, Hélène. "36 vues du Pic Saint Loup." Groupement National des Cinémas de Recherche. 2010, http://www.gncr.fr/soutien_fichefilm.asp?id=4003 (accessed October 7, 2009).
———. "Entretien avec Jacques Rivette: Compléments de Programme." In *Histoire de Marie et Julien*. DVD. Arte-Vidéo, 2004.
———. *Jacques Rivette, secret compris*. Paris: Cahiers du Cinéma, 2001.
Fried, Michael. *Absorption and Theatricality: Painting and Beholder in the Age of Diderot*. Chicago: University of Chicago Press, 1980.
Fulchignoni, Enrico. "Jean Rouch with Enrico Fulchignoni: Ciné-Anthropology." In *Ciné-Ethnography: Jean Rouch*. Ed. and trans. Steven Feld. Visible Evidence 13. Minneapolis: University of Minnesota Press, 2003. 147–87.
Gordon, Mel. *Lazzi: The Comic Routines of the Commedia dell'Arte*. New York: Performing Arts Journal Publication, 1983.
Grassin, Sophie, and Gilles Médioni. "Entretien avec Jacques Rivette." *L'express*, February 3, 1994.
Green, Miranda. *Celtic Goddesses: Warriors, Virgins and Mothers*. London: British Museum Press, 1995.
Guérif, François. *Le cinéma policier français*. Paris: Éditions Henri Veyrier, 1981.
Gunning, Tom. *The Films of Fritz Lang: Allegories of Vision and Modernity*. London: BFI Publishing, 2000.
Handyside, Fiona. "Rohmer à la plage: The role of the beach in three films by Eric Rohmer." *Studies in French Cinema* 9.2 (2009): 147–60.
Higgins, Lynn A. *New Novel, New Wave, New Politics: Fiction and the Representation of History in Postwar France*. Lincoln: University of Nebraska Press, 1996.
Hillier, Jim. Introduction. In *Cahiers du Cinéma. 1960–1968: New Wave, New Cinema, Reevaluating Hollywood*. Ed. Jim Hillier. Cambridge, Mass.: Harvard University Press, 1986. 1–24.
Hughes, John. "John Hughes On (And With) Jacques Rivette: Introduction by Jonathan Rosenbaum." *Rouge* 4 (2004). http://www.rouge.com.au/4/index.html. (accessed August 23, 2010). Rpt. of "The Director as Psychoanalyst: An Interview with Jacques Rivette." *Rear Window* (Spring 1975): 3–10.

Ionesco, Eugène. *Notes and Counter Notes: Writings on the Theatre*. Trans. Donald Watson. New York: Grove Press, 1964.
Ishaghpour, Youssef. *Opéra et théâtre dans le cinéma d'aujourd'hui*. Paris: Éditions de la différence, 1995.
James, Henry. *The Other House*. 1897. London: Rupert Hart-Davis, 1948.
Jameux, Dominique. *Pierre Boulez*. Paris: Fayard, 1984.
Jardonnet, Evelyne. *Poétique de la singularité au cinéma: Une lecture croisée de Jacques Rivette et Maurice Pialat*. Paris: L'Harmattan, 2006.
Jordan, Isabelle. "Entretiens avec Céline et Julie: I: juliet berto, II: dominique labourier." *Positif* (October 1974): 19–30.
Jousse, Thierry. "Théâtre de la cruauté." *Cahiers du cinéma* 413 (November 1988): 24–25.
Kernodle, George R. "Wagner, Appia, and the Idea of Musical Design." In *Total Theatre: A Critical Anthology*. Ed. E. T. Kirby. New York: E.P. Dutton, 1969. 9–19.
Le Clec'h, Guy. "Échec à l'inquisition, mais ta partie n'est pas jouée: Une 2ème chance pour *La Religieuse* de Rivette." (Interview with Jacques Rivette). *Figaro littéraire,* April 6, 1967.
Lellis, George. *Bertolt Brecht, Cahiers du Cinéma and Contemporary Film Theory*. Ann Arbor, Mich.: UMI Research Press, 1982.
Lemke, Sieglinde. "Primitivist Modernism. 1998." In *Primitivism and Twentieth-Century Art: A Documentary History*. Ed. Jack Flam and Miriam Deutch. Berkeley: University of California Press, 2003. 409–13.
Lesage, Julia. "Celine and Julie Go Boating: Subversive Fantasy." *Jump Cut* 24–25 (1981): 36–43.
Levinson, Julie. "Celine and Julie Go Story Telling." *French Review* 65.2 (December 1991): 236–246.
Liandrat-Guigues, Suzanne, ed. *Jacques Rivette: critique et cinéaste. Études cinématographiques* 63. Paris: Lettres modernes /minard, 1998.
Loubinoux, Gérard. "Le chant dans le chant: A la recherche d'une mémoire mythique." In *Opéra, théâtre: une mémoire imaginaire.* Ed. Georges Banu. Paris: Éditions de l'Herne, 1990. 77–89.
Maeterlinck, Maurice. "Livret original intégral." *Pelléas et Mélisande: L'avant-scène opéra* 9 (Mars-Avril 1977): 30–82.
Mandelbaum, Jacques. "'36 vues du Pic Saint-Loup' : La leçon de modestie de Jacques Rivette, de retour aux sources de son art." *Le Monde,* September 8, 2009, http://www.lemonde.fr/cinema/article/2009/09/08/36-vues-du-pic-saint-loup-la-lecon-de-modestie-de-jacques-rivette_1237519_3476.html (accessed January 2, 2010).
Marie, Michel. *The French New Wave: An Artistic School*. Trans. Richard Neupert. Oxford: Blackwell Publishers, 2003.
Markale, Jean. *Women of the Celts*. Trans. A. Mygind, C. Hauch, and P. Henry. Rochester, Vt.: Inner Traditions International, 1986.

Matheson, William H. *Claudel and Aeschylus: A Study of Claudel's Translation of the Oresteia*. Ann Arbor: University of Michigan Press, 1965.
Ménil, Alain. "Mesure pour mesure: Théâtre et cinéma chez Jacques Rivette." In *Jacques Rivette: critique et cinéaste*. Ed. Suzanne Liandrat-Guigues. *Études cinématographiques* 63. Paris: Lettres modernes /minard, 1998. 67–96.
Mérigeau, Pascal. "Rencontre avec Jacques Rivette: Balzac, son scénariste préferé." *Nouvel observateur* (March 22, 2007): 64–65.
Miller, Henry. *The Tropic of Capricorn*. New York: Grove Press, 1961.
Moindrot, Isabelle. "Mémoire ardente lyre." In *Opéra, théâtre: une mémoire imaginaire*. Ed. Georges Banu. Paris: Éditions de l'Herne, 1990. 17–21.
Monaco, James. *The New Wave: Truffaut, Godard, Chabrol, Rohmer, Rivette*. New York: Oxford University Press, 1976.
Morrey, Douglas, ed. *Jacques Rivette*. Spec. issue of *Australian Journal of French Studies* 47, no. 2 (May–August 2010): 121–221. Burwood, Victoria: Monash University, 2010.
Morrey, Douglas, and Alison Smith. *Jacques Rivette*. French Film Directors, Ser. Manchester: Manchester University Press, 2009.
*Music Academy Online*. Ed. David Schwartz. 2007. http://www.musicacademyonline.com/composer/biographies.php?bid=96 (accessed March 28, 2010).
Naremore, James. "Films of the Year, 2008: The Duchess of Langeais." *Film Quarterly* 62.4 (Summer 2009): 20–33.
Nichols, Roger. "*Pelléas* in Performance I—A History." In Nichols and Smith. 140–68.
Nichols, Roger, and Richard Langham Smith, eds. *Claude Debussy: Pelléas et Mélisande*. Cambridge, U.K.: Cambridge University Press, 1989.
Nicoll, Allardyce. *The World of Harlequin: A Critical Study of the Commedia dell'Arte*. London: Cambridge University Press, 1963.
*The Oxford Dictionary of Music*. Ed. Michael Kennedy. 2nd ed. Oxford: Oxford University Press, 1994.
Pirandello, Luigi. *As You Desire Me (Come Tu Mi Vuoi): A Play in Three Acts*. Trans. Samuel Putnam. New York: E.P. Dutton, 1931.
Powrie, Phil. *French Cinema in the 1980s: Nostalgia and the Crisis of Masculinity*. Oxford: Clarendon Press, 1997.
Rivette, Jacques. "The Genius of Howard Hawks." Trans. Russell Campbell and Marvin Pister. In *Cahiers du Cinéma. The 1950s: Neo-Realism, Hollywood, New Wave*. Ed. Jim Hillier. Cambridge, Mass.: Harvard University Press, 1985. 126–31. Rpt. of "Génie de Howard Hawks," *Cahiers du cinéma* 23 (May 1953): 16–23.
———. "Letter on Rossellini." Trans. Tom Milne. In *Cahiers du Cinéma. The 1950s: Neo-Realism, Hollywood, New Wave.* 192–204. Rpt. of "Lettre sur Rossellini." *Cahiers du cinéma* 46 (April 1955): 14–24.
———. "Notes on a Revolution." Trans. Liz Heron. In *Cahiers du Cinéma. The 1950s: Neo-Realism, Hollywood, New Wave.* 94–97. Rpt. of "Notes sur une révolution," *Cahiers du cinéma* 54 (Christmas 1955): 17–21.

———. "'Towards a Semiotics of Cinema': Barthes in interview with Michel Delahaye and Jacques Rivette." Trans. Annwyl Williams. In *Cahiers du Cinéma. 1960–1968: New Wave, New Cinema, Reevaluating Hollywood*. Ed. Jim Hillier. Cambridge, Mass.: Harvard University Press, 1986. 276–85. Rpt. of "Entretien avec Roland Barthes." *Cahiers du cinéma* 147 (September 1963): 20–30.

———. *Trois films fantômes de Jacques Rivette: Phénix,* suivi de *l'an II* et *Marie et Julien*. Foreword. *Mode d'emploi*. By Hélène Frappat and Jacques Rivette. Paris: Cahiers du Cinéma, 2002.

Rivette, Jacques, and François Weyergans. "Entretien avec Pierre Boulez." *Cahiers du cinéma* 152 (February 1964): 19–29.

Rodowick, D. N. *The Difficulty of Difference: Psychoanalysis, Sexual Difference and Film Theory*. New York: Routledge, 1991.

Romney, Jonathan. "Don't Touch the Axe." *Sight and Sound* 18.1 (January 2008): 67–68.

Rosenbaum, Jonathan. Rev. of *Celine and Julie Go Boating,* dir. Jacques Rivette. *Chicago Reader* Movie Review. http://onfilm.chicagoreader.com/movies/capsules.

———, ed. *Rivette, Texts and Interviews*. Trans. Amy Gateff and Tom Milne. London: BFI, 1977.

———. "*Tih-Minh, Out 1*: On the Nonreception of Two French Serials." In *Movies as Politics*. Berkeley: University of California Press, 1997. 303–17.

———. "Work and Play in the House of Fiction: On Jacques Rivette." *Sight and Sound* (Autumn 1974): 190–94. Rpt. in *Placing Movies: The Practice of Film Criticism*. Berkeley: University of California Press, 1995. 142–52.

Rosenbaum, Jonathan, Lauren Sedofsky, and Gilbert Adair. "Phantom Interviewers over Rivette." *Film Comment* (September–October 1974): 18–24.

Rosenbaum, Jonathan, Gilbert Adair, and Michael Graham. "Les Filles du Feu: Rivette x 4." *Sight and Sound* (Autumn 1975): 234–39.

Rouch, Jean. "On the Vicissitudes of the Self: The Possessed Dancer, the Magician, the Sorcerer, the Filmmaker, and the Ethnographer." In *Ciné-Ethnography: Jean Rouch*. Ed. and trans. Steven Feld. Visible Evidence 13. Minneapolis: University of Minnesota Press, 2003. 87–101.

Sartre, Jean-Paul. *Sartre on Theatre*. Ed. Michel Contat and Michel Rybalka. Trans. Frank Jellinek. New York: Pantheon Books, 1976.

Sellin, Eric. *The Dramatic Concepts of Antonin Artaud*. Chicago: University of Chicago, 1968.

Serrière, Marie-Thérèse. *Le T.N.P. et nous*. Paris: José Corti, 1959.

Shafto, Sally Gately. *UT Pictura Cinema: The Strange Adventure of Jean-Luc Godard*. Ph.D. diss., University of Iowa, 2000.

Shelton, Marie-Denise. "Primitive Self: Colonial Impulses in Michel Leiris's *L'Afrique fantôme*." In *Prehistories of the Future: The Primitivist Project and the Culture of Modernism*. Ed. Elazar Barkan and Ronald Bush. Stanford, Calif.: Stanford University Press, 1995. 326–38.

Silverman, Kaja. *The Acoustic Mirror: The Female Voice in Psychoanalysis and Cinema*. Bloomington: Indiana University Press, 1988.
Simsolo, Noël. "Entretien avec Jacques Rivette." *La saison cinématographique* 226 (1969): 85–92.
Skorecki, Louis. "Un Amour de Rivette." *Libération* (February 10, 1989): 28–29.
Smith, Alison. "The Author and the Auteur: Jacques Rivette and Luigi Pirandello." In *Jacques Rivette*. Ed. Douglas Morrey. Special issue of *Australian Journal of French Studies* 47, no. 2 (May–August 2010): 184–95.
Smith, Richard Langham. "The Play and its Playwright." In Nichols and Smith. 1–29.
———. "Tonalities of Darkness and Light." In Nichols and Smith. 107–39.
Smith, Winifred. *The Commedia dell'Arte*. New York: Columbia University Press, 1964.
Stein, Louis. *Beyond Death and Exile: The Spanish Republicans in France, 1939–1955*. Cambridge, Mass.: Harvard University Press, 1979.
Thirion, Antoine. "Étourdissant." *Cahiers du cinéma* 621 (March 2007): 10–11.
Thomas, François. "Les Films 'parallèles': musique et son directs." In *Jacques Rivette: La règle du jeu*. Ed. Daniela Giuffrida and Sergio Toffetti. Turin: Centre Culturel Français de Turin / Museo Nazionale del Cinema di Torino, c. 1991. 165–69.
Thomson, David. *The New Biographical Dictionary of Film*. New York: Alfred A. Knopf, 2009.
Tourneur, Cyril. *The Revenger's Tragedy*. Ed. R. A. Foakes. London: Methuen, 1966.
Touzot, Jean. *Jean Cocteau*. Lyon: La manufacture, 1989.
Truffaut, François. "A Certain Tendency of the French Cinema." In *Movies and Methods: An Anthology*. Ed. Bill Nichols. Vol. 1. Berkeley: University of California Press, 1976. 224–37.
Turim, Maureen. *Flashbacks in Film: Memory and History*. New York: Routledge, 1989.
Verlaine, Paul. "Fêtes Galantes." In *Oeuvres poétiques*. Paris: Éditions Garnier Frères, 1969.
Vexler, Felix. *Studies in Diderot's Esthetic Naturalism*. Ph.D. diss., Columbia University, 1922.
Wagner, Richard. "Opera Affirms the Separation of the Arts." In *Total Theatre: A Critical Anthology*. Ed. E. T. Kirby. New York: E.P. Dutton, 1969. 2–5.
Wiles, Mary M. Personal interview with Jacques Rivette, June 1999.
Wiles, Mary M. Personal interview with Jacques Rivette and Véronique Manniez, December 2009.
Williams, Alan. *Republic of Images: A History of French Filmmaking*. Cambridge, Mass.: Harvard University Press, 1992.
Wood, Robin. "Narrative Pleasure: Two Films of Jacques Rivette." *Film Quarterly* 35.1 (Fall 1981): 2–12.

# Index

Page numbers in italics indicate illustrations.

Mary M. Wiles is a lecturer in cinema studies at the University of Canterbury, Christchurch, New Zealand.

Books in the series
Contemporary Film Directors

*Nelson Pereira dos Santos*
Darlene J. Sadlier

*Abbas Kiarostami*
Mehrnaz Saeed-Vafa
and Jonathan Rosenbaum

*Joel and Ethan Coen*
R. Barton Palmer

*Claire Denis*
Judith Mayne

*Wong Kar-wai*
Peter Brunette

*Edward Yang*
John Anderson

*Pedro Almodóvar*
Marvin D'Lugo

*Chris Marker*
Nora Alter

*Abel Ferrara*
Nicole Brenez, translated
by Adrian Martin

*Jane Campion*
Kathleen McHugh

*Jim Jarmusch*
Juan Suárez

*Roman Polanski*
James Morrison

*Manoel de Oliveira*
John Randal Johnson

*Neil Jordan*
Maria Pramaggiore

*Paul Schrader*
George Kouvaros

*Jean-Pierre Jeunet*
Elizabeth Ezra

*Terrence Malick*
Lloyd Michaels

*Sally Potter*
Catherine Fowler

*Atom Egoyan*
Emma Wilson

*Albert Maysles*
Joe McElhaney

*Jerry Lewis*
Chris Fujiwara

*Jean-Pierre and Luc Dardenne*
Joseph Mai

*Michael Haneke*
Peter Brunette

*Alejandro González Iñárritu*
Celestino Deleyto
and Maria del Mar Azcona

*Lars von Trier*
Linda Badley

*Hal Hartley*
Mark L. Berrettini

*François Ozon*
Thibaut Schilt

*Steven Soderbergh*
Aaron Baker

*Mike Leigh*
Sean O'Sullivan

*D.A. Pennebaker*
Keith Beattie

*Jacques Rivette*
Mary M. Wiles

The University of Illinois Press
is a founding member of the
Association of American University Presses.

---

University of Illinois Press
1325 South Oak Street
Champaign, IL 61820-6903
www.press.uillinois.edu